TIM BURTON

AN UNAUTHORIZED BIOGRAPHY
OF THE FILMMAKER

TIM BURTON

AN UNAUTHORIZED BIOGRAPHY
OF THE FILMMAKER

Ken Hanke

RENAISSANCE BOOKS
Los Angeles

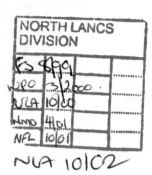
07830151

Library of Congress Cataloging-in-Publication Data
    Hanke, Ken.
        Tim Burton : an unauthorized biography of the filmmaker / Ken Hanke.
          p. cm.
        Filmography: p.
        Includes bibliographical references and index.
        ISBN 1-58063-046-4 (hardcover : alk. paper)
        1. Burton, Tim, 1958– . 2. Motion picture producers and directors—
United States—Biography. I. Title.
PN1998.3.B875H36   1999
791.43'0233'092—dc21
    [b]   99-18746
                                          CIP

10 9 8 7 6 5 4 3 2 1

Design by Susan Shankin

Distributed by St. Martin's Press
Manufactured in the United States of America
First Edition

Just about everybody

Under the sun

Should have a book dedicated to them.

To those souls who never had this pleasure,

I, in all sincerity,

Now dedicate this one.

ACKNOWLEDGMENTS

*Special thanks to the following persons
for making this book possible:*

Larry Billman, Philip Chamberlin, John Cocchi, Dolores Fuller,
Bill Givens, Jeanne Hanke, Shonsa Hanke, Tony Hudz, Dan Kamin,
Gary Litavis, Tim Lucas, Museum of Television and Radio
(Jonathan Rosenthal—Research), Justin Minch, Greg Pitt, Adam Resnick,
Barry Rivadue, David J. Skal, Seth Poppel Yearbook Archives,
Nathan Stein, Allan Taylor, Bryan Theiss, Richard Valley, Bill Warren,
Lucy Chase Williams, and to my editor on this project, Jim Parish.

CONTENTS

PREFACE

I CAME TO TIM BURTON'S WORK IN A SOMEWHAT roundabout manner. Like most people, my first exposure to Burton was *Pee-Wee's Big Adventure* in 1985, but I didn't go to see the movie because of any interest in the film itself, or the filmmaker. Rather, I was interested in hearing the Danny Elfman score. I was then—and am now—a major admirer of Elfman's work, and his contribution to *Pee-Wee's Big Adventure* was the entire attraction so far as I was concerned—at least until I saw the film.

In all honesty, I was anticipating another ill-advised attempt to stretch the sort of thing that might be mildly amusing for five minutes on *Saturday Night Live* into a feature film. It didn't take long to prove that this was not the case at all. Instead of the forced and even tedious television knockoff I had expected, I found myself confronted with the screen work of an almost impossibly inventive and fresh (in both senses of the word) talent.

I was a Tim Burton fan from the onset and was dismayed when the movie did not immediately produce the brilliant career I was so certain lay in front of this unheard-of filmmaker. Of course, once *Beetlejuice* appeared three years later, my original view of Burton's unique abilities was more than justified—and the rest of the world quickly caught up with those of us who had been so impressed with his debut work. By the time *Batman* was released in the summer of 1989, Tim Burton was as famous and admired (and, of course, attacked) as any filmmaker of modern times, and I found myself being asked to review the film for *Films in Review*.

However, it wasn't until *Edward Scissorhands* (1990) that I even flirted with the notion of writing something more in-depth about Burton and his work.

·This, for me, was the film that made clear not only what Burton was all about, but was the first movie I had ever seen that specifically seemed to speak to my own generation's childhood on its own terms. Burton appeared to have tapped into the malaise of the last of the "baby boomers" of suburbia of the early and mid-1960s, a subgeneration no one else seemed to even realize existed. Burton had not only recognized its existence, but depicted its world with alarming accuracy—both in realistic and fantasticated terms (something that was doubtlessly underscored for me by the film's exteriors being shot near where I had experienced those years myself)—and was creating a mythology to go with it. I felt immediately connected to this filmmaker in a way I had rarely encountered, and it was this that prompted the idea of exploring both the man and his work in greater detail—an idea that only found expression in 1992, right after the largely hostile reaction that had greeted *Batman Returns,* when *Films in Review* agreed that Burton was a worthy candidate for a career article. The resulting two-part examination of the director and his work up through that film was, in many ways, the genesis of this book. The more I saw Burton's work and the more I learned about him, the more I felt that of all current filmmakers, he was most worthy of a detailed biographical study—and the most intriguing.

In researching Burton with such a book in mind, one thing quickly became apparent in the seemingly contradictory nature of what I would call the tongue-tied eloquence of his interviews: He was also one of the most frustrating of all public figures. Despite the obvious validity of many of his remarks about his works and life, there was always a slight sense that he was virtually reading from a scripted set of responses, that he was almost himself playing a character.

There must, I thought, be more here than Burton was allowing us to see, even though the people I spoke with who knew him or had worked with him assured me that his legendary shyness was very real, despite the fact that his apparent innocence was almost certainly exaggerated, and that he really was just as awkward with words as he appeared. To a great degree, this did not surprise me. In fact, it reminded me a great deal of the subject of an earlier book of mine; Ken Russell, another distinctly *visual* artist who, while more verbal than Burton, can be similarly vague when talking about his work, and whose greatest eloquence and most revealing personal observations are found within his work. Specifically, I was reminded of a moment in Russell's film *Mahler*

(1974), where Gustav Mahler is asked to explain the "meaning of it all," and responds, "If I could tell you the answer in words, there'd be no need for me to write music." Perhaps if Burton could effectively verbalize the things he wanted to say, there'd be no need for him to make movies. And therein lay the crux of the matter—if one took the things that Burton said and looked at them within the context of his work, then something more revelatory occurred: a more complete picture of both man and artist. Where an artist—a genuine artist such as I am convinced Tim Burton is—may be less than wholly forthcoming in his personal statements, he is inescapably more open in what he says in his art. Between the two lies much of the truth, even if that often raises as many questions as it gives answers. What emerged from this approach was certainly a different picture of Tim Burton than the simplistic, if appealing, one that is usually associated with him. It is at once a more complex and darker, even sometimes disturbing, image, but it is also a far more human and real one.

INTRODUCTION

The Dark Side of Childhood and the Suburban Myth

PALE, ALMOST PAINFULLY THIN, AND, AS MANY HAVE
noted, "haunted-looking," his hair a tangle of black wisps that never seem to
have made the acquaintance of a brush, his heavy-lidded eyes suggesting sleepy
distractedness, Tim Burton looks more like a consumptive waif than he does
one of the most popular and powerful film directors in Hollywood today. And
yet that is exactly who and what Tim Burton is, proving either that looks can
be deceiving, or that on rare occasions, the meek do indeed inherit the earth—
or at least Hollywood. For a time, it seemed as if this strange-looking fellow
could do no wrong. He churned out hit movie after hit movie. Indeed, *Batman*
(1989) broke all records in its amazing popularity. Burton himself has always
dismissed his success and popularity as something that just "happened," which
seems more than a little disingenuous, but there is no getting around the fact
that he has somehow managed to craft an unusually personal body of work in
an abnormally high-profile, profit-driven setting, and it is apparent that at least
some of his ability to do this lies in the image he projects of himself—the self-
absorbed, haunted artist, who works solely on instinct without an understanding of—let alone an eye on—such things as profit margins.

Tim Burton himself may only look haunted, but his films most certainly
are haunted. They are all possessed by the specter of his childhood. Perhaps all
artists draw to some degree on their youth. Possibly, the very nature of creative

endeavor is an extension of childhood, a kind of intellectualized play where the fantastic imaginings of youth are made real. If this is true, then Tim Burton is an artist who has extended that kind of creative play further than anyone else has dared, and in ways that lesser mortals would never have considered.

Because all of his films have been fantasy-oriented (except for *Ed Wood* [1994], which is about the fantasy of making big-screen fantasies), often involving children or adolescents, there has been a critical tendency to think of his work as geared toward children and the director himself as childlike or at least uniquely in touch with "the child inside him." This concept caused a nasty backlash with the frequently terrifying *Batman Returns* (1992). Burton himself has rejected and professed a distaste for this glib assessment. "I don't know any children. I don't have any children and I don't like the phrase 'remaining like a child,' because I think it's kind of retarded," Burton told interviewer Mark Salisbury in 1994. Moreover, to describe as childlike the man who helmed *Batman* and *Batman Returns,* Warner Bros.' "big movies" of their respective years, is slightly ludicrous. Burton is a shrewd operator who maneuvered to participate in the franchising of his *Beetlejuice* (1988) film in its incarnation as a children's cartoon show (1989–92) and who has a $5 million "pay or play" contract (meaning he collects that amount whether or not the movie is ever made) for *Superman Lives*. Despite his obviously naive side and his much-touted private nature and inherent shyness (all things that seem slightly exaggerated in a myth of his own creating; rather as if, in his public life, he plays a film-industry character called Tim Burton), Burton is an artist who quickly learned to be a savvy Hollywood businessman in the bargain. Alternatively, Burton is an artist who was smart enough to know his limitations as a financial mover and surrounded himself with people who can ensure that he doesn't take a beating in any deal he signs. It's almost as if an extremely personal filmmaker—an Ingmar Bergman or a Woody Allen or a Ken Russell—had mystifyingly been crossed with a Steven Spielberg—an idea as unorthodox as Burton's screen works themselves, yet peculiarly apt for this unique person.

On the surface, in fact, megasuccessful Spielberg would appear to be a fair comparison to Burton. Both are children of the suburbs. Both are self-confessed movie brats. Both have been professionally successful beyond anyone's wildest imaginings. Both deal largely in fantasy. And both seem to have a preoccupation with childhood. However, there the similarities end. Indeed, the two are a study in contrasts, and possibly the reason lies in one simple fact—Spielberg, born in 1946, is twelve years Burton's senior. Spielberg's rather roseate-tinged sitcom vision of suburbia is of a wholly different era. Burton's darker and more realistic, yet not unaffectionate, onscreen view is clearly fueled by the same vague feeling of imminent destruction that permeates the music of his frequent collaborator, composer Danny Elfman. The view is skewed by a young childhood marked by the anarchic discontent of living with the idea that at any moment the Soviets were going to blast the United States out of existence. Perhaps the most chilling aspect of that time is not one of the recognized Cold War classics like *Dr. Strangelove* (1964) or *Fail-Safe* (1964), but rather the low-budget exploitation picture *Panic in the Year Zero* (1962). In this movie, the moment the bombs fall on Los Angeles, the daughter in the picture says, "I thought when it happened. . . ." (significantly, not *if,* but *when*). Burton would have been at the impressionable age of four when fear of nuclear war with Russia was common in the U.S. Never specifically addressed—as yet—in any of Burton's films, this phobic, even paranoid atmosphere clings to his every depiction of childhood, and doubtless has bearing on the streak of morbidity that permeates all of his films.

In another sense, Burton's motion pictures to date are less about childhood than they are a reaction to it—and it is not a positive reaction. This group of films is subversive in presenting childhood as a kind of living hell where the only immediate escape lies in fantasy. This is not to say that Tim doesn't romanticize childhood. He does, but not in any orthodox or conscious manner. He romanticizes it by making the fantasy aspect of it a reality. He turns a bleak suburban childhood into a dark myth where the imaginings of a lonely or misunderstood child become a grand reality. That old house we all were convinced as children was haunted suddenly is a Gothic mansion on camera and it *is* haunted. The strange man in the big "haunted" house whom one rarely sees and who might be anything actually *becomes* the mad scientist we, as kids, hoped he was.

Burton fulfills for filmgoers the things that could only exist in the imagination. In Tim's world of childhood, it is possible to revive a beloved dead dog by playing Dr. Frankenstein in your attic; it is possible to be in southern California (or Florida, standing in for it) and have snow. He re-creates the childhood of imagination, and he does so without the usual condescension of an adult and without making it cute and precious. The youngsters in a Burton film do not cavort in the adult-imagined manner of what childhood "should be" in the *Leave It to Beaver* sitcom mode; rather, they take themselves deadly seriously, which, realistically, is a great deal nearer the truth. As a result, Burton's short films like *Vincent* (1982) and *Frankenweenie* (1982), and his features like *Edward Scissorhands* (1990), are among the most interesting movies ever made about childhood and children, especially children of the suburbs. Whether Tim likes the accolades or not, he genuinely *does* have the gift of conjuring up childhood from the perspective of a child.

The very fact that the adult Burton admits to knowing no children is key to this. It's the honest view of his own growing-up, not the maturation adults like to imagine is going on with their own children or their friends' offspring. In this respect, Burton makes films that children actually enjoy and identify with as opposed to movies that are "good" for them in the manner of a *Skippy* (1931) or *The Yearling* (1946) or *Old Yeller* (1960). In essence, Burton's screen work does not preach to children about how their lives ought to be.

Possibly, Burton's lack of concern over presenting a "balanced" adult view of the world is also why film critics are often puzzled by Tim's work. He is almost universally praised as a stylist—and appropriately, since he is probably the most visually stylish filmmaker in American film today—but is frequently faulted for a telltale lack of narrative ability and dramatic coherence. While it must be admitted that one of his films (ironically, his biggest commercial success), *Batman,* suffers from what can best be described as a luxuriantly unhurried pace, Burton's movies offer fairly straightforward narratives and are not terrifically experimental in construction. Moreover, while he has provided the story in some cases and obviously has largely controlled what ends up on the screen, Tim has yet to write his own screenplay. The key here—the reason a critic like Robin Wood has tagged his work as "more distinctive than distinguished"—lies primarily, I think, in Burton's choice of subject matter.

The standard observation that Burton's films are invariably about outsiders or even freaks is certainly on the mark, but it doesn't entirely explain the perception that Burton lacks the ability to create high drama onscreen. Certainly, Burton is not the first filmmaker to take the perspective of the outsider in his filmmaking. Director James Whale (1889–1957), whose work clearly influenced Burton, made a career of depicting cultural and social alienation with *Waterloo Bridge* (1931), *Frankenstein*

(1931), *Bride of Frankenstein* (1935), *Show Boat* (1936), and no one has ever suggested that his characters were unsympathetic. What attracts us to Burton's characters, on the other hand, is their obsessions—or rather the *nature* of those obsessions.

From Burton's very first feature, *Pee-Wee's Big Adventure* (1985), this focus on studying excessive behavior is made evident. It's a film about a man obsessed with a bicycle, of all things. Clearly, it is not the most universally comprehensible obsession—at least as concerns an adult—and certainly is not the strongest theme for a feature film. Yet Burton is happy to accept it rather than question it. This is much the same from film to film in one way or another. Why does Lydia Deetz (Winona Ryder) dress all in black and put forth a morbid worldview in *Beetlejuice*? Within Burton's world, this moroseness is comprehensible—after all, Deetz is Tim's onscreen alter ego, and adolescence is hell—but on her own, divorced from the film that surrounds her, she just *is*. We are given the background on why Bruce Wayne has become obsessed with fighting crime in *Batman,* but not why he has chosen the somewhat extravagant path of dressing up like a bat to do so. (While it can be argued that the previous Batman films—and to a lesser extent, the comic books—did not explain this, either, Burton's otherwise psychological approach to the character makes its absence here both notable and personal.)

And so it goes. No explanation is offered for his screen characters' peculiar ways of approaching life. Burton gleefully accepts his characters' peculiarities and expects his audience to do so as well. On the whole, the viewers do. The critics, on the other hand, are apparently not so quick to accept this attitude on the part of the filmmaker. Burton's apparent lack of psychological depth—which, more charitably and correctly, might be read as Burton's nonjudgmental point of view—makes easy fodder for criticism.

Another unique and, to some, troubling aspect of Burton's movie output lies in the fact that—unlike others of the generation of movie brats (which, for better or worse, will be the case from here on: directors whose primary influences are earlier directors)—he is less concerned with evoking the films of the past than he is with presenting his *idea* of those bygone entertainments. The look of his very first screen effort, the stop-motion short, *Vincent* (1982), is certainly drawn from the German Expressionist classic, *The Cabinet of Dr. Caligari* (1919), but it was drawn from it secondhand. Burton admits to never having seen the film, but he had, of course, seen scene stills from it in "monster" magazines and books on horror movies. The result is that *Vincent* translates the Caligari look into Tim's *idea* of that look. It is at once Caligari and yet uniquely Burton—a subjective interpretation of a half-informed memory. His next film, the short *Frankenweenie* (1982), is much the same. The look of this film is inspired by James Whale's classic *Frankenstein* (1931), but Burton's version gives the viewer the *idea* or the *memory* of the earlier film rather than a literal re-creation. In some quarters, this causes Burton to be viewed as sloppy, suggesting that he doesn't do his home-work properly to reproduce slavishly the look of his film "models." The central misunderstanding here is that, for Burton, these movie predecessors are not models; they are influences. If there are any models at all, they are the skewed memories of photographs and movies that stuck in Burton's mind—the ideas that these images and moods and stories conjured up for him.

In many respects, Burton is the most selfish of all contemporary film-makers, in that he tends to use movies to his own ends. He employs film less to explore the outer world than to investigate his own inner one. Two of his entries—*Vincent* and *Edward Scissorhands*—are overtly autobiographical (at least as concerns the main characters) in their aims. They show us, without explana-tion, without analysis, two stages of Tim's life: childhood and adolescence. To some degree, *Frankenweenie* and *Beetlejuice* also fit this mold—the first relating to childhood, the second to adolescence. *Ed Wood* (1994), on the other hand, is both a biopic on the notorious director (1924–1978) and Burton's first attempt at examining his own adulthood. Similar resonances of self-examination are inherent in the two Batman pictures as well, but in a subtly different, less overt manner. It may be no accident that Tim's most recent film, *Mars Attacks!* (1996), is both his least introspective and his least successful—both commercially and artistically. In a very real sense, it would seem that Burton really has only one subject—himself. Fortunately, that subject is an extremely interesting one.

But who exactly is this frail, wild-haired, haunted-looking fellow who makes these unique, introverted feature films that are at once so loved by many and so dismissed by others? Is he really the sensitive artist that has been portrayed so fre-quently? Or is that merely a pose? How does he command the loyalty of so many of the biggest names in a creative industry not much known for loyalty? How has he managed to carve out an impossibly personal and defiantly quirky body of work within the confines of the most mainstream venues of establish-ment Hollywood? These are some of the questions I seek to answer in this book.

1 | BATMANIA

It's a guy dressing up as a bat,
and no matter what anyone says, that's weird.

TIM BURTON, 1994

JUNE 22, 1989. IT WAS THE EVENING BEFORE THE opening of Warner Bros.' big summer release, the much-anticipated *Batman*. The studio had much riding on the success or failure of this elaborate film. Not only was it their most important picture of the year, it had escalated in price from an already hefty $30 million price tag to an almost unbelievable $48 million.

Films based on comic books have always been dicey propositions. Manage to capture the comic-book fans *and* the general public—as had been done with the first *Superman* films in the late 1970s—and a huge box-office hit is assured. Alienate either faction, and you have a disaster. Bob Kane's 1938 comic-book hero, Batman, had already seen several cinematic incarnations by 1988: two 1940s serials; a popular, albeit deliberately campy, television series in the mid-1960s; and a none-too-successful feature film that brought the TV series and its stars to the big screen in 1966. These efforts, whatever their merits, reflected a simpler time and a simpler point of view. Not only had the world and the movies changed mightily by the time the new *Batman* came to fruition, but so had the comic itself. Always the darkest and most unsettling of the comic-book heroes (not surprising, since Kane had been largely inspired by the character of the Bat in Roland West's bizarre 1926 film, *The Bat*—and that character was an insane master criminal, just this side of a homicidal maniac!)—the character became even darker as the world of the comic book deepened and became increasingly complex over the final decades of the twentieth century.

The Batman movie had been in gestation for years—first owned in 1979 by producers Benjamin Melniker and Michael Uslan, with a script by Tom Mankiewicz of *Superman* (1978) fame. Obviously, the idea at that point was to cash in on Mankiewicz's previous success with the Man of Steel. However, in many respects, Superman is a much simpler character, in that he is pure fantasy in a much lighter vein. Batman, on the other hand, is grounded in reality, and a distinctly *noir* reality at that. As a result, no one seems to have known quite how to approach the project as a major feature film, and it remained quagmired in Hollywoodland limbo.

It was then acquired by the flamboyant team of Jon Peters and Peter Guber. Peters, a former hairdresser, had gained fame and a degree of notoriety when he was hired to do Barbra Streisand's hair on *For Pete's Sake* (1974). He and Streisand quickly became an item and in the bargain, he became her producer, a role he both relished and excelled at. Forming a partnership with Peter Guber (Peters would be the hands-on producer of the team and Guber would work behind the scenes), he established himself as a major power to reckon with in Hollywood, and, by many accounts, not a wholly scrupulous or pleasant power. Throughout the 1980s, Peters and Guber had attached various directors, including Joe Dante and Ivan Reitman, to the Batman screen project. However, nothing materialized until they tapped into a shy, fragile-looking young filmmaker who was developing his own unique filmmaking style and a cult following with moviegoers. That man was Tim Burton.

Burton was at once the most obvious and the most unlikely choice to direct *Batman*. His first feature film—*Pee-Wee's Big Adventure* (1985), starring the decidedly offbeat Pee-Wee Herman—though not well-received critically, had been likened to a cartoon and achieved a healthy box-office success. A rising director such as Burton, with an acknowledged visual sense and a penchant for the unusual, was certainly a logical choice for *Batman*. At the same time, Tim was known to be quirky. He was in Hollywood, but not *of* Hollywood. He was at the very least an eccentric. Burton didn't play by film-industry rules, seemed unaware of demographics and marketing, and could sometimes appear downright inarticulate in interviews and meetings. In their book on Jon Peters and Peter Guber, *Hit and Run* (1996), Nancy Griffin and Kim Masters refer to Burton, not ineptly, as "a haunted-looking fellow with a pale face framed by a nest of black hair. He dressed in black and rarely spoke in complete sentences." In that regard, he was not quite what Warner Bros. had in mind as the most imposing candidate to helm such a huge and important movie production in the studio lineup.

Two things intervened on Burton's professional behalf—Peters and Guber, along with studio executive Mark Canton, liked him and respected his abilities as an artist, and his second feature film, *Beetlejuice* (1988), became a freak (in more senses than one) hit. Tim had been offered the Batman project prior to the success of *Beetlejuice*. He and screenwriter Sam Hamm had worked out a script that had been well received by studio honchos. However, it wasn't until *Beetlejuice* was clearly a success that the studio gave Burton the go-ahead on actually filming the coveted, expensive-to-make *Batman*. By the time shooting commenced at Pinewood Studios in England in October 1988, Burton was beginning to regret his victory.

He might have known what to expect. "Horror" stories about working with the demanding Guber and Peters were not uncommon, and Burton had already experienced considerable interference in the matter of the "final" script. The original script that he and Sam Hamm had presented was deemed in need of serious revision. Worse, while it was still in rewrites, the epic entry was pushed into production to meet the 1989 summer release deadline, leaving Tim at the helm of a movie that hadn't been clearly finalized. "As Burton stood on the back lot at Pinewood Studios outside of London, gazing at sets that filled nearly ninety-five acres and nine soundstages, he was overwhelmed. He had four months to make a special-effects extravaganza that had to make every kid want to wear a Batcape next Halloween," wrote Griffin and Masters in *Hit and Run*. More attuned to smaller projects, co-workers he knew and responded to, and far less studio pressure, Burton was certainly bound to feel swallowed up by the massive project. The enormity of the responsibility was undeniable and many of Jon Peters's blustering and bullying antics were foreign to Burton's sensibilities. The most surprising aspect of it all was that Burton didn't break under the strain.

Ironically, Peters himself, whom Burton liked personally, helped get him through the taxing production. There was something about Burton that made the normally explosive producer take an almost paternal tack with the film-maker. Peters adopted a protective attitude toward the director on the set, though not at the expense of getting Tim to push the film more and more toward what Peters, as producer, envisioned. Key scenes were rewritten or reworked the night before shooting them. One of the most famous scenes in the film—the encounter between Batman (Michael Keaton) and the Joker (Jack Nicholson) in Vicki Vale's (Kim Basinger) apartment—was done in this fashion. Not only were new screenwriter Warren Skaaren, Burton, and Peters in on its creation and construction, but, in a successful demonstration of the collaborative nature of film, so were Michael Keaton, Jack Nicholson, and Kim Basinger. Burton later admitted it was one of the best scenes in the feature, but the experience had been far from enjoyable.

The movie's climax was similarly reworked, though on a much larger basis—including the construction of a $100,000 thirty-eight-foot-tall model of the Gotham City cathedral in which the action takes place—and with some-what less happy results. Here Tim and his stars found themselves adrift, impro-vising an ending to the film at the last minute, trying to satisfy the demands of the story, of Peters, and their own ideas of what the film should ultimately be. Burton knew instinctively that if his big breakthrough film had a climax that didn't work, he and the film were sunk. The pressure was unbelievable and it is little wonder that Burton later referred to the entire experience of making the film as "torture."

Once the movie was in post-production in 1989, Jon Peters worked up one of the most original and impressive (some, including Burton, might say *overbearing*) ad campaigns in the history of Hollywood filmmaking. This was in part to quiet the objections of Batman fanatics, who were skeptical of the pro-ject in general, and of the license they felt it was taking with their beloved hero, not to mention the almost universal criticism of the unlikely hero status of comedian Michael Keaton cast in the title role. It was essential to minimize the vocal negativity of diehard traditionalists. This Peters did brilliantly with Anton Furst's stark Batsymbol poster design, heavy media saturation, endless merchan-dising tie-ins, and the very untraditional original Coming Attractions trailer, which was nothing but a jumbled collection of scenes without a musical track. Anyone who didn't know about *Batman* well in advance of its opening must have been living in a cave. With all the hoopla, *Batman* had become *the* anticipated event of 1989. For his part, the young director, whose professional future was riding on the project, kept well away from the hype and viewed the huckstering of his film with an uneasy mixture of amusement and disgust.

Burton also refrained from getting involved with the producers' and studio's own anticipation of the film's opening. When reports started to filter in that people were actually camping out in front of theatres on the night of June 22, Tim was conspicuously absent from the circle of people being informed of the unusual event. Instead Burton quietly stayed away from it all. No one that night, however, was prepared for the fact that *Batman* would gross $42.7 million in its first weekend, and over $100 million by the time the first week was over. Suddenly Tim Burton had become the most successful director in Hollywood. He was not yet thirty-one.

2 | BACKYARD GOTHIC

*If you weren't from Burbank, you'd think it was
the movie capital of the world with all the studios
around there, but it was and still is, very suburban.
It's funny, the areas around Burbank have gotten
less suburban, but somehow Burbank still remains
the same. I don't know how or why, but it has this
weird shield around it. It could be Anywhere, U.S.A.*

TIM BURTON, 1994

NAMED AFTER A LOS ANGELES DENTIST, DAVID BURBANK,
who had founded a sheep ranch there in 1867, Burbank was conceived and
developed by the Providencia Land, Water, and Development Company in 1867
and was incorporated as a city in 1911. It subsequently became an industrial
center and, more famously, home to Warner Bros., Columbia Pictures, Walt
Disney Productions, and NBC-TV. In point of fact, Burbank out-Hollywoods
Hollywood in terms of studios, though its principal claim to fame probably lies
more in its suburban realm, and the negative image lodged into the public consciousness in the 1960s by Johnny Carson on TV's *Tonight Show* and *Rowan &
Martin's Laugh-In,* with their constant barrage of derisive references to "beautiful downtown Burbank."

And, in truth, Burbank is just about as bad as every joke that has been made at its expense—"undistinguished" may be the kindest adjective. It is the transitional point between the San Fernando Valley (Van Nuys, Sherman Oaks, Studio City) and the San Gabriel Valley (Glendale, Pasadena, Sierra Madre). The Hollywood Hills stand on the south side of the San Fernando Valley, making the area surrounded on the north by large mountains and on the south by a smaller range. The Hollywood Hills are at the tail end of the Santa Monica Mountains, ending more or less with Mount Hollywood, famed location of the Hollywood sign. Looking at the sign from Hollywood, Burbank is, somewhat fittingly, behind it.

Beyond its status as an outpost of the entertainment industry, Burbank, when Burton was growing up there, was essentially a company town for Lockheed Aviation, which housed its famous "skunk works" at the Burbank Airport. All in all, the town's other businesses existed to support—and in turn were supported by—Lockheed or the studios, though the latter were generally a world apart from the everyday world of Burbank. In the days since Burton's childhood, the giant aviation factories have closed down and moved to nearby Lancaster, on the edge of the Mojave Desert, though the Burbank Airport, once the company airport for Lockheed, remains a busy place, serving as a relief airport for LAX.

When Tim Burton entered the world (as Timothy William Burton) in Burbank on August 25, 1958, it was into this echt-1950s world of suburbia that he came. Burbank, in 1958, was not yet a cultural joke. Indeed, it was scarcely known to most of the world, since the movies then—and to a large degree even now—meant only one thing: Hollywood. Burbank was a small town within a big one and largely reflected the Eisenhower-era world of mass conformity with its standardized houses and lockstep mentality. Everyone was largely expected to do and believe and behave the same way. Anything outside a fairly rigid set of largely unquestioned rules was considered suspect or worse. This, after all, was the end of the era of Senator Joseph McCarthy and the extensive witch hunts for supposed Communists festering in America's underbelly. It was simply safer to play it safe—and the more you were like your neighbor, the safer you were, and the more your neighbors were like each other (and like you, of course) the more *you* were validated.

Everyone being alike—as in the world of Burbank, California—tends to endorse the idea that you must be okay, too. "Nobody did anything. No one would ever say he was an *atheist,* they'd say they were *Protestants.* You'd never do anything to reveal yourself," Burton told *Village Voice* columnist Gary Indiana in October 1994. Burton's parents, Bill and Jean, were very much a part of this world. A former minor-league ballplayer for the Los Angeles Cardinals' farm team (Burton thinks his father left the game due to injuries), Bill now worked for the city—in Parks and Recreation—and Jean ran a cat-oriented gift store, Cats Plus, which specialized in knickknacks that in some way depicted the feline form. If this was a sign of eccentricity on her part, it was certainly of the mildest and most respectable kind, not to mention a somewhat precious and kitschy variety.

There seems to have been little or no real sense of family in the Burton household, at least from Tim's perspective. When asked about his father in a 1991 interview for the *New York Times Magazine,* he commented, "I'm not close to him. It's been a source of confusion. I'm just something of a remote person in some ways. I've had an incredible desire to get out of the house from an early age." His feelings about his mother are equally detached: "I don't know. It sort of freaked me out several years ago, realizing I don't know a whole lot about my parents, don't even know some of the basic facts, like where they were born."

The degree to which this vagueness about his family roots is literally true is certainly open to question. However, there is no getting around the fact that Tim was an unusual and detached child. In one of his rare public statements about his son, Bill Burton told *Newsweek* of the time Tim saw some lumber and a dead tree propped against a gray wall outside the window during a remodeling project on their Burbank home. "God, you've got a great view!" was his immediate response to this rather dismal image. "My wife and I looked at each other. It was just a dead tree against a gray wall. But he was deadly serious," Bill Burton commented. He was unable to comprehend the attraction, despite the obvious similarity of the stark gray and black imagery to some of his son's artwork. At the time of *Batman,* in an April 1989 *New York Times Magazine* piece, Jean Burton commented on her son's apparent alienation from the family: "I know he feels there were painful conflicts between us. I think they were all from within. Tim was awfully tough on himself in many ways."

It was a world of joiners—Elks Clubs, Moose Clubs, Rotary Clubs, Boy Scouts, Little League. . . . The whole concept was one of *belonging*. And Burton was never much of a joiner. He admits to having played some sports (significantly, pointing out that this was *not* forced on him by his athletic-minded father), but the only evidence of him being a part of a group is during his sophomore and junior years at Burbank High, when he was on the Water Polo Foothill League! Even there, Tim seems curiously out-of-place—half the size of his teammates and staring sullenly at the camera in the group photos, looking for all the world like the living embodiment of the outsider.

In 1950s' Burbank, everything was geared toward holding together a facade of stability and so-called normalcy. This is not surprising when it is taken into consideration that this was also the era of the idea of imminent nuclear war. A great many people, perhaps most, felt that World War Three was waiting in the wings and that they would shortly be incinerated, or, worse, left to the lingering death of radiation. It may seem like distinctly ostrich-style behavior, but keeping that surface of normalcy intact acted as a kind of denial to keep the death threat at bay. It worked well enough for those of Bill and Jean Burton's generation, but the effect soon palled on their children, paving the way for the 1960s' explosion of nonconformity and contempt for the Babbit-minded world of the suburbs. Burton would later tell *Premiere* magazine that Burbank was "a visually wonderful, hellish place. . . . When you're a kid you think everything is strange, and you think *because* you're a kid everything is strange. Then when you get older, you realize it *is* strange."

Tim was just coming to conscious realization of the world around him in the early 1960s, a massively confusing time under any circumstances, but particularly so for a young child. On the one hand, it was the era of the comforting image of order and conformity with a large part of the world, especially in suburbia, pretending they were living in an episode of *Leave It to Beaver* or *Father Knows Best*. At the same time, these pleasant fantasies were existing right next to constant television news of Russian premier Nikita Khrushchev pounding a table at the United Nations with his shoe and vowing, "We will bury you." When a child went to school in the United States in those days, he or she was given instructions on what to do in case of nuclear war, which seemed a very real possibility at the time. The signals were decidedly mixed—everything was just wonderful in the best of all possible worlds—except, of course, that the whole thing might be blown to bits at any moment!

It is no wonder that this should also be the era that horror movies were making a comeback and had become immensely popular with children, with the advent of television's reshowing of the old Universal Pictures classics (and not-so-classics) of the 1930s and 1940s starting in 1957, and the birth of horror fan Forrest J. Ackerman's *Famous Monsters of Filmland* magazine back in 1958. These films and magazines were not only mildly subversive, but they created a sense of fantasy and demystification of (possibly even a denial of) death in their reanimated corpses, vampires, and zombies.

In his brilliant essay, "Him and Me: A Personal Slice of the Dracula Century," David J. Skal (six years Tim's senior) writes about the appeal of horror in those years: "A few weeks before Halloween 1962, when I was ten years old, the threatened prank of the season wasn't toilet-papered fences, but the deployment of nuclear warheads, aimed at the American mainland from Cuba. I had been looking forward to growing up, but President Kennedy's grim announcements on television strongly indicated that this might not be in the cards. While waiting for my untimely incineration, I went to the library and pored over the pictures of fallout shelters in magazines. The people inside them looked like ordinary suburbanites, but more monastic. . . . The fallout shelter was a lot like a crypt, where people existed in a strange half-life poised precariously between consumer nirvana and nuclear oblivion. They were something like vampires, I realized, atomic-age undeath shielding itself from a nasty nuclear sun." But then came the realization that came to most children of the time: "We didn't have a fallout shelter, but I liked the idea of not having to die." As a result, Skal adopted the fantasy of becoming a vampire or some similar immortal creature. It was a more effective solution for a child than the older generation's games of denial. It had an immediacy and an assurance lacking in that more subtle approach.

Burton—a withdrawn, and naturally sensitive boy—was very much a part of this world at an early and even more impressionable age than Skal. He made his own adjustments to the era. The attraction to horror films was immediate for him. An unusually perceptive child, as is often the case with creative children who observe from the sidelines, Tim was quick to see the facade of his suburban existence. "I grew up around people who were afraid to do anything, and hid behind these masks of normality, just falling into line, not saying anything on their own, but just sort of together, like the angry villagers in *Frankenstein*," Burton later told reporter Gary Indiana.

What is particularly telling about this assessment is his likening of the people he grew up around to the "angry villagers in *Frankenstein*," since, in other places, Burton has clearly stated his identification with the misunderstood monsters in the old horror films. It suggests that he not only felt out of place in his surroundings, but downright shunned and even threatened. "The houses [in Burbank] are close together, but there's a weird feeling of 'What's going on next door?' I remember there was no real communication, but if there was ever a tragedy, if there was a car accident out front, people would come out of their houses, and it would be like a block party. It's not something I can relate to, really—this blood lust. It's like a way to make yourself feel alive," Tim told *Premiere*, by way of explaining some of the behavior he depicted later in *Edward Scissorhands*, which is perhaps his most direct comment on the subject of suburbia.

It is also more than a little intriguing to find the director describing people hiding behind "masks of normality," since Burton appears to have taken this concept to heart and inverted it in his own life, hiding much of himself behind what might be called a "mask of eccentricity." Burton might have complained about the people in his childhood—"You'd never do anything to reveal yourself"—yet, except in his art, that could very well be said of Burton himself, since there is so much of his personal life and history that he simply never discusses or reveals to anyone, and much of what he says in interviews is so similar that it begins to sound like a rehearsed script. If an interviewer departs from that script—such as asking a question about his brother, Daniel—the result is a blanket refusal to speak on the topic.

The only relief Tim found to his existence in this land of ticky-tacky box houses and people playing at being "normal" lay in the horror films on television and in the second-run movie houses. Fantasy of all sorts appealed to him, especially the Japanese Godzilla films ("For a while I wanted to be the actor who played Godzilla") and the Ray Harryhausen stop-motion films like *Jason and the Argonauts* (1964). However, what held the most attraction, what spoke to Burton directly was the array of colorful horror films of Vincent Price, especially the adaptations of Edgar Allan Poe stories that Price made for moviemaker

Roger Corman. "Growing up in suburbia, in an atmosphere that was perceived as nice and normal (but which I had other feelings about), those movies were a way to certain feelings, and I related them to the place I was growing up in," explained Burton. "Vincent Price was somebody I could identify with. When you're younger things look bigger, you find your own mythology, you find what psychologically connects to you," he added. Indeed. It is peculiarly apt that Burton should refer to mythology, since in not too many years Tim would be crafting a mythology of his own, to which an astonishing number of people would psychologically connect, just as he had connected with the Price movies.

Beyond the expected retreat into the self and the identification with the macabre, Burton found solace in his imagination. As it happened, the Burton home was situated near a cemetery—boasting the presumptuously pompous name Valhalla—that served as a weird playground for him and his few friends, who dubbed themselves "the Graveyard Club." Even this, however, was fueled by his imagination, since Valhalla is anything but the sort of Gothic graveyard found in Tim's movies. Instead, it is one of those huge, low-maintenance "memorial parks" where headstones are forbidden in favor of flat markers and the odd memorial statuary. Probably because of the military connection to Lockheed, many of the memorials are war-themed, with the cemetery's center-piece being "the Portal of Folded Wings," where several aviation pioneers are buried. Only through the horror-movie filtering of his mind could this in any way relate to his own visions.

At the same time, Tim went through a self-confessed stage of being some-what destructive (not to mention delighting in terrifying the neighborhood children with his antics). After that period he found an unusual escape by doing exactly the opposite, thanks to his perception of creativity as the ultimate sub-versive act in his world. "It's really hard to do anything. I grew up in this puri-tanical 'American dream' kind of thing where everybody's supposed to be normal and people attacked anybody who tried to make anything," Burton commented. It is not surprising, then, that that would be exactly what he would do—try to make something. In Burton's case, this "something" turned out to be movies.

Among modern moviemakers, a childhood including a bout of backyard filmmaking is not in itself unusual. Even filmmakers from earlier generations dabbled in this. Orson Welles played about with film long before becoming a filmmaker. Ken Russell made a little horror film while still in school. The typically ambitious Steven Spielberg is said to have made a feature-length remake of *The War of the Worlds* (1953) as a youngster. Burton, however, differs from all these in that none of his predecessors seem to have thought of filmmaking as an act of rebellion, which he clearly—at least subconsciously—did. And unlike Spielberg, he didn't set out to copy something he admired, but crafted his own variations on the ideas of the pictures he'd seen and admired. "There was one we made called *The Island of Dr. Agor*. We made a wolfman movie and a mad-doctor movie, and a little stop-motion film using model cavemen," he told interviewer Mark Salisbury. From the onset, it's apparent that all of Burton's projects would be filtered through his personal sensibility.

Tim himself makes no bones about the amateurishness of his childhood films, nor about the fact that he soon learned to use this unusual hobby to help coast through high school. An indifferent student and a self-confessed non-reader, he discovered that making a film on a book or a topic was easier than actually reading the works in question and discussing them, and was a sure way to a good grade. The effort and the novelty alone are enough to dazzle a teacher, especially in those precamcorder days. Nonetheless, it is obvious that these backyard doodles were an expression of Tim's interests and personality. He may joke about bluffing his way through a high-school psychology project by loosely matching visual images to the title track from shock-rocker Alice Cooper's *Welcome to My Nightmare* album. However, the choice of material to express his view of his own psychology is certainly telling, not to mention that it evidences a youthful fascination with the kitsch and pop culture that would ultimately permeate his professional films. It may be true that, as a child, he never seriously considered filmmaking as a viable way to make a living; however, it may just be part of his public persona as someone to whom things simply come, with no actual planning. Regardless of where the truth lies, there's no denying that Burton's themes and subject matter were already being established in his preadulthood years, if only in the crudest of forms.

Whether or not he harbored notions of becoming a filmmaker, Burton did not set off on that course in a direct manner. Instead, he concentrated his energies on his talents for drawing in a uniquely quirky style. (Burton was obviously influenced by artist-designer Edward Gorey, whose dark, weird, and funny illustrated books achieved instant cult status in the 1960s, and whose gray-and-black sets for the 1970s Broadway revival of *Dracula* were especially similar to Tim's work.) Drawing was easier, slightly profitable, and, of course, cheaper than making films. Tim turned out seasonal (especially Halloween!) window designs for some Burbank shops, and in eighth grade managed to win a community design award (and ten dollars) with a drawing that graced Burbank's garbage trucks for a year.

It was also still very much an act of rebellion for Burton. "If you look at kids' drawings, they all have this naive spirit. In the school system I grew up in, that got pounded out of you, so by age thirteen a kid says, 'Oh, I can't draw,' or whatever. I shielded myself from that, and punched through it. Because I couldn't draw, either. If I had listened to those people, I'd have ended up like everybody else. 'I can't do this, I can't do that,'" he commented to Gary Indiana in the *Village Voice* in 1994. Impossible though it is to seriously imagine Tim ending up "like everybody else," his point is a valid one and his obvious anger at the idea of dealing with a system where the point seems to be to remove all traces of individuality and creativity is certainly justified.

His years at the remarkably uninspiring Burbank High School—a typical 1920s-style rambling series of dreary brick buildings surrounded by asphalt parking lots and drab, treeless playing fields—did little to bring Burton into the mainstream of society, despite his stint on the water polo team. Not that Burton was entirely without support or encouragement in his art. His parents were, at least, vaguely indulgent (though Tim, at one point in his teens, did leave home in search of more amenable arrangements with his grandmother).

The exact cause of this family rift remains unclear and is one of the many areas of his life that Burton refuses to address publicly. The never-identified "friends" who helped him make movies as a youth were obviously not really in tune with him, since they are not distinct enough in his mind to rate names or personalities. Also, there is no suggestion that any of them were ever more than convenient acquaintances who merely passed through Tim's childhood without significant impact.

Tim's younger brother, Daniel, himself a professional artist, is never referred to by Burton in his talks with the media. This avoidance is done to such an extent that the director invariably comes across as an only child (apart from *Edward Scissorhands,* the characters in Burton's films tend to be only children, or so at odds with their siblings that they might as well be). On one of the few occasions Burton has even spoken of his brother, it was merely to comment that he hadn't talked to him in two years. Tim's reticence on this topic—like so many others—has only served to give rise to strange speculations about their relationship, the most bizarre of which is the totally unfounded notion that all of Burton's ideas are pilfered from Daniel, who is therefore kept in the background.

Strained family relations and the lack of any close friends certainly plagued Tim in his artistic ambitions. However, at least one teacher at Burbank High actually encouraged him in his art, and because of this, upon graduation in 1976, the eighteen-year-old managed to get a scholarship to the Disney-founded California Institute of the Arts (CalArts). It was there that he decided to become an animator.

3 | THE DISNEY WAY

I couldn't draw those four-legged Disney foxes.
I just couldn't do it. I couldn't even fake the Disney
style. Mine looked like roadkills.

TIM BURTON, 1994

THE CALIFORNIA INSTITUTE OF THE ARTS—OR CALARTS,
as it is familiarly known—in Valencia, California, about twenty-two miles north-
west of Burbank, is a private educational concern offering bachelor of fine arts
(BFA) and master of fine arts (MFA) degrees. The school, incorporated in 1961,
was the first such degree-granting institution in America designed for performing and visual-arts studies. CalArts was established by Walt and Roy Disney
(of the Disney Studio) and a merging of two existing schools, the Los Angeles
Conservatory of Music (founded 1883) and the Chouinard Art Institute (founded
1921). Originally based in Los Angeles, CalArts moved to its present location in
November 1971, by which time it offered degrees in five areas of the arts: art,
film and video, music, theater, and dance. The campus—a modern, sleek, and,
not surprisingly, somewhat Disneyesque collection of buildings on well-mani-
cured grounds—occupies sixty acres that overlook the city of Santa Clarita and
is surrounded by the San Gabriel, Tehachapi, and Santa Sussana Mountains,
making the location nothing if not scenic.

In 1975 a $14 million endowment from the Walt Disney estate helped set up a special program for training animators for their filmmaking TV studio. It was a shrewd move on the Disney Studio's part, since it had lost much of its direction since Walt Disney's death in 1966. The sense of innovation and creativity that had been its hallmark had stagnated in an era of production executives who spent more time trying to second-guess a dead man ("How would Walt have done this?") than actually accomplishing anything creative or fresh. What they did produce onscreen was often half-baked and tentative. There was little sense of inspiration, only an increasingly feeble attempt to retread the studio's past successes. What better way to inject new life into the studio than by tapping into the best and brightest at CalArts?

After a year (1976–77) of drifting around the school's film department, Tim moved into the Disney program, apparently thinking that a career as an animator might not be a bad life choice. Very clearly, he viewed animation as less risky and far-fetched than any idea of becoming a full-fledged live-action movie director. Plus, the Disney program offered the possibility of immediate employment if he was picked by their review board to join the studio. In retrospect, it seems to have been a wholly pragmatic decision on Burton's part. Despite his dabbling in stop-motion animation in his childhood films, his fondness for the movies of Ray Harryhausen, and his love of drawing, there is no evidence that Burton had any significant interest in nor passion for traditional forms of screen animation. Beyond this, the idea of Tim Burton, the intentional outsider and nonconformist, deliberately placing himself in the hands of one of the most regimented corporations of all time is a ludicrous notion on anything but a "practicality" basis. Joining up with Disney and the conformity it represented was Burton's halfhearted version of, "Grow up, get a haircut, get a job."

At first, it seemed that Disney's desire to acquire fresh talent and new ideas into the studio might play in Burton's favor. However, if Tim's attempts at submitting to a regimented mindset were halfhearted, Disney's commitment to doing anything significantly new and different seemed to go little beyond lip service. The stated desire to expand their horizons in this manner soon turned into an effort to annex these young animators and shape them into the studio ideal—"the Disney Way"—of what an animator should be. It was a bid to tap into youthful talent, but not utilize it much—a kind of corporate pussyfooting that offered the illusion of moving ahead while playing it safe.

The Disney Studio, however, was not concerned with degrees as such. The review board was just as likely to pull a promising freshman out of CalArts and offer him a job on the lot as they were to wait and choose from the crop of graduating seniors. In Burton's case, this was very fortunate, since the scholarship his high-school artwork had garnered him (to the extremely pricey school) had been rescinded in his third year there. It is unlikely Tim would have been able to finish school had Disney not chosen him to become an animator on the strength of his submission piece, a brief bit of pencil test animation (essentially a rough sketch cartoon) called *Stalk of the Celery*. (It was a work Burton dismissed later as "stupid.")

Burton suddenly found himself a fully employed animator at work on Disney's *The Fox and the Hound* (1981). It was the lot's latest attempt to repeat what they perceived as Walt Disney's formula: a rather saccharine, eighty-three-minute narrative about the childhood friendship between the two natural enemies of the title and how it plays out as their tendencies emerge. It features the voices of such decidedly non-Burtonesque performers as Sandy Duncan and Mickey Rooney.

At the studio, Tim was assigned to Disney staffer Glenn Kean, an animator of the old school. Upon discovering that his new acquisition's talents didn't run toward drawing "cute fox scenes," Kean assigned the newcomer to dealing with more distant shots—the long shots where detail wasn't so important. The results for Burton were far from pleasant. His attempt to force himself into doing something he neither believed in, nor identified with, resulted in a significantly unpleasant period where he has spoken of sleeping upward of fourteen hours a day—ten at home and another four at work. This psychological escape mechanism—technically called hypersomnia—is a classic symptom of a serious form of depression. Burton openly hated the entire experience of animating someone else's ideas. He later commented to the *Washington Post,* "And let me tell you, hearing Sandy Duncan's voice in slow motion for a year is not my idea of fun. It's like Chinese water torture. I just couldn't do it."

This, and Tim's generally erratic behavior (he took to sitting in a closet or hiding under his desk to avoid dealing with anyone), did little to help Burton form any strong ties to his co-workers. Overall, his depression and his unusual talents came across only as strangeness. He was still very much the outsider, and probably the only thing that saved him from being fired was the generally confused atmosphere of a film studio in search of a direction in the late 1970s.

Some measure of salvation came the following year when the studio decided that perhaps Burton's talents might be put to better use as a "conceptual artist" and not as an animator. Instead of trying to draw other people's ideas, Burton would be allowed to have a shot at creating the ideas themselves. This at least afforded him a degree of creative freedom. The only problem was that nothing ever came of his efforts. They were admired, even praised, but that would be the end of it. "It was a very weird relationship, because on the one hand they let me get away with murder, but it was like, 'Don't tell anybody,'" Burton noted of this period in his career. These brilliant ideas (including the one that would become *Tim Burton's The Nightmare Before Christmas,* [1993]) were going nowhere at an alarming rate (Burton had spent a year coming up with ideas and designs that were never used); and what good is all the artistic freedom in the world if no one ever sees it? Burton may often appear as if he doesn't court popular acceptance, but without some kind of an audience there can be no real sense of validation. The idea of an artist who doesn't need an audience is too absurd to seriously contemplate.

In an ill-advised effort to blend the old and the new (the Disney hierarchy was not about to commit themselves to anything all that daring at this point) and to find something for Burton to do, they teamed Burton with "old school" artist Adreas Deja to design what would become one of the studio's few animated financial disasters, *The Black Cauldron* (1985). It was not a collaboration in any sense of the word. Deja did his usual thing and Burton let his fertile— and too-long-untapped—imagination run free, and never the twain did meet. Not surprisingly, it was Deja's work that ended up in the eighty-minute effort. Burton's was considered, as always, just a little too "weird" to be of any "commercial" use. This kind of conceptual work that went nowhere did have a payoff, though—in the form of the admiration of two of the Disney higher-ups, producer Julie Hickson and head of creative development Tom Wilhite.

They sensed that Burton's originality might be worth exploring, at least tentatively, in the search for a sense of direction.

In his spare time, Burton had been working on a children's book he called *Vincent*. It was a kind of homage to his beloved Vincent Price, whose movies had meant so much to him in childhood—an homage and perhaps a chance to exorcise childhood demons. At the very least, a film version of it, such as Hickson and Wilhite suggested, would allow him to present his first vision of childhood as he saw it, to the world at large. Three years had been spent at Disney and nothing that could truly be called Burton's had come of it. Now, armed with a minimal $60,000 of Disney money and the use of the Disney facilities, thanks to his new benefactors, he had the chance to create something on-camera wholly his own. The results were little short of phenomenal—five minutes of the essence of Tim Burton.

Teaming for the first time with Disney animator Rick Heinrichs, Burton brought his little story of seven-year-old Vincent Malloy peculiarly to life in *Vincent* (1982). As a rule, animated films are either traditional "cel" animation in which a series of drawings are photographed a frame at a time to give the illusion of movement, or they are three-dimensional stop-frame animation where jointed models are carefully moved between single-frame shots to produce the same effect. In an unusual move, Burton opted to combine both forms and the starkest of black-and-white imagery, producing something just a little unlike anything previously seen by filmgoers.

"There's something about three-dimensional animation that I've always found in certain instances to be more powerful, more real. I've never liked animation just for animation's sake. I think it should serve whatever the story is," Burton explained in an interview for the special laserdisc edition of *Tim Burton's The Nightmare Before Christmas*, further commenting on its earlier use in *Vincent*: "Well, *Vincent* is something where I wanted to experiment, using stop-motion, but techniques usually fall into one category—like we're going to do all claymation or stop-motion. What we liked to do was use lots of different techniques—even use some two-cel animation mixed with the three-dimensional to give it this slightly different, maybe more graphic qualities." Thematically, it was unlike much that had been seen before. Certainly, it bore little relation to anything ever bearing the Disney name.

On the surface, *Vincent* is merely a slightly twisted story about a boy who escapes from the boredom of his all-too-ordinary middle-class existence by imagining he is Vincent Price, much to the chagrin of his mother. Burton even appears to play by certain animation fantasy rules in adopting the very typical cartoon approach of presenting the adults in the little film as nothing more than a pair of legs and never the whole person, carefully depersonalizing these "extraneous" characters. In Burton's hands, however, this cliché takes on added significance—in the case of Vincent Malloy (and Burton), they are depersonalized to begin with, less real than the fantasy elements that otherwise fill the short subject. Consciously or not, Burton adapted a cartoon convention and then subverted it simply by giving it a meaning. It was but one of several telling aspects packed into the movie's five minutes.

Frankly autobiographical—Burton's claim that the big-eyed, wild-haired Vincent onscreen was not deliberately made to look like himself is the only thing about the entire project that doesn't ring true—*Vincent* is a charming and apt self-portrait in miniature and one of the first times that anyone had dared to depict the inherent cruelty and viciousness of a child on the screen. True, there had been monster children in the movies before this; the little horrors of *These Three* (1936), for example, and its remake, *The Children's Hour* (1962), not to mention the homicidal child of *The Bad Seed* (1956). (Television had been even more to the point in certain episodes of the classic *The Twilight Zone* and *Alfred Hitchcock Presents,* both of which very likely formed part of Burton's mindset.) However, these were unmistakably *not* films for children and were also by no means intended to picture anything but an aberrant child.

For all intents and purposes, *Vincent* was in part a children's film and its protagonist was not some warped horror, but rather a fairly common depiction of a child of Burton's generation. Without anyone realizing it, Burton had just dragged Disney up to date. The precocious and precious sitcom-cute children that had populated Disney films long after they had any relation to reality (if they ever did) were replaced now by something very real—and to the studio, unsettling. (It's unlikely anyone on the lot quite understood why, instead seizing on the film's overall weirdness and its striking *Cabinet of Dr. Caligari* images as the reason for their unease.) The idea that a nonvillainous, nonmonstrous child of seven should dwell on the morbid and the fantastic, play with the idea of turning his dog into a monstrous zombie, and even fantasize about dipping his frightening aunt in a vat of hot wax to add her to his "wax museum" (à la Vincent Price's *House of Wax* [1953]) was indeed abhorrent to them. It had no connection to anything Disney.

Just how little the studio understood or felt at ease with the film is clearly demonstrated by their efforts to convince Burton to change its ending. The movie short climaxes with young Vincent feigning death—with a wholly typical child's flair for the dramatic—as a preferable alternative to his mother's insistence that he go out and play in the sun, or, in other words, go pretend to be like a traditional, Disney-style seven-year-old. Tim stops here. The studio, apparently concerned that viewers would think Vincent actually dead, wanted a "happy ending" grafted onto this when they saw the finished work. Worse, they wanted an ending where Vincent is snapped out of his morbidity and becomes Disneyized, "normal," by having his father (conspicuously absent from the rest of the film) suddenly invite him to a ball game. Not only would such an ending have been absurd—Vincent would surely rather *really* die than go to a ball game—it would have subverted the entire cinematic concept. That was not what mattered to the studio. What mattered to them was that it would restore the status quo. Amazingly—and probably only because it was an inexpensive and dubiously marketable short film—they did not insist on the changes and left the project alone. However, they quietly consigned it to near oblivion, relegating it to the more "artistic" film-festival circuit, where it received good press and awards in its limited showings in Seattle, Chicago, and London.

Looked at today, *Vincent*, for all its intrinsic merit, seems almost like a preview of the films that follow—both thematically and stylistically. Many of the designs and fantasticated creatures would reappear in *Pee-Wee's Big Adventure* (1985), *Beetlejuice* (1988), *Batman Returns* (1989), and *Tim Burton's The Nightmare Before Christmas* (1993). The preoccupation with childhood as a kind solitary hell enlivened only by the richness of one's own imagination and creativity recurs in various forms in every Tim Burton film that comes after *Vincent*. And, of course, there is Vincent Price (1911–1993), Burton's beloved horror icon, who would make one of his final cinematic appearances in *Edward Scissorhands* (1990).

Securing Price's services as narrator of *Vincent* was probably the high point of Burton's early moviemaking career. Here was validation in the extreme!

Price read the storyboards Burton and his producers sent him, understood the idea at once, and accepted the assignment. "I was so struck by Tim's amateur charm. I mean *amateur* in the French sense of the word: in love with something. Tim was in love with the medium and dedicated to it," Price explained.

What bigger boost could there have been to this tongue-tied filmmaker than the endorsement and participation of his childhood hero? Scarcely anything could have touched this—at least, as it turned out, since Price was everything Burton imagined him to be. (Burton's own claim that "there's a reason why you respond to certain people on the screen—there's some sort of light there, they project something beyond even what their character is" is a charming bit of poetic thought that may well be exactly right.) Had Price, the veteran star, been less, it's impossible to say what sort of negative impact it may have had on Burton both as an artist and a human being. The experience completely altered Burton's worldview for the better: "I imagine it will always be the most amazing thing that ever happened, because it was a real validation. It sounds kind of corny, but it made me feel good and continues to make me feel good about what life has to offer."

Whatever misgivings Disney may have had about *Vincent* in particular, there was no doubting the talent of this strange young man, and Burton still had his adherents, especially Julie Hickson. She and Burton had not only meshed creatively, but personally. Through their professional association, the pair became romantically involved, so her interest in promoting Burton and his career took on a different aspect.

The five-minute *Vincent* proved Burton could do something, but it had the same built-in brick wall that had been encountered by Richard Lester when he made his award-winning short, *The Running, Jumping, Standing Still Film* (1960)— it was so very different that response was along the lines of, "It's brilliant and when we need a feature film like it, we'll let you know." Proof of talent is one thing. Answering the question of how to channel this talent into a full-fledged career is another matter. In Burton's case, especially within the Disney Studio environment, the answer did not seem to be forthcoming.

4 | THE REAL WORLD AS CARTOON

I left cartoons because they take so much time,
and there's a greater challenge in applying animation
ideas to live action.

TIM BURTON, 1989

THE DELIBERATELY INGENUOUS ATTITUDE TIM BURTON
constantly applies to his directorial career—that it just grew out of itself organi-
cally—may be good public relations and contribute nicely to the Burton myth;
however, it is scarcely supported by the facts. The critical praise for *Vincent* had
not actually led to anything, and he was in need of a project to follow it up.
Moreover, he wanted to branch out, get away from animation and work with
live actors. He wanted to apply his vision to the real world and transform it
into something his own. Burton knew this was not going to be an easy transition, but it was certainly a deliberate one on his part. This is at once evidenced
by Burton's own words concerning his rarely seen TV film, *Hansel and Gretel*
(1982), for the fledgling Disney Channel: "I had this idea of doing *Hansel and
Gretel* using only Japanese people and giving it a little bit of a twist. I had a
bunch of drawings and they let me do it." There is certainly no indication in
that statement that he was asked to do the film and every indication that it was
Burton himself who actively pitched the project to the cable network.

Actually, the idea was a shrewd one on his part—an inexpensive entry for an outlet desperately in need of product, a project just unusual enough to capture attention (one is reminded of Adolphe Menjou as the flamboyant theater director in *Gold Diggers of 1935* [1935], and his boasts of a production of *A Midsummer Night's Dream* "with an all-Eskimo cast!") and to be remembered. Best of all, it would be a project that would be seen rather than admired and shelved. In this Tim was but partly right.

His revisionist *Hansel and Gretel* was okayed, it was remembered, and it was seen. However, it was only seen once and *then* shelved. Even today, it remains the one inaccessible Burton work. One cannot but wonder if, at this point, it isn't deliberate on Burton's part. Tim has never spoken ill of the TV project, but has referred to the performances of his nonprofessional cast as "amateurish." It should be remembered that he had not previously dealt with actors, professional or otherwise, and the handling of performers is a part of the art of directing—perhaps the most subtle and undervalued part, because it is the least obvious. As a result, the little film was a very clever way of getting a feel for dealing with *people* in front of the camera. The next time at bat, Burton not only would have a solidly professional cast, but at least some idea of how to direct them. They wouldn't think him a total incompetent, and they would be sufficiently professional to cover his inexperience. This might have been partly instinctual on Burton's part, but to suggest that it was all largely accidental is asking for a level of credulity difficult to muster.

The rewards of *Vincent* and *Hansel and Gretel* were far from immediate. Burton went back to marking time, but while he did this, he and Julie Hickson were planning the groundwork for his first "real" movie. It would still be a short film, though Burton has expressed his belief that with a little more time and money, it could have been expanded into a feature-length production. However, it would have real actors, solid production values, and be shot on film, as opposed to the TV videotaping technique employed on *Hansel and Gretel*. The project was called *Frankenweenie* (1982).

Frankenweenie marked Burton's debut as a serious director of actors, and he managed to underpin the film with the solid support of performers like Shelley

Duvall, Daniel Stern, and reliable character actors Paul Bartel and Joseph Maher. He imbued this thoroughly charming suburban take on *Frankenstein* with a measure of professionalism and gloss that helped put it over the top artistically. The naturalness of young Barrett Oliver as Victor Frankenstein was another asset, even if some of the supporting cast were a bit more awkward in roles that, admittedly, were little more than rough sketches by its creator.

The story line is simple, but perfect for the piece. Young Victor Frankenstein is a backyard filmmaker (referred to as "another Alfred Hitchcock" by his parents, an accolade neatly dismissed by Victor as "that fat guy on television") whose beloved dog (and star), Sparky, is run over by a car. The devastated child decides—on the strength of a grade-school science lesson involving making a dead frog jump with electricity—that he will resurrect his pet. This he does with all the élan and gravity of a prepubescent Colin Clive (of James Whale's 1931 *Frankenstein*), but his creation is not a monster in any sense, despite the fact that the neighbors, faced with this somewhat unlikely situation, feel otherwise. When they frighten the reanimated Sparky, he panics and runs, and they turn into a mob, tracking him and Victor to an abandoned miniature-golf course. The pair take refuge in the course's windmill hazard, which is accidentally set ablaze. Sparky rescues Victor and then expires from the exertion, only to be revived by a jolt from the neighbors' cars when they see the error of their ways. It paves the way to a happy ending where Sparky meets a girlfriend in the form of a poodle with a Bride of Frankenstein coiffure.

The brilliance of *Frankenweenie* is not in its savvy re-creation of bits and pieces from Whale's *Frankenstein*, though this is clearly the model for much of its look. This is not a satire, nor is it a quick knockoff. Consciously or otherwise, Burton offers us a childhood view of the world as filtered through an imagination fed on movies like *Frankenstein* and *Bride of Frankenstein* (1935). Like *Vincent,* the short is clearly fantasticated autobiography, but with a very significant advancement. Where *Vincent* drew a very obvious line between its hero's fantasy world and the real world, *Frankenweenie* completely blurs any distinction between the two universes. The result of this seemingly casual approach is a strangely organic work quite unlike anything previously done, and quite the most incisive portrait of a mid-1960s childhood imaginable. It is childhood as it appears to a child, not as an adult would like to imagine it.

Its undeniable merits to one side, the most remarkable thing about *Frankenweenie* is just how much it defines Tim Burton, his childhood, his perception of that childhood, and, perhaps most of all, how very much it constructs the myth that Burton has surrounded himself with personally.

In one sense, Tim obviously re-creates his old neighborhood with its nearby cemetery (here transformed into a very cleverly designed pet cemetery, where the various tombstone shapes relate to the deceased animal; e.g., a cross that appears to be formed by two bone-shaped dog biscuits) and proliferation of miniature-golf courses (here, a mysterious and spooky affair that figures cleverly in the plot). The very interesting aspect is the off-the-cuff manner in which he effortlessly incorporates these bits of childhood gothic into the very real tapestry of a solidly real, satirically idealized suburbia. If there is any gasp at all from the viewer, it is one of sheer delight, not one of disbelief. The reason is simple—Burton spoke directly to his own generation and, in many ways, to those that followed. There is an innate sense of recognition, a feeling of, "Yes, this is how childhood seemed."

No one had done anything like this before. No one had seen anything like this. And that, of course, would be precisely the problem in the eyes of the Disney people. The deadly earnestness of childhood, the mysteriousness of the everyday object transformed into something it resembles by a child's imagination, the fantasy play of, in this case, being a "mad scientist" that isn't play at all, were fresh, vibrant, and startlingly real—largely because Burton just presents them as a given reality in *Frankenweenie*. When everyday objects like Christmas reindeer, old fish tanks, cast-off bicycles, swing sets, kitschy lamps, and purloined toasters become workable parts of Victor's mad scientist laboratory, the result isn't shocking because of its incongruity, but because of its familiarity, tapping into a collective consciousness of the mysteries of childhood. What imaginative child, having just seen Whale's *Frankenstein* on television and then going to a miniature-golf course and seeing one of the familiar windmills, would not conjure up images of Dr. Frankenstein and his monster creation in their life-and-death tussle atop the burning building in that film? However, it took an adult of Tim's particular genius to *remember* that feeling and to create something from it.

As a picture of Burton's own childhood, there are clearly areas in *Frankenweenie* where he rewrites history. The Frankenstein house has far more relevance to TV's *Leave It to Beaver* than anything Burton has suggested about his own childhood home. He has described the latter as boxy, and has related stories of his bed-room windows being blocked in by his parents. This is hardly the sort of house pictured in *Frankenweenie*. Then, too, the onscreen parents are obviously some-what idealized. They are pictured as indulgent and distracted, which certainly squares with the facts of much of Burton's childhood, However, neither Daniel Stern's Ward Cleaveresque father nor Shelley Duvall's June Cleaverish mother (all pearls and perpetual chocolate-chip cookies) do anything to suggest the kind of undercurrents that drove Burton to go live with his grandmother while still in high school. Just as clearly, Burton never intended this to be a literal ver-sion of his life. Instead he slyly opted to send up on-camera the sitcom-perfect world his parents' generation attempted to wish into existence or pretended *did* exist, when that didn't quite work.

On a purely technical level, *Frankenweenie* is a little marvel. Burton's delib-erate use of the kind of studio-bound gothic with its painted-canvas skies and utterly stylized settings that marked Whale's *Frankenstein* was both delightful and slightly shocking as he re-created them on the Disney soundstages and jux-taposed these scenes with location shooting for the suburban neighborhood itself. It was shocking because it recalled techniques not used in film for years, but which were once fairly common. What no one knew at the time, of course, was that Burton was about to make them common again, at least where his own screen work was concerned.

Apart from *Frankenweenie*'s notable achievements, both on a technical level and in the realm of its re-creation of a certain era of childhood, it boasts the thematic implications with which Burton has come to be so closely associated. Despite Victor having an apparent circle of friends—typically nameless, and looking for all the world like a generic Disney mix of kids that were foisted on the film—Victor is very much alone in the world. His backyard filmmaking effort, *Monsters from Long Ago,* has only one cast member—his dog Sparky. His experiments are conducted without assistance and the results are kept to him-self. Once the screen story is under way, in fact, the obligatory children vanish from the scene and only one, rather unpleasant little girl (whose primary func-tion is to scream upon seeing the revived Sparky) remains. The story's neigh-bors themselves are at the very least odd, and certainly incomprehensible in their actions. Most notably, they are ready to turn from their vaguely eccentric normalcy into a bloodthirsty mob as soon as they encounter something—in this case, Sparky—that is out of their concept of the world as it should be. Given some of Burton's subsequent statements, it isn't hard to believe that he feels they are attacking Victor as much as his creation, simply because he dared to create anything. In this cinematic presentation, Burton effectively—though affectionately and none too harshly—attacks the very core audience at whom the Disney product is aimed. Small wonder they didn't know quite what to do with the completed twenty-five-minute film.

Another inherently unsettling area of the offering—and a theme that Burton touches on again and again in subsequent works—is what it consciously leaves out of the story of *Frankenstein*. There is no moral. Burton's Frankenstein is not punished for daring to emulate God. Indeed, God doesn't enter into it at all. No one even suggests that this creation of life might be an affront to God, only that it's out of the ordinary and needs removing. The reaction is essentially no different to what they might have done if an "undesirable" family had moved in down the street. These people are clearly the basically nonreligious "Protestants" of Burton's childhood. Family films that don't at least pay lip service to some notion of religion—especially in a context that normally does so—are certainly not the sort of thing one expects to find bearing the Disney Studio logo!

Somewhat surprisingly, Disney actually liked *Frankenweenie*. They liked it well enough to plan to release it with their reissue of *Pinocchio* (1940). Burton was ecstatic. At last, something of his was actually going to be seen—and what better exposure than as the opening act for an established Disney classic? What, indeed. No one, however, had reckoned on the Motion Picture Association of America's rating board, who screened *Frankenweenie* and promptly slapped a PG (Parental Guidance) rating on it. The rating rendered Burton's film useless as a companion to the G-rated *Pinocchio*, since no theatre chain would book a General Audience–rated feature with a short film bearing a harsher rating. Everyone was stunned. What was wrong with *Frankenweenie*? There was no real violence, no nudity, no swearing. So what could have earned it a PG? The answer was simple. The whole tone of the film was wrong for children. It was too dark. It was too morbid. It was too weird. More likely than not, it was just too true to childhood to sit well with the board.

Disney might have fought the MPAA and they might have won, or at least negotiated some compromise (though it is impossible to imagine what it might have been, short of grafting a cautionary message onto the film). However, at this juncture, Burton's supporters on the Burbank lot found themselves out and a new regime of executives took control of the studio. "Officially," they liked *Frankenweenie,* but they were not willing to bother themselves about it. Why should they? It was an inconsequential, fairly inexpensive, movie short. And, as anyone who has ever dealt in the power side of the arts knows, there is nothing so dead as the preceding administration's projects. It's a lose-lose situation. If it fails, the new regime is blamed. If it succeeds, the old regime wins the credit. Disney did release *Frankenweenie* in Great Britain as the opener for the PG-rated *Baby: Secret of the Lost Legend* in 1985. However, that did nothing for Burton's standing. In essence, *Frankenweenie* suffered the same fate as *Vincent.* It was shelved and forgotten and consigned to oblivion until 1992, by which time Tim was too powerful and too popular to ignore and the short film finally appeared on videotape.

Burton was understandably disappointed, and quickly becoming disillusioned with the motion-picture industry. He had made three films and, ultimately, none of them had received much exposure. Even by the time *Beetlejuice* came out in 1988, the handling of Tim's creative output was a sore spot with him. "*Vincent* and *Frankenweenie* going unreleased has been a constant source of frustration to me. Disney owns both films. *I* can't even get a copy of them," he complained to *Starlog* magazine. At the time, he was certainly burnt out with Disney, so when Shelley Duvall offered him a chance to direct an episode of her *Faerie Tale Theatre* for the Showtime Cable network, he leapt at the opportunity to try something different for someone—virtually anyone—else.

Aladdin and His Wonderful Lamp was not one of Burton's wiser choices creatively. The Mark Curtiss–Rod Ash teleplay was weak and even such performers as Robert Carradine (as Aladdin), Leonard Nimoy (as the Evil Magician), and James Earl Jones (as the Genie) could not do much to bring any real life or substance to it. Burton's staunchest supporters want to find something to admire in the forty-seven-minute offering. They tend to settle on aspects of the production design, which does manage to incorporate a number of standard Burton touches. However, basically the video film is a poor showing, impossibly cheap and cursed by the limitations of being a three-camera video work and knocked off in a week's time. Tim's inexperience with actors is much more obvious here than in *Frankenweenie,* and the whole thing comes across as utterly impersonal and completely disposable. Ironically, since it was made specifically for children, it is the only Burton work that might be said to condescend to children. The performances have all the sense of commitment one expects from grown-ups not trying very hard, since their audience is none-too-critical. It was, however, industry work. It wasn't done for Disney, and it did get seen. Ironically, though, it was Burton's largely unseen *Frankenweenie* (sometimes in Hollywood, good word of mouth about a film almost no one has seen can be more valuable than a demonstrably brilliant work) that would really open the door for him. It was all thanks to the most unlikely star ever to come along in the Hollywood firmament.

5 | KINDRED SPIRITS

I know I am, but what are you?

PAUL REUBENS

in *Pee-Wee's Big Adventure* (1985)

OF THE MORE INEXPLICABLE PHENOMENA IN THE 1980S, near the top of the list is Pee-Wee Herman, the brainchild (or brainless child) of Paul Reubens (born August 27, 1952), who played his bizarre creation on TV to the very hilt. At one time or another, Herman has been likened to virtually every classic comedian from silent-film comic Harry Langdon (to whom Pee-Wee *does* bear a certain physical resemblance) to musical comedy star Eddie Cantor. (In fact, the biker-bar sequence in *Pee-Wee's Big Adventure* actually recycles a Cantor routine from *Roman Scandals* [1933], when Pee-Wee tries to escape being harmed by murderous bikers by injecting his own suggestion, "Let him go," into their nefarious plans for his demise.) Nevertheless, Herman's persona was—and remains—largely unique.

Unlike the classic screen comics such as Chaplin or Laurel and Hardy, Pee-Wee Herman—he of the high-pitched voice and bow tie—was never meant to be attractive, or grounded in reality. Rather, the character is like an extended in-joke with most of the humor stemming from the viewer being part of a select circle. In the mid-1980s it was impossibly hip to be a fan of Pee-Wee, who first burst onto the scene in 1981 with the cult TV hit *The Pee-Wee Herman Show*. In turn, it spawned a Saturday-morning children's TV show, *Pee-Wee's Playhouse,* in 1986, a singularly peculiar success that defied all the odds by being "stupid" enough to appeal to children, while simultaneously being sufficiently savvy to draw a much older crowd. The TV show was an almost schizophrenic mix of kiddie material and pretty adult innuendo comedy, centered around Reubens's fanciful creation.

Dressed in a gray suit with a red bow tie, sporting a hairdo that the mid-1950s Jerry Lewis might have rejected, obvious lipstick, rouged cheeks, and behaving like a demented five-year-old with an impossibly grating voice, Pee-Wee Herman was designed first and foremost to catch attention (which he did) and hold it, by the sheer force of his outrageousness (which he also did). He made a virtue of being deliberately irritating in a manner that made him subversive: "I want the show to be really wacky, so when kids are finished watching they will be filled with creative energy," he told *Time* magazine, in a statement designed just to delight any parent hoping for a little peace and quiet. Perhaps his most bizarre attribute, though, was his sexuality. What *was* this strange man-child? For all intents and purposes, Pee-Wee Herman was essentially sexless, but his very outfit was at cross-purposes with this image. He may have been the perennial child and the living embodiment of the "nerd" as hero, but why, then, did he choose to wear the most indelicately-tailored tight trousers since the early days of the Beatles and the Rolling Stones? If the character and his antics seemed childish, the bulge in his form-fitting pants constantly hinted at something far less innocent.

Having captured a large following on TV, it was natural that Reubens would be offered a chance to take his Pee-Wee character to the big screen. This eventuality transpired thanks to the interest of Warner Bros. studio production executive Bonni Lee (who had seen a print of *Frankenweenie,* thanks to a copy of it being in the hands of one of its staunchest supporters, horrormeister Stephen King, who was convinced Burton was going to be an important filmmaker) who insisted on screening the short for Reubens. Immediately, the TV star knew exactly who he wanted for a director—Tim Burton. This was a very shrewd choice on his part. For one thing, there was an obvious similarity between them in terms of senses of humor. Then, too, Reubens would be better able to control a first-time director and assure that his screen debut would not be Hollywoodized into something other than the original concept.

Moreover, Reubens's childishness and his affinity for kitschy art was remarkably in tune with Burton's. Producers Robert Shapiro (whose production outfit, Aspen Film Society, was spearheading the project) and Richard Gilbert Abramson were quick to agree.

Tim was himself immediately drawn to the script for *Pee-Wee's Big Adventure* (by Phil Hartman, Reubens, and Paul Varhol) for two extremely simple reasons. First, he could relate to the Pee-Wee character—especially as concerns the obsession over an object (in this case a bicycle), the value of which is vague to the world at large—and second, the script scarcely told a story at all. Both of these aspects are worth considering in some depth to understand Burton the filmmaker. The admission that he could identify with the Pee-Wee character, whom he has referred to as being in a state of "permanent adolescence," is a contradiction of his own objections to being perceived as remaining in touch with the "child inside." Of course, people in general and artists in particular are more than entitled to a bit of self-contradiction, but whether he likes it or not, Tim demonstrates over and over again that he most certainly *has* kept contact with the "child inside" and, in particular, with his own childhood.

Every one of his films touches on this—for that matter, so do his works outside of movies. However, in this instance, part of that sense of identification with the Pee-Wee character has less to do with specifics, than with the more generalized aspect that the character simply behaves as he wishes without regard for how this behavior might be viewed. Pee-Wee is very simply himself at all times and demands to be taken on those terms. This is central to Burton's own views and allows him to thumb his nose at suburbia once again—a little more pointedly this time by taking an alternate path. This round, instead of the neighbors not understanding and wanting to remove the nonconforming element (as they did in *Frankenweenie*), they pretend it isn't there at all.

No one in the entire feature film ever questions Pee-Wee's appearance or his behavior, giving them the appearance not so much of tolerance, but of willful blindness. It is on exactly the same level as pretending that you don't know that the old lady down the street is a terrible lush, or that the man three doors down cheats on his wife. So long as the surface is maintained, everything is fine. Pee-Wee takes this a step further, though, by deliberately assaulting their senses in this cinematic excursion. It is one thing to ignore the strangeness that goes on behind closed doors; it is another to ignore a bright red house with Santa's reindeer on the roof 365 days a year and a yard filled with eccentric statuary, not to mention Pee-Wee himself! By crossing that line, Burton and his co-conspirators make their point. The suburbanites who can ignore the largely unseen, only seem mildly self-deluded; the ones who can ignore a house like Pee-Wee's seem downright mentally defective. However, it is very much the same thing.

The script's lack of much of a story is another matter. For this particular project, the dismissal of a story line in favor of a series of loosely connected and fantasticated incidents works beautifully. (Indeed, one of the things that ruins the non-Burton sequel, *Big Top Pee-Wee* [1988], is the fact that here Pee-Wee is totally submerged in an ocean of plot.) The film is allowed literally to unfold in a series of ever-more-inventive vignettes, in a refreshing manner that has the good sense to make the viewer feel "in" on the joke. However, this one film's approach would tag Burton with a not-entirely-deserved stereotype as a brilliant visualist who cannot tell a coherent story on-camera.

With a script in place and Burton and Reubens in seemingly unshakable accord, *Pee-Wee's Big Adventure* lacked only one element to emerge as the perfect Tim Burton debut feature. That element arrived when the studio allowed Burton his choice of music composer. Burton chose Danny Elfman, lead singer, songwriter, and guiding force behind the high-energy rock group Oingo Boingo. To call that choice auspicious would be one of the great understatements of all time. It was—and is—nothing less than a match made in heaven; their collaboration has been likened to that of Alfred Hitchcock and Bernard Herrmann, as well as Fellini and Nino Rota—and *Pee-Wee's Big Adventure* allowed Elfman to evoke both! And yet, it is also one of the most unlikely teamings imaginable, despite a not-dissimilar stance to what Kevin Allman in *Details* magazine called a "suburban malcontent." Where Burton is the shy, seemingly inarticulate introvert, Elfman is the exact opposite: outgoing, well-spoken, a lovably natural ham, and very over-the-top.

Although both are deliberate outsiders, Elfman has always been more confrontational and contentious. In forming his rock group (an offshoot of brother Richard's The Mystic Knights of the Oingo Boingo), Danny went out of his way to create something almost unworkable by simply requiring far too many musicians (a total of seven rather than the usual four) to be economically viable, and following this up by mixing the sounds of rock, punk, and 1930s jazz—all wrapped up in an impossible name! "I wanted to piss everybody off! If anybody banded together as a movement, I was against them and I wanted to offend them," Elfman told an interviewer later. The almost patented and curiously sexless innocence of Burton's worldview, however, found a strange soul mate in the wild-man author of such outrageous songs as "Nasty Habits" (a satiric jibe at kinky masturbatory practices behind closed curtains), "Little Girls" (a take on a penchant for young girls and the legal ramifications—"The little girl was just a little too little"), and "Wild Sex in the Working Class" (a factory worker keeps going by fantasizing about the similarities between sex and the movement of the machinery he tends). Intriguingly, one of the very few public references Burton has ever made on the topic of sex is when he likened the magic Elfman experienced doing his first film score to an individual's first sexual encounter.

Born May 29, 1953, Danny Elfman was five years Burton's senior and that separation of a few years allowed him to add a level of conscious intellectual observation to the time period that formed and still haunts the filmmaker. Elfman, whose influence extends beyond music, added a layer of sophisticated savvy that Burton's previous work had lacked. While not an active participant in the making of *Pee-Wee's Big Adventure,* there are clear indications that Elfman's work had been in mind long before his arrival: Several aspects of the film's set design—notably the nightmarish skeleton silhouettes in Pee-Wee's house—are pure Elfman and might have been taken from an Oingo Boingo album cover. In a way, this is not surprising, since Elfman's rock music had always boasted a cinematic edge, the result of a lifelong interest in the movies ("If you had asked me in high school, I would have told you I wanted to be a cinematographer. Anything but a musician," Elfman has noted).

Elfman's partnership with Burton was immediately both unusual and idyllic. "Rather than telling me exactly what he wants orchestrally, Tim will show me a scene and describe the feeling he wants to get across. Then I'll go to the studio and try to find that feeling in music," Elfman explains. And from the very first notes that grace *Pee-Wee's Big Adventure,* it is obvious that Elfman has a special knack for connecting to just what Burton requires to accompany his film's visuals and dialogue. Elfman's quirky scoring is the musical equivalent of

Burton's particular cinematic and thematic style. It takes the familiar and uses it to push the envelope, always going just a little bit farther than seems completely logical, but never quite teetering over the edge.

Elfman's movie scores for Burton are not secondary items. They are not background scores in the usual sense, but are on an almost equal footing with the films—in fact, the scores are rarely used as *background* at all. In more cases than not, the scoring takes over mostly when the talking stops and the Burton imagery and Elfman score hold sway.

Burton's basic claim that he had been a fan of Elfman's music from seeing the band play in Los Angeles clubs is probably true to a degree. However, it also seems more than likely that he was familiar with Richard Elfman's quirky film, *Forbidden Zone* (1980), an utterly unique work, fueled by equal measures of Max Fleischer's *Betty Boop* cartoons and outrageous sexuality (almost everyone in the movie will have sex with almost anyone—and anything—with little or no prompting). Danny Elfman not only wrote songs and a smattering of incidental music for his brother's feature film, but appeared in it in the unlikely guise of a lecherous Satan redefined as Cab Calloway, performing a wigged-out and lyrically altered version of "Minnie the Moocher." *Forbidden Zone* became a quasi-underground hit (and also made the *Village Voice*'s ten best list for the year). Despite the picture's overt sexuality, which is certainly antithetical to Burton's own work, it is something that would undoubtedly appeal to every other aspect of his mindset, with its references to old cartoons, outrageousness, and a breathtaking blend of live-action and animation. That *Forbidden Zone* would play a key role in Burton's attraction to Elfman as the composer for his project seems inevitable.

With the script, the star, and the composer lined up, in accord, and ready to go, *Pee-Wee's Big Adventure* was an almost flawless first-time Hollywood feature filmmaking experience for Burton. The film's modest $6 million budget (the wholesale use of Los Angeles and easily accessible nearby locations, and the staging of the film's biggest scene on the Warner Bros. lot itself, helped here, making the only real location expense the famous visit to the Alamo in San Antonio, Texas) kept the studio from interfering with the shoot. Their one concern was Tim's ability to helm a feature, and they hedged this bet by surrounding him with veteran technicians, who could be relied on to get him through the experience.

6 | BURTON UNBOUND

There are a lot of things about me you don't know
anything about, Dotty—things you wouldn't
understand, things you couldn't understand, things
you shouldn't understand.

PAUL REUBENS
in *Pee-Wee's Big Adventure* (1985)

FROM THE VERY OPENING SHOT, IT IS OBVIOUS THAT
Pee-Wee's Big Adventure is not going to be an ordinary movie, especially for its
era. Even before the screen credits unfold, Elfman's jaunty circus music is on the
soundtrack, while the credits themselves are almost Woody Allenlike in their
aggressive plainness, something that is completely at odds with the kind of
grabbing flashiness that marked Hollywood films in the mid-1980s.

Once the film proper is under way, the viewer is mystifyingly greeted
with the image of the Eiffel Tower, which turns out to be part of a charming,
animated billboard for the "Tour de France" bicycle race. As the camera continues to pull back, the bicyclists themselves race into view down a road that is
clearly nowhere but southern California. Into this throng of professional riders
on racing bikes comes Pee-Wee, garbed in his standard outfit, riding a clunky,
1950s-style bike and handily blowing away his competitors as he breezes past
them to the finish line. His triumph is captured in a breathless crane shot, all
decked out in confetti, streamers, balloons, unreal sunshine, Pop Art colors, and

Elfman's mockingly triumphant music. Burton and company are working overtime to keep the experience consciously about the movie; almost as if the viewer, at first being urged to suspend disbelief, is subsequently *dared* to attempt any such suspension. It quickly transpires that this is a dream sequence when Pee-Wee's rapturous victory vanishes as his alarm clock goes off. The tone and willfully nonstructured structure is immediately established—the picture has actually started with a pointless digression. It is merely the first of many, and one of the tamer ones at that.

This flight of fancy only serves to propel us into the most fantastic and pointlessly joyous excess imaginable, the world of Pee-Wee's house. Filled with toys and Rube Goldberg gadgets, the home exists for no other reason than to delight its owner-occupant. That none of Pee-Wee's gadgets seem to work quite right matters not in the least. The bizarrely elaborate equipment that is supposed to result in an animatronic Abraham Lincoln flipping its creator's morning flapjacks may only result in a pancake-encrusted ceiling, but the mere enjoyment of the concept completely entrances him and the viewer. It deftly suggests that the rest of us are missing a big slice of life simply because we are too inhibited to enjoy everything for its own sake. Pee-Wee's wide-eyed exuberance is immediately nothing less than liberating.

There is, however, another side to this scene. It becomes evident as soon as Pee-Wee's most cherished possession—his vintage custom bicycle (stored in a hidden recess in a hedge and unveiled with all the ceremony that befits what is effectively Pee-Wee's costar)—comes into play and his annoying rich friend, Francis (Mark Holton), makes a bid to have his father buy the bike for his birthday. The dialogue consists entirely of childish insults (mostly centering on the phrase, "I know you are, but what am I?"). However, the image is suggestive of something else altogether, since both Pee-Wee and Francis are grown men playing at being little boys. Once more, the thrust is at suburbia, reducing the kind of petty squabbling inherent in these small inner communities to the level it really is—overgrown kids fighting over the most unimportant and even ridiculous issues. It is impossible to watch this film sequence and not come away with our own self-importance being a little less intact.

Happily skipping from vignette to vignette, the nine-minute feature then follows Pee-Wee to a 1960s-style shopping center where he carefully—to the point of overkill—chains his beloved bicycle to an animatronic clown outside a theatre that is tellingly showing a "Cartoon Cavalcade." The air of the sixties—the childhood era of nearly all of the movie's creative force—is unforced, but clearly there, only slightly skewed. It is a comic version of the kind of mix-and-match time frame that David Lynch would use to sinister effect the following year in *Blue Velvet*, and which Burton would continue to perfect with each of his succeeding screen works.

The actual children in the film move through this world, but are not part of it, speaking in 1980s slang and dressed in contemporary clothing. The marvelously 1960s-style Chuck's Bike-o-Rama only *looks* like the kind of mom-and-pop outfit that proliferated during Burton's youth, since it transpires that Chuck (Daryl Roach) himself is a black man with a thick West Indies accent ("Oh, yes. Dat's me. Dey call me Chuck"). The world of Pee-Wee, like the world of Tim Burton, is still there *under the surface,* and it is this world that Burton chooses to see and to inhabit and to present to the viewer, while carefully suggesting a realization that it isn't quite true in any but a subjective sense.

Interestingly, and tellingly, it is here that the thrust of Pee-Wee's—and, by extension, Tim's—adolescent nature comes into view, when cute bicycle mechanic Dotty (Elizabeth Daily) attempts to get him to go on a date with her. Sexual panic immediately sets in. In an effort to extricate himself from any possible embarrassment on the topic, Pee-Wee tells her, "There are a lot of things about me you don't know anything about, Dotty. . . . things you wouldn't understand, things you couldn't understand, things you *shouldn't* understand." (There is, of course, an additional resonance to this in light of Reubens's 1991 arrest on an indecency charge in a Sarasota, Florida, porno theatet, but it might also be applied to Hollywood's perception of Burton himself, and it certainly has bearing on the overall tone of Tim's work.) Interestingly, this brief flirtation with even the *idea* of sex is followed by the "punishment" of finding that his bike has been stolen, thereby tacitly suggesting a connection between sex and something bad.

Stylistically, the discovery of the theft of the bicycle shows both Burton and Danny Elfman at the height of their cinematic powers. The movie suddenly turns Hitchcockian—melodramatic angle shots and distorted images crowd the frame, the friendly animatronic clown is now menacing and taunting and Elfman serves up Bernard Herrmann–inspired shrieking strings! This is the sort of moment that the picture's aggressive nonstructure allows, of course, since there is nothing all that startling about such a work slipping in and out of other styles. The truly remarkable thing about this, though, is that it is both funny and effective in overplaying the importance of the basically mundane situation, while obviously taking Pee-Wee's personal plight very seriously indeed. This is reinforced by the subsequent police investigation where it becomes evident that the theft of his bicycle may be important to him, but rates rather far down the scale where the authorities are concerned.

Having thus wandered into what passes for the plot—or more correctly, the situation—*Big Adventure* happily speeds along from one incident to another as it follows Pee-Wee's singular escapades in pursuit of his stolen bicycle. Suspicious (correctly so, it turns out) that Francis is behind the theft, our hero explores this avenue of attack. When this fails and he alienates his friends because of his erratic behavior and all-consuming obsession about the bike, Pee-Wee seeks the guidance of a patently phony fortune-teller (Erica Yohn), who tells him that his stolen property has been stashed in the basement of the Alamo! This sends Pee-Wee on the road where he has a series of strange encounters: getting picked up by a convict (Judd Omen) on the run ("You know those little 'Do Not Remove Under Penalty of Law' labels they put on mattresses? Well, I cut one off!"); riding the rails with a Walter Brennan–type hobo (Carmen Filpi), whose incessant singing of American folk songs finally drives him to jump off the train; accepting a lift from a burly lady truck driver who turns out to be the ghostly Large Marge (Alice Nunn); having a quasi-romantic encounter with a waitress, Simone (Diane Salinger), whose dream is to live in France; earning the wrath of her inhumanly gigantic boyfriend (Jon Harris). . . .

One of the many big-screen highlights in this 1985 entry is the tour of the Alamo itself, conducted with nitwitt perfection by *Saturday Night Live*'s Jan Hooks. It works perfectly, as does much of the film's mood and humor, because it is so grounded in reality—as anyone who has ever gone on any such guided tour knows all too well. Pee-Wee, however, visibly expresses the disdain for this kind of overly perky, idiot tour yammering that the rest of us are too polite to do in real life, making the sequence very satisfying indeed for viewers.

When it turns out that not only is there no bicycle to be had, but that the Alamo doesn't even have a basement, Pee-Wee becomes involved with the waitress's vengeful boyfriend and seeks refuge by masquerading as a rodeo performer (he wins, of course). Later, he runs afoul of bikers with whom he ultimately makes friends by dancing to the Champs' "Tequila" (a hit song from Burton's and

Reubens's childhoods, which the film briefly threw back into the limelight). Finally he discovers that his bike is being used in a movie at Warner Bros., and he returns to Burbank (naturally) to reclaim his property.

Sneaking onto the studio lot, Pee-Wee dresses like one of the nuns in the impossibly saccharine movie that features his bike, and, seizing a chance, proclaims, "I'm starting a paper route right now," and pedals off through the studio with ever-angrier crowds from various productions in hot pursuit. Beautifully and breathlessly staged, the studio chase sequence is essential Burton in that it presents a film studio *not* as it is, but as Burton would wish it to be in his view of a "perfect" world. (Who but Burton, for whom both Godzilla and Christmas are of iconic importance, would craft a screen chase in which a man in a Godzilla suit would end up riding in a sleigh with Santa Claus?)

Ultimately Herman is propelled out of the studio and into suburban Burbank, where he rescues the stock from a burning pet store and is proclaimed a hero. (It is difficult not to conclude that the fact that the animals rescued from the burning store include everything *but* cats is a very deliberate poke at Burton's mother's love for them.) As a result, Warner Bros. not only forgives him for destroying several major productions (including a Godzilla movie, complete with Japanese crew, that looks suspiciously like *Monsters from Long Ago* in *Frankenweenie*), but the studio also decides to turn Pee-Wee's story into a film (starring James Brolin and Morgan Fairchild as Pee-Wee and Dotty!), which premieres at a drive-in theatre with most of the film's cast in attendance. In a parody of Spielberg's famous bicycles-across-the-moon image from *E.T.: The Extra-Terrestrial* (1982), Pee-Wee and Dotty ride off into the night on their bicycles. Had it taken itself seriously, *Pee-Wee's Big Adventure* might have been called Fellini-esque in its plotting (and, indeed, the drive-in sequence is accompanied by Elfman's evocation of the score for the Italian filmmaker's *8½*).

Warner Bros. was very pleased with the results and gave the feature a combination classy/sideshow launch with a premiere at Mann's Chinese Theatre and a follow-up carnival party with amusement-park rides, sword-swallowers, et cetera, on the roof of the nearby Holiday Inn, which was perhaps more in keeping with the movie's intent and the personalities of its creators. In his "The Great Life" column, in the August 7, 1985, issue of the *Hollywood Reporter*, George Christy devoted nearly the entire page to the premiere, which attracted such luminaries as Steve Martin, Victoria Tennant, Eddie Murphy, Rodney Dangerfield, Jim Brooks, Carol Kane, David Lee Roth, Alice Cooper, and the man who could be said to have started it all, Stephen King. Producer Shapiro and the other Warner Bros. representatives received nothing but warm congratulations on the movie, while trade reporter Christy singled out Burton (pictured with an uncommonly broad grin on his face) for praise: "The other star is Tim Burton. . . . Tim hits a bull's-eye with sight gags (some are reminiscent of Laurel and Hardy), and zeroes in on comic-strip characters with a vengeance." He even calls the film "a comedy act for all ages." Everyone involved had reason to be ecstatic.

Shot for a scant $6 million, *Pee-Wee's Big Adventure* was released in August 1985 to what can only be called mixed reviews. The movie did make Pat Dowell's (reviewer for National Public Radio) "ten best" list for the year, while *USA Today* tagged it a "demented masterpiece." David Edelstein championed the film in the *Village Voice* and, more surprisingly, Pauline Kael (*The New Yorker* magazine) came down on its side. More typically, it was called the "absolute worst movie of the year" (*Richmond Times-Dispatch*); "for, about, and by second-graders" (*People* magazine); and "tirelessly coy" (Vincent Canby, *New York Times*). Burton's success as a director hardly seemed assured with this sort of press. However, the mainstream reviewers proved only one thing—by and large the critics simply didn't understand what they were reviewing at all. (It would not be the last time that Tim's intentions were misunderstood or distorted by the community of critics.)

Fortunately, in this case box office counted for more than good reviews and Warner Bros. quickly found themselves with a freak hit on their hands. Their minuscule $6 million investment would go on to gross a staggering $45 million in tickets purchased. Tim Burton had arrived—or so it seemed.

One major change in Burton's personal life occurred just at this career point. According to a *Vanity Fair* article, "Tim Burton's Hollywood Nightmare," when *Pee-Wee's Big Adventure* was released, he ended his long-standing relationship with Julie Hickson, who had been instrumental in getting his early works at Disney made at all. Neither Burton nor Hickson will comment on the event or its causes. In fact, Burton never refers to any romantic involvement during this period of his life.

7 | INTO THE MAINSTREAM

I, myself, am *strange and unusual.*

WINONA RYDER
as Lydia Deetz in *Beetlejuice* (1988)

DESPITE THE SURPRISING COMMERCIAL SUCCESS OF
Pee-Wee's Big Adventure, Tim Burton was still looked upon as something of an
oddity in the Hollywood film business, especially since the movie clearly was
part of that freakish area that studios never quite seem to grasp (as every
attempt to set out to deliberately make one so clearly attests): the cult hit. Tim
himself was not always helpful with his "professional inarticulate" persona,
which, not without reason, worried film studios. Perhaps he was just as strange
as his screen works. Viewed from this standpoint, what they had was this odd,
frequently noncommunicative director in his late twenties with two largely
unseen short films, two almost-equally-obscure TV works, and a fluke cult hit.
He was himself not a terribly prepossessing figure, nor was his body of work.
All of this resulted in a gap of three years before his next feature film reached
movie screens. Fortunately, by then he was sufficiently secure financially so that
the question of merely living from day to day did not seriously enter the picture, nor did it drive him to accept just any assignment that came his way.

While waiting for something to come along, Burton turned his talents to a
new version of the classic Ray Bradbury episode of *Alfred Hitchcock Presents,*
"The Jar" (1986), for the revamped version of the TV series (complete with

colorized Alfred Hitchcock intros) for NBC-TV. The new rendition, which aired on March 16, 1986, was written by Michael McDowell, and moved the story from a rural setting and a sideshow carnival, to the contemporary art world. The half-hour entry featured Griffin Dunne as an unsuccessful artist, mercilessly savaged by the critics and cheated on by his wife (Fiona Lewis), until he runs across "the jar" of the title. The jar—a large apothecary affair—contains an indescribable, amorphous mass, floating in a blue liquid (a prologue set in Nazi Germany suggests that the contents are a human head), which exerts a mysterious fascination on those who view it. As a result, Dunne is catapulted to fame, at which point his wife loses her power over him and her paramour (who decides that Dunne is more capable of advancing his career than she is at this point). She tries to rid herself of the hated jar, accidentally knocking it over in the process. Caught by Dunne, he murders her, and her head takes the place of the original contents of the jar.

Burton has expressed great dissatisfaction with "The Jar," even though he was able to cast his old *Frankenweenie* cohort Paul Bartel in the role of a snobbish art critic, as well as securing the services of Elfman—here in collaboration with Oingo Boingo guitarist Steve Bartek—for the score. All in all, the episode is only an interesting footnote to Tim's career, and its major import lies in the odd resonances to Burton and his life. The idea of the wife who is willing to attach herself body and soul to whomever can best advance her career seems peculiarly apt to an artist who is himself trying to advance his career. Perhaps the most telling aspect of it is the gradual transformation of Dunne's nerdy artist into more and more of a Burtonesque figure as the story progresses. By the time Dunne's character, in a homicidal rage, surprises his wife, he has become a dead ringer for the director, wearing one of Burton's signature floral-pattern shirts, his hair going wildly in every direction. Once again, Burton hints that, like Pee-Wee Herman, there are things about him that we don't know, couldn't know, and *shouldn't* know—something far darker and more unsettling than the optimistically quirky filmmaker he has been pigeonholed as.

Whatever the shortcomings of "The Jar" may be (and mostly its failings stem merely from it not being a full-blown Burton work; there is little wrong with it on its own terms), it is certainly more central to Burton's career than his services as executive producer on the Steven Spielberg–produced TV series,

Family Dog, an animated CBS-TV series that viewed the world from the point of view of a dog. Burton became involved at the behest of former Disney colleague Brad Bird, and he seems mostly to have functioned on the project during its preliminary design stage, despite his executive-producer status. The series, which lasted on air from June to July of 1993, was neither a commercial nor critical success, and did nothing to advance the career or prestige of anyone involved. In essence, Burton spent the three years between *Pee-Wee's Big Adventure* and *Beetlejuice* spinning his artistic wheels.

Yet it was clear that there was something here—and something that Warner Bros. are willing to work with, at least to the extent of letting Burton and screenwriter Sam Hamm develop the long-awaited *Batman,* though by no means were they prepared to okay the project. (They knew that *Pee-Wee's* core audience was the youth market—the same base market to which a comic-book film must inevitably be aimed.) Instead, it was now up to Burton to prove himself a viable filmmaker to the studio honchos. Could he be trusted to turn out a solidly commercial movie?

Not surprisingly, the Hollywood mindset had already proven a major stumbling block. The success of *Pee-Wee's Big Adventure* immediately stereotyped Burton, who was besieged with scripts that attempted to duplicate its perceived formula. A chance to break free from this rut arrived in the guise of Michael McDowell's script, *Beetlejuice* (1988), a property held by record mogul David Geffen's fledgling film company, which, fortunately, had a distribution arrangement with Warner Bros. Better still, McDowell had worked with Burton previously on "The Jar." "Nearly every script I was offered had the word *Adventure* somewhere in the title. One project fell through and *Batman* was still on hold. I was freaking out until the script for *Beetlejuice* came along," confessed Burton, in a rare moment of candor at the time.

From the onset, everyone knew that the approach to Burton's second feature-film project had to be different. Regardless of its merits, *Pee-Wee's Big Adventure* had a definite and downright defiant "Take it or leave it" feeling to it (Burton's concept, stating, "This is Pee-Wee, believe him or not"). That's a perfectly fine attitude for a movie that stands no chance of becoming a mainstream hit. Moreover, it had no real plot, merely a premise on which to hang a series of comedy sequences. If Burton was to move outside the cult realm, he had to come up with a more user-friendly product—something with which a large chunk of the filmgoing public could identify and relate. *Beetlejuice* was designed very much with this in mind, while in no way trying to compromise those things about Burton's work that made it unique.

McDowell's screenplay was a nearly perfect choice for this task. It had been significantly altered in rewrites with co-producer Larry Wilson and writer Warren Skaaren, and liberally added to. ("Many of the cast come from an improvisational background, so I felt it would serve to balance the movie if much of what the actors did was created on the spot. We didn't throw out Michael's script. We just embellished it a lot," Burton told *Starlog* magazine in 1988.) Being a supernatural comedy about ghostly doings (it might best be described as Thorne Smith, of *Topper* fame, on acid), it allowed Burton free rein in the fantasy department. He could become as visual, unrealistic, and stylish as he wanted without anyone worrying too much about it. Questions of logic and reality don't matter so much in fantasy, and fantasy is the key element here. What no one expected was the curious turn the screen fantasy would take.

The initial assumption by the studio and the publicity department was that *Beetlejuice* would be a more or less "traditional" ghost comedy. In other words, "Think *Ghostbusters*." In point of fact, what they finally got was about as far removed from the 1984 megahit as could be imagined. The standard premise—dating back at least to the 1915 play, *The Ghost Breaker*—of pitting a comic hero against a supernatural phenomenon was nowhere to be found. Instead, the specters take center stage and become, by and large, the characters with whom the audience is clearly supposed to identify. The premise may owe something to *Topper* (1937), but the execution is entirely its own. For openers, the film's principal ghosts are far more "normal" than the human beings who surround them. By the time the movie was nearly in its final stage of editing, it was decided that perhaps the best approach toward marketing it was to simply let its creators—Burton and McDowell—express their own takes on just exactly what sort of movie they'd made. "I don't see it as a horror movie at all. I'm almost afraid to say what it is," McDowell said, while Burton commented, "Well, it's kind of intellectual and kind of stupid. It's not really a flat-out anything."

These statements, made late in the production, indicate an easier birthing process than the reality of the situation reflected. The studio had reservations that McDowell's script was too dark. As it progressed in development, nearly everything done by McDowell, Larry Wilson, and Burton came to be questioned by the Warner Bros. front office. Instead of a creative endeavor, *Beetlejuice* was becoming an endless round of corporate meetings and nitpicking nightmares. Enter script doctor Warren Skaaren, who, with Burton, was finally able to wrestle the script and the studio to the ground. Even then, as Burton has noted, much of what met with the studio executive's approval was significantly altered during the actual shooting. By and large, however, Burton managed to come up with something that at least *appeared* to be a reasonably straightforward script of the sort that Hollywood understands.

One of the first things that so notably sets *Beetlejuice* apart from *Pee-Wee's Big Adventure* is the relative normalcy, even attractiveness, of its onscreen leads, Alec Baldwin and Geena Davis, as Adam and Barbara Maitland. There is nothing even remotely freakish about them, and it's obvious that they are to some degree a concession to a presumed public taste—rather like MGM giving the Marx Brothers a romantic lead for the audience to "care about" in the 1930s. It didn't really work then and it didn't work much better in 1988, but it pleased the studio and calmed their fears about the project's more *outré* aspects, of which there were an abundance. Burton has always tended to defend the Maitlands as a necessity for the madness of the others to play against, but the feeling that they are there more to keep the front office at bay than anything else is impossible to shake.

Almost as surprising as the quirky script is the film's cast. Well-known now, Geena Davis, Alec Baldwin, Catherine O'Hara, Jeffrey Jones, and Winona Ryder were all far from being household names in 1988. The closest thing the film had to box-office insurance on the star level was Michael Keaton in the title role. Keaton had not been Burton's first choice (the kitsch-minded director had wanted Sammy Davis Jr., but no one at the studio was interested in *that* idea), but the two quickly found themselves in rapport and a long working relationship resulted. Interestingly, Burton claims never to have seen Keaton onscreen prior to *Beetlejuice,* yet it is hard not to identify the Beetlejuice character as a ghoulish version of the character the comedian/actor had played in Ron Howard's *Night*

Shift (1982), the role that first brought Keaton to the public's attention. Some of the rest of the cast were decidedly quirky choices, especially talk-show host Dick Cavett (in a thankless role that he mysteriously stalks through as if in a perfectly vile mood) and singer Robert Goulet, whose participation hints at Burton's growing penchant for casting popular figures from his childhood, often in an unusual and even against-type fashion.

Armed with this script and a cast he could work nicely with, Burton was given a ten-week shooting schedule (including location work in Vermont), and $13 million—his first "straight" feature was now off and running. The shoot itself was not without its own share of problems. The medium-sized budget only allotted a million dollars for the film's special effects, which, owing to its nature, were numerous. This, however, suited Tim, who had no intention of having the effects themselves steal the show, nor any desire to produce a too-slick product.

Burton's basic idea of effects work was—and has continued to be—firmly grounded in the classic stop-motion work of artists like Ray Harryhausen. In essence, he wanted effects that were amusing and fairly simple and more likely to produce an audience outcry of, "Wow, that was neat," as opposed to the more distracting, "How did they do that?" At the time, Burton explained, "We went big and more personal with them. What people will see are effects that are, in a sense, a step *backward*. They're crude and funky and also very personal." This was true, but also they were "floor effects," or, in other words, illusions that are achieved live on the set, more in the manner of a magic act than what is thought of as a cinematic approach. This does add a certain sense of reality to the illusion, but it also complicates the handling of a sequence by locking the movement of the performers into a fairly narrow range.

Moreover, the method Burton chose for his effects is a time-consuming process ("We couldn't get that damned tombstone to crumble on cue," Burton noted) and often an infuriating one: "The intent was to do them quick, funky, and fun. You can only take that so far when you've got ninety adults standing around getting pissed off because a mechanism isn't doing what it's supposed to do. Much of the stuff we did worked live, but 'Let's do it in post-production' was a phrase you heard frequently on this show," explained Burton. To a degree, he was being candid, but, in another sense, he was being rather ingenuous, since fixing this kind of problem with this kind of effect in post-production usually means editing around it, something that is borne out by the finished product. However it was ultimately done, Burton achieved his aims and became—in part thanks to the similarity between these effects and the famous transformation of Large Marge the truck driver and the animated Tyrannosaurus rex in *Pee-Wee's Big Adventure*—the first filmmaker whose special effects themselves have a distinctly personal look. And without question, the effects in *Beetlejuice* are distinctly Burton-looking, regardless of the small army of technicians employed to execute them.

The film's premise is simple enough: The Maitlands are killed in a car accident (ironically in a hypersafe Volvo with their seatbelts fastened!) when they swerve to avoid hitting an alarmingly cute little dog and crash through a picturesque covered bridge. They fall to their deaths only *after* the dog in question unbalances the floorboard on which their car is perched. It is hard to imagine that Burton didn't feel a tinge of satisfaction at this jab at conformity in its dullest incarnation. On that score, though, it was only an overture to the opera about to come! What is remarkable is that the studio allowed it to happen at all.

Killing off the leads and turning them into ghosts was not especially novel, despite the cleverness of the presentation. However, what is distinctly more unexpected is to land them immediately in the film's version of the hereafter—trapped in their own home by the fact that stepping out-of-doors immediately propels them onto the surface of Saturn (a hostile, Dali-esque desert landscape) and places them at the mercy of giant, cartoonish, but nonetheless menacing, carnivorous sandworms. Equally out of the ordinary is the fact that the couple's only source of information on their plight is a book, *Handbook for the Recently Deceased*, which appears out of nowhere and is of doubtful practical value in any case ("This thing reads like stereo instructions"). This much, however, is still essentially a setup for the crux of the movie.

The plot proper gets under way when the Maitlands' house is sold to an upscale New York family, the Deetzes. Actually, the Deetzes en masse are not the problem; Charles (Jeffrey Jones) and daughter Lydia (Winona Ryder) are fine. He wants to live the simple life (or at least make a pretense of it), while she—a singularly gloomy figure all in black—seems to be of the view that she can be morbid here as well as anywhere else. (She reaches the decision that her new surroundings are satisfactory when she comes face-to-face with a large spider in its web.) The problem is Delia Deetz (Catherine O'Hara), Lydia's stepmother, who is there only under protest and intends to convert the house into a trendy showplace—"or else I will go insane *and take you with me!*"

This she plans, much to the horror of the Maitlands, with the aid of her pretentious and prissy interior-designer friend, Otho (Glenn Shadix), happily traipsing through the house, making snide comments on its decor and contents ("Save me from L. L. Bean!"), spraying sample colors, and generally creating designer havoc to the mounting fury of the house's spectral owners. "We're not entirely helpless, Barbara. There's a word for people in our position—*ghosts*," decides Adam, inspired to frighten the Deetzes into absenting the premises. The idea sounds promising, but not only are they invisible to Delia and Charles (the handbook explains that the living usually won't see them), but they aren't very good at spooking. Most of their antics go unnoticed (indeed, Charles inadvertently scares *them* at one point), except by Lydia, who can see them. (The handbook explains that "live people ignore the strange and unusual," but, as Lydia explains, "I myself *am* strange and unusual.")

Enter Beetlejuice—"the afterlife's leading bio-exorcist"—via a TV commercial advertising his services as a specialist in ridding ghosts of unwanted humans; all one needs to do is say his name three times. Not certain they want to become involved with this obvious huckster, Adam and Barbara decide that before utilizing his services, they will follow the instructions for help in the handbook. This lands them in the fantastic bureaucracy that, according to the movie, *is* the afterlife—a messy, cluttered, confusion of endless filing systems and waiting rooms, all controlled by suicide victims (still bearing the stigmata of the means of their demise). The Maitlands' particular case is in the hands of Juno (veteran character actress Sylvia Sidney), a no-nonsense chain-smoker with a slit throat from which her constant cigarette smoke wafts. She warns them against using the services of Beetlejuice ("He does *not* work well with others") and bundles them off to try again.

Their second onslaught against the newcomers is no more successful than the first. Lydia mistakes their moans for the sexual antics of her parents ("Cut it out! I'm a child, for God's sake!" she yells, pounding on the wall) and is hardly more impressed when she sees them, decked out in designer sheets with eyeholes!

"I'm not scared of sheets. Are you gross under there? . . . Like all bloody veins and pus?" she forthrightly asks them. Learning that they want to frighten her parents out of the house, she laughs, but agrees to try to plead their case.

This tactic does not work with Delia, so the Maitlands finally unleash Beetlejuice. They are not much impressed by his manic style (when asked for his credentials for the job, he starts off with an impressive list of supposed schooling before sliding into ever more outrageous and vocal claims—"I've seen *The Exorcist* about 167 times," and, "You're talkin' to a dead guy!" Beetlejuice also uses overt rudeness (such as constantly looking up Barbara's skirt and copping the odd feel).

Opting against his help, the Maitlands decide to try something a little more flamboyant on their own, which they do during a swanky dinner party being held by Delia for some of her New York friends. Taking possession of their unwanted guests' bodies, Barbara and Adam make their victims sing like Harry Belafonte and dance about the room to Calypso music, before causing the shrimp cocktails to turn into hands that pull them face-first into the salad bowls. It is certainly an inventive haunting (scarcely something with which one would credit the Maitlands). However, it is also ineffective, since rather than horrifying anyone, it delights the Deetzes, especially enterprising Charles, who sees a way of cashing in on this by way of a ghost-themed amusement park.

The Maitlands, of course, have no desire to become ectoplasmic performing seals for Charles Deetz and hide from their would-be exploiters. They have, however, forgotten that Beetlejuice has been unleashed, and he launches a full-scale assault on the Deetzes in the form of a banister that turns into a Beetlejuice-headed snake until Barbara thrusts him back into the netherworld by reciting his name three times.

Even this latest turn of events is not enough to dissuade Charles, who attempts to carry out his theme-park scheme with the aid of Otho's expertise as a medium. He conjures up the Maitlands against their will for the benefit of potential spectators. Seeing that the experience is taking its toll on the hapless ghosts, Lydia promises to marry Beetlejuice if he will save them, which he does. Lydia is then saved from this bizarre union (the ring for which is still attached to a severed finger) by Barbara's intervention on the back of a Saturnian sandworm, which devours Beetlejuice. The grateful Deetzes turn the house back to its former state and they all agree to live there in harmony. It is decidedly unusual screen material made even more unusual through its many creative digressions, which are the core of its appeal.

On a purely personal level, the most striking thing about *Beetlejuice* lies in the fact that Tim Burton has, as is often the case, given himself an onscreen alter ego. In this case, the character that clearly fulfills this function is Lydia Deetz, an adolescent girl. There can be no doubt that she is Burton's onscreen self—she dresses all in black (a common Burton affectation) and her black hair is generally pulled upward in a version of Burton's own unruly mop. Her attitudes are also drawn purely from Burton's adolescence, as is her preoccupation with photography. When her dad promises to construct a darkroom for her in the basement she dramatically counters by saying, "My whole life is a darkroom—one big dark room." When, late in the film, Beetlejuice refers to Lydia as "Edgar Allan Poe's daughter," the image of her as a female Tim Burton is complete.

In many respects, the onscreen character of Lydia is more a portrait of Burton than any offered so far. The tension between her and her parents has far more relation to Burton's own life than the rather cozy depiction of the Frankenstein family in his earlier *Frankenweenie*. Her status as a misunderstood loner is certainly unquestioned, and yet there is a resonant depth to Lydia that is missing from all previous Burton movie characters. On the one hand, she clearly revels in her differentness and her morbidity (reworking a suicide note for maximum dramatic impact!), but there is an undercurrent of deeply disturbing and sad loneliness in Lydia. It is a loneliness that is at first assuaged by her contact with the Maitlands. At the ending, the film also indicates that her separateness may ultimately extend into the outside world where she is seen interacting with other children at school (the first instance where she has been around anything other than adults). The implication that Burton himself, for all his claims of being content to be his solitary self in his own adolescence, would have wished he might have fit in a little better, been a little more "normal," is hard to ignore. It is certainly borne out by subsequent onscreen characters, notably his most autobiographical one, *Edward Scissorhands*.

Similarly, Lydia's seeming aversion to sex or at least the overtly sexual is strikingly in keeping with Burton's apparent view of the matter—as when she pounds on the wall when she thinks her parents are in the throes of passion, or when, seeing the Maitlands in their sheets and mistaking the image for some sexual peculiarity on the part of her parents, she yells, "Sick! Sexual perversion! If you guys are gonna do that weird sexual stuff, do it in your own bedroom!" Burton and sex are not something that go well together on-camera.

Another aspect of the degree to which Burton seems unable to deal with sexuality in adult terms is evident in the hypersexuality of Beetlejuice. Unlike Lydia, he is anything but repressed. However, his take on sex is also strictly adolescent, expressing itself only in rude gestures, looking up skirts, copping quick feels, and indulging himself in the anonymous couplings offered by the Dante's Inferno Room whorehouse. This locker-room mentality about sex is as far as Burton has managed to travel on the subject. It is a subject with which he is clearly not comfortable—unless it is wrapped in the essentially sexless romanticism of the Maitlands, where the specter of the act of sex itself is never even approached. A review of the literary endeavors of three filmmakers—Burton, Oliver Stone, and Gus Van Sant—in the October 1, 1997, issue of *Harper's Bazaar,* says of Burton's book, *The Melancholy Death of Oyster Boy and Other Stories* (1997), "Burton remains mercifully presexual"—an assessment that could pretty much be applied to his work straight down the line.

Naturally, Danny Elfman is back as Burton's "house composer" for *Beetlejuice,* and his contribution to the film is perhaps of even greater importance than on *Pee-Wee's Big Adventure*. It is certainly a much more elaborate and integrated score (it almost *has to be* more integrated, since the film itself is). The score is also more functional, since it is often the key to the tone of the film, giving the audience guideposts to Burton's intentions in this often unorthodox narrative.

The slightly mocking tone of the score in the opening scenes, for example, is the only clue the viewer is given that these idyllic moments are not to be taken at face value, that this picture-postcard happily-ever-after world isn't real. Similarly, Elfman's almost campy use of odd orchestrations and instruments (including a tambourine) is essential in undercutting the film's darker aspects. If the movie deftly skitters on the edge of comedy and grotesqueness, Elfman's music is always there to keep the playful intent in the foreground. The soundtrack is otherwise unusual and personal in the choice of Harry Belafonte songs as the Maitlands' music of choice. In part, this is merely an outgrowth of Burton's use of "Tequila" in *Pee-Wee's Big Adventure*—hits from the director's childhood—but it is also a direct reaction to the pop soundtrack (and attendant soundtrack-album merchandising tie-in) that was popularized, milked to death, and taken to ridiculous extremes by Lawrence Kasdan's *The Big Chill* (1983).

The release of *Beetlejuice* in March 1988 was greeted somewhat more kindly than *Pee-Wee's Big Adventure*. However, it was by no means an unqualified critical success. Roger Ebert (*Chicago Sun-Times*) so completely missed the point of the whole thing that the most positive aspect of his review singles out the one thing most everyone else objects to—the blandness of the Maitlands. "It's hard to describe what makes the opening scenes so special. Alec Baldwin and Geena Davis, as the young couple, seem so giddy, so heedlessly in love, that they project an infectious good cheer. The local folks are so gosh-darn down-home they must have been sired by L. L. Bean out of *The Prairie Home Companion*. The movie is bathed in a foolish charm," he wrote. Seemingly, he was oblivious to the fact that all this down-home foolish charm was a satirical put-on! A more common complaint was that the film was "uneven," that it was fine when Michael Keaton or Sylvia Sidney was onscreen, but suffered when they weren't. As with *Pee-Wee's Big Adventure*, Pauline Kael (*The New Yorker*) came to the film's defense, correctly noting that much classic comedy is uneven; "The best of W.C. Fields was often half-gummed-up, and that doesn't seem to matter fifty-five years later."

It hardly mattered what the reviewers said. The freak hit of *Pee-Wee's Big Adventure* was no longer so freakish when the $13 million investment on *Beetlejuice* brought in a whopping $80 million in gross revenues. Warner Bros. may not have understood Burton, the critics might not have known how to take him, but it was obvious that there was indeed a big audience out there for his very personal brand of quirkiness. With the success of *Beetlejuice*, Burton had without question grabbed the brass ring—and the prize redeemed with that ring was, of course, the biggest and most prestigious motion-picture production of 1989: *Batman*.

8 | GOING BATTY IN BRITAIN

Some of it is very much me. Some of it isn't.

MICHAEL KEATON
as Bruce Wayne in *Batman* (1989)

BATMAN WAS SOMETHING OF THE CARROT ON A STICK that Warner Bros. had been dangling in front of Tim Burton ever since *Pee-Wee's Big Adventure* had proved a hit in 1985. The beleaguered production had gone through ten scripts and ten writers before Burton and screenwriter Sam Hamm were allowed to have a shot at it while *Beetlejuice* was still under way, the studio having liked what it had seen of that film so far. The financial success of *Beetlejuice* clinched the deal. However, Burton quickly found himself more than a little out of his depth. It wasn't merely that Burton had no experience with action pictures (the chase sequence in *Pee-Wee's Big Adventure* hardly counts), huge stars, and gigantic budgets (not to mention the immense responsibility that goes with such budgets), but he wasn't even a comic-book fan, though he admitted to having always been intrigued by the Batman character. "I love Batman, the split personality, the hidden person," Burton told writer Mark Salisbury, further noting that he could relate to such a character, even identify with him. Burton saw this character who was—at the very least—two people at one time, as a kind of symbol of all America and the pretense of appearing to be one thing, while hiding the reality from the world.

Burton's inexperience with the screen genre was deftly brushed aside in a slightly gushing piece of public relations by producer Jon Peters, "He had humanness, lovingness, but he also seemed tough and strong. He had a passion for *Batman* and a desire to do something completely different with it." Burton certainly had a desire to do something different, but saying that he especially had a "passion" for *Batman* itself is open to analysis. This, however, may not necessarily have been a bad thing. A lack of reverence for the comic books (which, as Burton has pointed out, are constantly rewriting their own histories anyway) allowed Tim the kind of freedom of thought necessary to create something unlike any Hollywood comic-book film that had come before his *Batman*.

In Sam Hamm, Burton found the perfect partner to help him realize his vision of the superhero as deeply disturbed and schizoid. "I think Tim's the first director out there to be filtering junk culture through an art-school sensibility," commented Hamm at the time. The statement was very much on the money. Beyond doubt, Burton was interested in taking a pop-culture icon and *exploring* it, rather than exploiting it for its own sake. He was out to create a work that addressed the issue of why we are drawn to this long-popular character. As much as it is a Batman movie, *Batman* quickly becomes an entertaining work *about* Batman, not just an adventure with the character. In short, it was to be one of the first entirely character-driven action pictures.

A more radical idea could scarcely be imagined. Burton was quick to point out that Batman is not a superhero. He has no special powers. He cannot transform himself into anything. He doesn't fly. He's "just" a crimefighter who, for some inexplicable reason, insists on dressing as a bat. This, in fact, was Burton's primary rationale behind the casting of Michael Keaton. The newly designed Batman suit (easily the most elaborate such costume in any comic-book film) came with carefully sculpted musculature. Why, Burton reasoned, would a brawny, bodybuilder type feel the need to wear such a thing? This immediately ruled out the standard action-hero figures. Burton wanted someone who would be completely transformed when he put on the suit. "I'd considered some very good square-jawed actors, but I couldn't see them putting on a Batsuit," Burton explained.

Far from square-jawed, but capable of projecting a sense of intensity *and* bookishness, Michael Keaton was cast by Burton amid much protest from comic-book fans, who saw Keaton only as a comedic actor. "You look at Michael and you see all sorts of things going on inside," Burton reasoned, showing an immediate grasp of something that had escaped the notice of the traditionalists: When Bruce Wayne assumes the role of Batman, his only means of expression are his eyes. Without intensely expressive eyes, no amount of heroic jawline or rippling muscle is going to make the character work. Moreover, there is no need for the character himself to be a hulking mountain of a man. Batman has always been more of a thinking man's superhero, heavily reliant on scientific gadgetry in his battle against crime. In this regard, Burton and Hamm merely take things one step further.

From the very onset, one thing Burton wished to avoid was pandering to the public's apparent taste for vigilantism, personified by the crypto-fascist tone of so many "outside the law" heroes. To this end, he and Hamm—and later, production designer Anton Furst—keep the tactics and motivations of their hero constantly in question. Without a doubt, Batman is the hero, but much of what he does is questionable from a number of standpoints.

For example, immediately following the scene of Batman's first major bout of vigilantism at the Axis Chemicals plant, he is carefully framed so that the single word AXIS, in gigantic red neon letters, looms over him, deftly suggesting a connection between his actions and those of the totalitarian governments of World War Two. Similarly, the dangers inherent in these actions are brought home when they result in transforming the evil Grissom's (Jack Palance) henchman, Jack Napier (Jack Nicholson), into the Joker. (The film is deliberately unclear as to whether Batman loses his grip on Napier, or *deliberately* allows him to fall, thereby allowing Batman to have actually *created* his evil doppelgänger.) All of this is what Burton had hoped to get onto the screen. To do that, he would certainly need that "strength" of which Jon Peters spoke so loftily. Against all odds, Tim largely managed to achieve his goals. What Burton probably never realized was that his helming this important screen project was due only to the legendary back-stabbing and dubious dealings of Peters and Guber, which had allowed him this freedom.

Long before Burton was ever associated with this movie project—before he had even made a film—Michael Uslan, a comic-book fanatic who had secured a position with D.C. Comics, had originated the idea of a "faithful" Batman picture. Unhappy with previous screen incarnations of Batman—

especially the camped-up 1960s Adam West TV series—D.C. president Sol Harrison agreed to let Uslan have the licensing rights to the characters, certain that he would preserve the character as depicted in the comics if his proposed series of Batman films ever got made. Uslan's concept was markedly different from Burton's in that he had no problem with the vigilante aspect of the character. As originally planned, when Uslan and his partner, Benjamin Melnicker, sold the concept to Peters and Guber at Casablanca Filmworks, Uslan and Melnicker were to have 40 percent of the profits, along with a measure of creative control.

In a November 6, 1980, memo cited in *Hit and Run* Uslan states, "No longer portrayed as a caped clown, Batman has again become the vigilante who stalks criminals in the shadow of the night." Two years later, Peters and Guber had aligned themselves *and their holdings* with Warner Bros., and their new deal did not seem to stick very closely to the agreement they'd made with Uslan and Melnicker, who found themselves increasingly ignored and shut out—so much so that by the time the project was about to go into actual production, they learned about it from an announcement in the trade papers. Moreover, they learned that their producer status had been "usurped" by Peters and Guber. Their complaints to Warner Bros. fell on deaf ears and the best they got out of the pact was executive-producer status, absolutely no artistic control, and a scant 10 percent of the profits. Indelicately put, they'd been had. However, without Uslan essentially being removed from the project, it is highly unlikely that Burton would have had the kind of freedom he required to create his highly revisionist *Batman*.

It was a long road from concept to the final film, and definitely not an easy one. For as long as anyone associated with the movie can remember, Jack Nicholson was the first choice for the Joker. Uslan had envisioned him in the key part from the earliest days of the project. Nicholson was *not*, however, Sam Hamm's first choice. Hamm wanted Ray Liotta and, while no one argued the potential strength of Liotta's performance in the part, Liotta wasn't a big enough name, nor did he have the crossover appeal they were hoping for with Nicholson. Nicholson was the key, so far as Jon Peters and Peter Guber were concerned, to unlocking the door to an audience older than that to whom a comic-book film (however revisionist) is inherently aimed. Very probably, Liotta would have helped to make a more integrated movie, but this was an occasion where commercial considerations won out. Also, Nicholson and his popularity helped offset some of the negative backlash concerning the controversial casting of Keaton.

The rest of the *Batman* casting was relatively simple. Despite the increased importance of female lead Vicki Vale (once the decision to jettison the character of sidekick Robin had been made), the part called for little more than beauty and the ability to project intelligence (without actually being given anything especially intelligent to do!). Originally, the assignment was handed to Sean Young, but when she broke her arm early in shooting, she had to be replaced. Burton's first inclination was Michelle Pfeiffer, but Keaton nixed this idea, since until recently he had been romantically involved with Pfeiffer and thought the experience of acting with her at that point might be awkward at best. Finally, this somewhat thankless assignment was given to Kim Basinger, who, despite receiving special advertising billing with a box around her name, was considerably less well served by the film than her male costars. Robert Wuhl landed the even more unprepossessing role of a reporter on the trail of "the Batman," who falls in love with Vale. Veteran actor Jack Palance was brought in for a fun-and-showy turn as a crime boss. Certainly the big casting coup in the supporting parts, however, was British actor Michael Gough in the role of Batman's faithful butler, Alfred. To him fell the task of humanizing the character of Batman, and he did so brilliantly—so much so, in fact, that Gough has been the one actor to have spanned all the *Batman* movie sequels that followed. Smaller parts were in the capable hands of performers such as Pat Hingle, Billy Dee Williams (another instance of Burton casting a former star from his childhood years), and William Hootkins.

Complicating the production was the acknowledged fact that the screenplay Hamm had worked out with Burton was still in need of further work when *Batman* started shooting. It is, of course, impossible for every vestige of a production to be entirely worked out prior to shooting. What works on paper may not work on film. Certain effects may not be possible as described. A location may dictate a change in plan. Beyond that, no creative filmmaker is going to allow himself to be so locked into a preconceived plan that he leaves no room for inspiration, invention, or happy accident. However, historically there are all manner of precedents (*Apocalypse Now* [1979] being a prime example) to illustrate that starting a film before the script is fixed, or at least very nearly so, is not the soundest of ideas. But with everything in place for production to begin and the studio wanting the film for its big 1989 summer release, there was little choice but to commence the shoot in October of 1988, with the idea that the script could be doctored by Warren Skaaren (who eventually shared writing credit with Hamm) while shooting went on. As it turned out, nearly everyone involved would have more than a little input before the production wrapped, and even at that, the finished product contained a snag or two—and one howler of a plot gaffe that the critics focused on.

Making Burton's task just that much more difficult, *Batman* was to be filmed not on his Burbank home turf at Warner Bros., but, for economic reasons, at Pinewood Studios in England. From the standpoint of being freed from the constant hounding of the Hollywood press as to just exactly was going on, this was, in Tim's estimation, a good thing. In every other respect, it was foreign in the extreme—to the extent that when the Californian Burton arrived for shooting, he hadn't thought of the difference in the weather and didn't even own a decent winter coat. Much as the film crew were baffled by the choice of the young and inexperienced Burton in general, this sort of absentmindedness convinced them just that much more that he was a singularly bizarre choice to helm the production (at least, until the film was under way).

If the late-fall weather wasn't enough to chill Burton to the bone, what he saw certainly would have accomplished that on its own. It is one thing to abstractly grasp that you are at the helm of a $30 million movie (a figure that would reach $48 million before things were over). It is quite another to come face-to-face with the sets for that movie, taking up no less than nine soundstages and almost the entirety of Pinewood's ninety-five-acre backlot, not to mention a crew of over three hundred technicians all waiting to be told what to do.

To put it bluntly, Burton was nearly paralyzed with fear of what he'd gotten himself into. Of course, he had a couple of extremely eccentric, personal hit films, but was he really up to the task of doing something on this grand a scale? Was he out of his league altogether? Had his earlier successes been flukes? What was a twenty-nine-year-old wunderkind doing thinking he could be responsible for this? Would a seasoned film crew even take him seriously? For that matter, wouldn't a powerhouse star like Jack Nicholson simply eat him alive and never pause to notice? According to Joe Morgenstern in the *New York Times Magazine,* Burton—innocently and in obvious awe—commented to a visitor to the set, "This movie's so monumental"—and there's no reason to believe he was being deliberately ingenuous. It *was* monumental and no one felt that more than he did.

Much as Warner Bros. had done in a general way with *Pee-Wee's Big Adventure,* they hedged their bets on Burton's inexperience with this kind of film in a specific sense: surrounding him with a crew who were far more used to dealing with action, large budgets, and all the attendant pressures. Production designer Anton Furst—the young designer of Neil Jordan's *The Company of Wolves* (1985) and *High Spirits* (1988), as well as Stanley Kubrick's *Full Metal Jacket* (1987)—and cinematographer Roger Pratt, who had shot Terry Gilliam's *Brazil* (1985), another film taking place in a kind of alternate reality, were Burton's choices. However, the rest of the crew was assembled largely by the studio and with a keen eye on their specific credentials for pulling off big-budget action epics. Burton's line producer was Chris Kenny, who had worked with Steven Spielberg on *Empire of the Sun* (1987). First assistant director Derek Cracknell boasted a long history with action pictures. Editor Ray Lovejoy had helped assemble movies as diverse as Peter Medak's *The Ruling Class* (1972) and Ridley Scott's *Alien* (1979), making him a perfect choice for Burton. Lovejoy had a background that not only included action and suspense, but also enabled him to understand Burton's sense of the absurd, as well as the more standard requirements of the genre. The elaborate action scenes were given over to action specialist (and director of *Rambo III* [1988]) second-unit director Peter MacDonald. Great backup, yes; but, in Burton's eyes, also a great deal of pressure—the last thing he wanted was to appear inept in front of a creative team of this caliber.

In the main, he needn't have worried. Rather than be contemptuous of his inexperience, most everyone—including the notoriously mercurial producer, Jon Peters—took to his apparent genuineness, decency, and innocence. Peters has spoken of Burton bringing out an instinct to mother him, and the same proved true of others. Ray Lovejoy told Joe Morgenstern, "You'd go over the wall with him. He's that kind of guy. You'll always be on Tim's side." Anton Furst, in whom Burton found the perfect person to make his idea of Gotham City a workable reality, was also quick to praise him on an artistic basis: "If you think about filmmaking as a multimedia thing, Tim's sense of psychology, of visual images, and music and sound is superb." In every sense, the production team that was assembled for *Batman* ended up being in Burton's corner, and in every case (with the possible exception of first assistant director Derek Cracknell, who refused to comment on him), they ended up being favorably impressed by Burton—both as an artist and as a human being. This is indeed rare on any movie. It is even rarer on a high-profile, big-budget, make-or-break block-buster. However, it proved true with Burton.

This is not to say that the making of *Batman* was an easy process. It was anything but that. No production of its enormous size is likely to be a day at the beach. Burton's inexperience with this genre of film and the pressures of its importance and expense inevitably showed through. At one point, he even ran from the set in tears, completely convinced that he simply couldn't make the movie. He had to be coaxed back into action by Jon Peters. Burton later con-fessed (as reported in *Hit and Run* by Nancy Griffin and Kim Masters, 1996) that there were times when he frankly had no idea what he was doing on the set or how to do it or even what the film was really about. He almost seemed to be moving through the project like a sleepwalker. He became sick with a severe cold during the shoot, as well, but kept pressing on with the filming, proving himself a professional.

The situation on *Batman* was such that Burton was completely vulnerable and constantly looking for a sense of validation and support. And this he found—or so it seemed at the time—when he took a break from shooting to attend a party in London. It was there that he met Lena Gieseke, a German painter, who appreciated his work and was sympathetic toward it and him. The two immediately hit it off—a rare thing for the usually reticent Burton, whose name had been romantically linked previously only with Julie Hickson, and that had not been a well-publicized fact.

The chemistry was so immediate between Burton and Gieseke that the pair married on February 24, 1989, while the film was still in production. A honeymoon with a filmmaker under pressure on a huge production is probably not the best way to start a successful marriage, but the pair seemed blissfully happy at the time. For journalists, it was simply a juicy nugget to add to the long list of incredible fortunes that had befallen Tim Burton: his unprecedented successes with his first two films, landing the biggest movie going (and largely on his own terms), and finding love, all at once. If anyone could be said to have it all at the same time, Burton seemed to qualify.

Another thing that Burton had, however, was a broken script that was going to have to be fixed. There were several problems, not the least of which were the film's climax and a key developmental scene, the first Joker-Batman encounter, involving the three stars. The solution to the latter was an all-night session involving Burton, Skaaren, Keaton, Nicholson, Basinger, and Peters. It was tense, tiring, and nerve-racking, but it resulted in what is perhaps the movie's strongest characterizational scene and the key moment in the picture that makes it clear to the viewer that Bruce Wayne/Batman is very nearly as mentally disturbed as his evil counterpart, the Joker. It is a facet of the main screen character that is touched upon elsewhere in the dialogue, but only made apparent in this one instance. Without this scene, *Batman* would have never worked as well as it does.

The climax, which also serves to bring into focus that dual nature of Batman and the Joker, was less easily achieved. The ending, as written, was neither exciting nor compelling—plus it killed off Vicki Vale. Jon Peters was not happy with that idea, especially since he and Basinger had become romantically involved during the shoot. Something "grand" was needed to liven it up to the level of the big finish required for the film.

The crumbling Gothic cathedral in which the finale's action takes place was not a part of the original concept, and production slowed while a forty-foot scale model was designed and constructed. Clearly inspired by the similarly out-of-place cathedral in Fritz Lang's *Metropolis* (1926) (where that film's villain unceremoniously drags the heroine), the set itself is the key to *Batman*'s climax, which becomes an extended and more psychologically motivated reworking of the end of *Metropolis*—with a passing nod to Alfred Hitchcock's *Vertigo* (1958) in the bargain.

"It was one of those nightmares where you feel big and small at the same time. Here you've got this big production with all these people waiting around, and you're supposed to shoot this sequence that's suddenly all wrong. I thought, 'My God, why didn't I see it to begin with? How did I let this happen?' Whatever the case, we didn't have it at first, but we came up with something good," Burton commented tactfully, since apparently he did not care for the new ending. And they did come up with "something good," though perhaps not quite the best solution imaginable in terms of pace, regardless of its epic grandeur. It was beautiful, and fully sound in terms of theme. However, it was a sequence that would turn around and bite Burton in the backside when the critics got ahold of it, and not entirely without cause. It is slowly paced, and that does suggest that Burton didn't fully understand the requirements of a big action picture.

Despite the fact that *Batman* emerged as an impossibly popular film, the climactic scene always tends to make audiences restless. Or perhaps Burton just didn't care. To the best of his abilities, Tim was determined to make an action picture *his* way, and the leisurely pace of the climax was part of that. It is clearly not accidental, as is evidenced by the fact that Danny Elfman's accompanying music for the sequence is aptly titled "Waltz to the Death," neatly summing up the approach being taken.

That Burton did not have quite the free hand on *Batman* that he had had on his first two films is driven home by the pop soundtrack that was foisted on him by the studio and the producers. Having successfully sidestepped the trendy pop-soundtrack-album tie-in approach on *Beetlejuice* (Harry Belafonte was represented with a couple cuts on the soundtrack album and his music is quoted in Elfman's score, but a separate tie-in album of songs did not happen), he would have to swallow his artistic objections on *Batman*. While Burton has stated that he had no problem—on their own merits—with the Prince songs he was handed, he was less than enthusiastic about their use in the film.

In the end, Burton managed to cleverly showcase two of the songs, while at the same time minimizing them and cutting them short, as if to say, "I will use them and use them well, but I will not be subservient to them." In both cases, this more flamboyant music is appropriately linked to, and even played by, the Joker. In the first and more interesting instance, the Joker uses it to accompany the sequence where he and his gang deface the contents of the Flugelheim Museum, allowing the scene to unfold like a marvelously perverse musical number. The second song's showcasing is more perfunctory in that it is merely the music used for the Joker's murderous "goodwill" parade.

Whatever their artistic merits in *Batman* may be, the songs undeniably served the film's publicity machine brilliantly, allowing additional promotion by the constant exposure of film-related Prince videos on MTV. The resulting consumer confusion over a film with *two* soundtrack albums—one featuring the Prince songs and the other consisting of Elfman's brooding score—was a small price to pay, at least so far as the marketing strategy was concerned.

But what of the film itself? What precisely did Burton get down on the screen and how did he manage to create an almost wholly personal blockbuster?

9 | BURTON BATS A HOME RUN

It's not exactly a normal world, is it?

MICHAEL KEATON

as Bruce Wayne in *Batman* (1989)

BURTON SETS THE TONE FOR EXACTLY WHAT SORT
of film *Batman* is to be immediately, before the credits proper are under way.
With the ominous Danny Elfman score brooding on the soundtrack over the
familiar Warner Bros. logo, the logo itself changes into something darker,
bleaker, than its normal self (beginning an astonishing Burton trademark: the
director actually personalizing the studio logos on his films, something he has
managed to do on each subsequent film—a somewhat bombastic touch that
nonetheless makes *every* frame of the film wholly Burton's). When the image
then dissolves into the opening credits, Burton's camera pans down from the
gloomy night skies of Gotham City and glides through a connected series of
strange, dark passageways of twists and turns in a mysteriously sinuous—and
significantly unhurried—traveling shot beneath the starkly-designed credits. It
only moves out and away from this object at the very end, to reveal we have
been prowling through the intricacies of Anton Furst's *Batman* logo. In itself,
this is another Burton touch, since it echoes the model work that opened
Beetlejuice, a device he would continue to employ and embellish in *Edward
Scissorhands* (1990), *Batman Returns* (1992), *Ed Wood* (1994), and, perhaps most

breathtakingly of all, in *Mars Attacks!* (1996). The opening credits have already established the tone—dark, unhurried, and finally mythic. The film itself is exactly the same; shot through with humor (though not as successfully as *Batman Returns* would be), the levity itself tends to be dark, and the film takes itself very seriously indeed.

Our first look at Anton Furst's Gotham City is a stunner, fully justifying the expense of the set and bearing out Furst's ingenious concept. "The philosophy was to start with New York in 1900 and conceive of it growing without zoning laws. Because of zoning, skyscrapers are stepped back as they go up. That lets light in. If you're corrupt, you build out as you get to the top. Our buildings cantilever forward as if they were trying to maximize their space. It makes for a very frightening complex," he remarked in a *Time* magazine article. He might also have noted that it gives an impression of a world in which the characters are constantly menaced by these buildings pressing down on them. Not inaptly, the look of Gotham has been likened to that of *Metropolis*, but there are also elements of *The Cabinet of Dr. Caligari* (1919) in its warped perspectives, and an overall sense of a 1930s WPA project that got out of hand and has since gone to seed in the film's depiction of urban decay.

Far more than *Pee-Wee's Big Adventure, Batman* is set in a deliberately nebulous time period. Some aspects of the film are perfectly modern or even futuristic. Others—such as the Joker's fleet of cars—date back to the 1970s, while still other touches seem to place the movie's action in the world of 1939, when the character of Batman first appeared. Speeches are given into period microphones, newspaper photographers shoot with old Graflex cameras and fire off flashbulbs (the newspaper office itself is a holdover from that era; the reporters come across like refugees from *The Front Page*), people use telephones that are fifty years old, they wear clothing straight out of an old gangster picture, and so on.

To add to the sense of a wholly separate world onscreen, there is a sense of the generic to many of the items seen in *Batman*. TV cameras, for example, are emblazoned with a 1950s graphic proclaiming, Action News, but no channel number is referenced; police cars are starkly labeled with the word POLICE and little else. The effect (aptly reminiscent of the approach taken by Roland West in *The Bat Whispers* [1931]) is both striking and vaguely unsettling, keeping the viewer slightly off balance.

The introduction of Batman within the film could scarcely be bettered. First glimpsed from a height as he looks down on a crime in progress—an effect given a weirdly unreal feeling by the dark figure of Batman being made darker (even his shadow is ink-black) and by the striking use of animation—he is then shown closer-up in the background of a shot of the criminals dividing the loot and discussing whether or not there really is a "Bat." They soon find out the truth to that when Batman quite literally descends upon them. A few shots and Batman collapses, only to rise again and send one of them crashing through a door before dangling the other over the edge of the rooftop. "I want you to tell all your friends about me," he tells the villain. "I'm Batman." With that, he flings the thug across the rooftop and then drops over the edge of the building and is gone. Everything about the approach works. There isn't a false move or a shot that runs too long.

Unfortunately, the opening is not matched by the scenes that follow. They are necessary to set up the story itself and are enlivened only by occasional flourishes of wit, usually in the dialogue, such as the pre-Joker Jack Napier commenting, "Decent people shouldn't live here. They'd be happier someplace else," when District Attorney Harvey Dent (Billy Dee Williams) promises to make Gotham City safe for them. There's also a nice touch when Alexander Knox (Robert Wuhl), the only reporter who believes that there is a "Bat" terrorizing the underworld, is handed a sketch of a bat in human form, which is signed and given to him by no less a personage than Batman creator Bob Kane himself. Undoubtedly, the highlight of these early scenes is the scenery-chewing villainy of Jack Palance's crime boss, Carl Grissom. Introduced to us after a breathtaking shot gliding up his art deco skyscraper, Grissom is the ultimate flashy, double-breasted-suit-wearing gangster. Everything Palance does livens the scenes he's in as Grissom happily sets up Napier to take a fall in revenge for playing around with his mistress.

Once the film hits the scene at Axis Chemicals, Burton the filmmaker regains his stride completely. The images are fresh, striking, and clearly evocative of their comic-book origins. The action and effects are superbly handled and remarkably coherent in a scene that could easily have slipped into confusion in light of the number of events happening simultaneously. With economy and lucidity, we are presented with Napier discovering he's been double-crossed, corrupt police detective Eckhardt (William Hootkins) giving instructions to have Napier shot on sight, the arrival of Commissioner Gordon (Pat Hingle), Napier trashing the chemical plant, the arrival of Batman, Gordon's first sighting of Batman, Batman's encounter with Napier, Napier's murder of Eckhardt, Napier's plunge into the vat of chemicals, Batman's escape, and the climactic shot of Napier's burned hand emerging from the river outside the chemical plant. Though undoubtedly guided to a great degree by the project's action specialists, Burton's grasp of the mechanics of the sequence is stunning and there can be little doubt that the scene is presented largely as he conceived it.

Quite as good, and more important in understanding Burton, are the scenes between Bruce Wayne and Vicki Vale at Wayne Manor. The sequences, like all those involving Wayne Manor, are the movie's only use of actual locations. Here is an instance where a standing structure is as completely fantastic as anything Furst might have imagined. Knebworth House, an oversized and slightly ludicrous example of the "stately homes of England," was already perfect for a depiction of the residence of someone so absurdly wealthy that he might indeed have a house containing rooms into which he has never ventured.

This location had already appeared earlier in *Batman,* as the site of the charity affair preceding the first Axis Chemicals sequence, but it is in this more intimate section—a secluded dinner between Wayne and Vicki Vale—that it truly makes its mark, its rambling vastness a cogent reflection on the essential emptiness of Wayne's existence. The sequences involving the couple at dinner are at once amusing—a meal for two across a good thirty feet of table where everything has to be said at least twice to be heard—and charming. In an off-screen remark during filming, Burton sums up the entire concept beautifully: "This is like a kid's idea of a first date." It is certainly in keeping with the naiveté of Tim Burton's notions of romance, and it's interesting to note that the date culminates with a slightly tipsy Vicki falling into bed with Bruce. This marks the only occasion in any Burton film where the main characters engage in sex in an outright manner. While it is possible that this interlude reflects the more adult romanticism of Burton himself being in love, there is a sense of unease about it that is brought home when, after the fact, Bruce first feels compelled to utilize a strange contrivance that allows him to sleep while hanging upside down like a bat, and then seeks refuge on a nearby sofa, leaving the bed to Vicki.

In a move that is out of keeping with the otherwise fairly straightforward narrative of the film (probably to minimize the actual sexual encounter between Bruce and Vicki), these scenes are crosscut with what are perhaps the most brilliantly achieved moments in the entire film on a stylistic level. The scene in *Batman* where an underworld medico (with an improbable shingle hanging outside his business that reads simply, Surgery!) examines his handi-work on Napier, all the while making excuses for the primitive conditions under which he is laboring and the extent of the injuries suffered, is one of the most assured pieces of filmmaking in Burton's entire career to date. It is done in classic horror-film style, deliberately evoking the specter of James Whale, with the camera laterally tracking through this surgery from hell before alighting upon Napier and the doctor, while the actual unwrapping of the bandages cov-ering Napier's face is obviously based on the unveiling of Peter Lorre in Robert Florey's *The Face Behind the Mask* (1941).

Bathed in shadows with stark pools of illumination and film-noir garish neon signs flashing outside the windows, the scene is a technical marvel. Burton also echoes classic horror films by carefully playing the viewer and not allowing Napier's Joker actual countenance to be so much as glimpsed, only the reac-tions to it—first the horrified doctor and then Napier himself. The latter smashes the mirror he's given, dissolves into bitter laughter that turns maniacal, rises from the operating chair, breaks a swinging lightbulb, and goes out into the world. Burton even has the nerve to extend this approach by keeping the Joker in shadow for as long as possible in the subsequent scene! Unfortunately, the impact of his accomplishment was diminished before *Batman* was even released, since the Warner Bros. publicity department just could not resist showing Jack Nicholson's Jokerface to the world.

The encounter between the Joker and Grissom that follows is very nearly as good on its own merits, with Palance's scene-stealing Grissom alternating between cold fear and gangland bluster. "Your life won't be worth spit!" he warns the Joker, who obviously intends to kill him. The Joker counters by finally stepping out of the shadows so that Grissom and the viewer finally encounter his perpetually grinning clown-white face, red lips, and greenish hair. Then, in a scene of almost balletic violence, he blasts away in the various poses of a trick-shot artist at the man who double-crossed him. The segment climaxes with the Joker bowing to a nonexistent audience for approval as he casually saunters offscreen—all backed by a sudden outburst of circus-style music from Danny Elfman.

As soon as the Joker has taken over for Grissom, the plot that makes up the bulk of *Batman* gets under way. Decked out in a startling flesh-colored makeup to mask his real appearance, the Joker attempts to blackmail the alliance of gangster groups into compliance by offhandedly electrocuting the one member who dares to question him. When the other groups set themselves up as being in control of Grissom's "businesses" in his absence, the Joker and his own minions attack the rival gangsters with murderous results. Unfortunately, the media seize more upon a possible connection between this gangland slaying and Batman, which fuels the Joker's enmity against his rival.

Despite the emergence of the film's basic, and deliberately simple, story—the Joker's plotted destruction of the inhabitants of Gotham for failing to recognize his "artistry"—*Batman* remains essentially character-driven, and in a remarkably shrewd manner that constantly emphasizes the similarities between Batman and the Joker. As the film progresses, layer upon layer of their duality is uncovered. No sooner does the Joker see a photo of Vicki than he, too, develops an attraction to her. His henchman informs him that she's involved with Bruce Wayne, which sets the groundwork for the film's famous Flugelheim Museum encounter and adds another level of conflict, though unknown to the Joker, between him and Batman.

In the meantime, the nature of the Joker's plan is revealed—the indiscriminate killing of Gothamites. Thus, the Joker casts himself as the premier "homicidal artist," who casually murders everyone in the Flugelheim Museum but Vicki.

There is more than a casual hint of Tim Burton's own subversive streak in this wholesale vandalism of the museum. However, this fact escaped the film's critics (many of whom thought the scene distasteful), as well as many Burton supporters, who remained oblivious to the clues scattered throughout his works from the beginning, that there are far darker undercurrents to his personality than the surfaces of his screen works might suggest. In the end, the scene is remembered more for Batman's timely intervention on Vicki's behalf, their escape on a fantastic wire-and-pulley system, and the splendid action sequence involving the Joker's men and the police in hot pursuit of the pair through Gotham City.

In one of *Batman*'s most beautiful and evocative sequences, Batman takes Vicki on a drive through a gorgeously mysterious, stylized forest and to the Batcave where he gives her the solution to the Joker's murderous methods. Finally she realizes that there's more to this meeting than an interest in passing on information. At first, it appears that Batman is expressing *his* romantic interest in her, an idea slyly sent up by a mocking cutaway to a flight of bats when he seems to put the make on her. However, it turns out, in the following scene, that his interest actually is in obtaining the roll of film she has that contains a photo of him with his mask pulled back.

The film's next key sequence is in the apartment where Bruce tries to explain his mysterious actions and apparent mood swings to Vicki—actually planning on revealing his other identity to her. He is interrupted by the arrival of his romantic "rival," the Joker. Bruce confronts the Joker by revealing that he knows the Joker's real identity. Nonchalantly lecturing the Joker about the history of Jack Napier, Bruce suddenly explodes into violence. The move is so quick and so unexpected that the viewer is shocked into that central awareness that the hero is, in his own way, just as bad as the villain of the piece.

Having made that point, the scene moves to another plot point as the Joker pulls a gun on Bruce. Soon it is revealed that the Joker (as Napier) had murdered Wayne's parents years ago. All the elements of the strange on-camera relationship between Batman and the Joker are now in place. It remains only to stage their final showdown, but not before the film's most notorious gaffe—when Alfred, Wayne's butler, blandly walks Vicki into the Batcave to see Bruce, completely destroying his cover!

That aside, the buildup to the showdown is nothing less than brilliant. Batman goes on the offensive, completely destroying the Joker's lair and Axis Chemicals, in a marvelously designed setpiece that is meant to pay homage to Mario Bava's *Danger: Diabolik* (1967). The reference to this earlier film is very direct as the Batmobile blasts its way through a door labeled Bay 4 in lettering so stylized that it reads "BAVA." (Very much an admirer of the Italian director, Burton much later told Bava actress Barbara Steele that he would love to remake Bava's horror classic, *Black Sunday* [1961], with Lisa Marie in the old Steele role.)

Any hopes Batman harbored that he finally might have destroyed the Joker are dashed when he spots his nemesis escaping in a helicopter, and flying off to the film's huge "goodwill" parade and Two Hundredth Anniversary Festival, where Batman once again thwarts his nemesis's evil plans.

It is at this point that the film reaches the actual showdown in the old cathedral—an idea that, while not an utter failure, obviously played better as an idea than in actuality. Running an improbable thirteen minutes, the sequence is just too slowly paced to quite work. The setup itself lasts a full four minutes before Batman even disposes of the Joker's henchmen. Astonishingly, *over eight minutes* of screen time elapses before the final confrontation and Batman's final slugging of the Joker, sending him over the edge of the building and soon thereafter to his death.

Part of the problem with the *Batman* finale is that it was never worked out properly before shooting. The seemingly interminable climb to the top of the bell tower, for example, was shot before Burton or anyone else quite knew why the Joker was taking Vicki up there. At the time, Nicholson wanted to know where he was going and why, and Burton had to confess that he didn't know. "I knew they had to go up to the bell tower and they better do something up there. That was always a given. But what?" Burton later admitted. He theorized that Jon Peters himself may have been responsible for the confusion surrounding the film's ending. "Hollywood is a very control-oriented place, and if people want to feel in control, a very easy way to bring control back to yourself is to create chaos. Because if you're the one creating chaos, then you're the one who has to fix it. And on some level, that may be true of Jon." Whatever the truth of that, Peters was clearly not responsible for the pacing of this key sequence. Part of the cinematic problem also rests on Burton himself, who may simply have gone too far in trying to make the film thoughtful and the ending too grand. If he feared the climax might seem too rushed and perfunctory, he certainly took care of that problem with a vengeance!

Commercially, it hardly mattered. Thanks in large part to Peters's unbelievable media blitz that created enthusiasm without resentment, *Batman* did a whopping $42.7 million in its opening weekend, breaking all box-office records up to that time, and then went on to break another record by crossing the $100 million mark in ten days. Burton and company had *the* Hollywood hit of all time on their hands. The question of exactly why is another matter.

What accounts for the success of *Batman*? Audiences were often noticeably fidgety during its duller stretches. Was it a hit because of Tim Burton, or in spite of him? Were audiences reacting to his thoughtful, somewhat gloomy take on the subject, or were they getting off on Jack Nicholson in a purple suit spouting punchy (and funny) one-liners? Burton himself harbored very little doubt about the film's popularity. "To me the success doesn't have much to do with the movie itself. If it hadn't been *Batman* and I'd make the exact same movie . . ." he told *Newsweek,* tellingly leaving the sentence hanging, indicating that the *Batman* name counted for far more at the box office than the name Burton did. Actually, the truth is probably somewhere in between. The mere fact that Burton had made a *serious* movie on Batman counts for something, but the fact that he was able to tap into the myth of the character counts for even more. And if there is one thing Burton knows how to do, it is to make myths. In a very real sense, the major characters in all his pictures—*Mars Attacks!* being the notable exception—attain a mythic stature in large part because the director himself treats them with a kind of respect that is largely unknown from any other filmmaker.

Critical reaction to *Batman* was largely mixed. The film was so tremendously hyped that a certain amount of critical backlash was inevitable. The usual charges—in some ways justified this time—were brought in, that Burton couldn't tell a dramatically coherent story. It is certainly true that *Batman* boasts far more thematic than dramatic coherence. It might also be said that the production has an overabundance of plot, but not much story. Sheila Benson in the *Los Angeles Times* said that "the film flops about" and claimed it was "disastrously short on the sort of wit that can make a gargantuan movie lovable." This may be viewed as saying it wasn't mindless enough to be enjoyably brain-dead summer entertainment. Vincent Canby of the *New York Times,* who had been a major detractor of *Pee-Wee's Big Adventure,* was equally unimpressed, deciding, "The film just meanders mindlessly from one image to the next." Roger Ebert of the *Chicago Sun-Times* was more disturbed by *Batman* than anything else, it seems. He apparently wanted to like the film and was enthusiastic about the design and the "haunting power" of its dark imagery, but found it "a triumph of design over story, style over substance—a great-looking movie with a plot you can't care much about." He found the museum sequence "vile," thought the entire proceedings unsuitable for children, seized upon the film flub scene where Alfred just blandly trundles Vicki into the Batcave, and, in short, found the film to be a "depressing experience." At the same time, he goes on record saying that it should "probably" be seen! Of course, critics can occasionally build a film so it attracts a viewership, but it's rare they can break one that has a presold popularity. Thus, it didn't matter much what anyone said about *Batman*. It was *the* cinematic event of the summer of 1989, no matter what.

Burton himself nursed ambivalent feelings about *Batman*. Bruce Wayne's lines about Wayne Manor—"Some of it is very much me. Some of it isn't"—could very well sum up his attitude on the project. From the outset, it was obvious that it would be less personal than his previous work. He knew from the start that some degree of compromise was going to be necessary for the chance to make a movie this expensive. However, in the main, he was satisfied that the overall film reflected his essential vision. "I read a lot that said it wasn't me. Actually, if there was a reason it wasn't me as much, it was time constraint. Everything happened very quickly. That's where I feel the most dissatisfaction. But I knew that going in," he told the *Los Angeles Times* for its Calendar section. Compromised or not, *Batman* has the distinction of having grossed over $475 million in box-office receipts, an additional $150 million in video sales, and even more in merchandising, pushing its total take to over $2 billion. That is no small accomplishment.

10 | BURTON GETS PERSONAL

Tim is Edward.

VINCENT PRICE, 1991

THE SUCCESS OF *BATMAN* PROPELLED BURTON FROM the ranks of cult director to superstar director. Suddenly it was cool to be weird, to be eccentric, to be out of step with the world at large. In Hollywood, anyone making a movie that grosses $100 million in its opening ten days could probably do anything short of mass murder (and even then it might depend on the victims) and still be considered cool. In that sense, Tim Burton was suddenly as cool as they come as the 1980s ended.

He at once recognized this and was baffled by it. He told *Newsweek* that it spooked him to go to parties and hear, "'Oh, you must be incredibly happy.' As if my happiness was based upon that. If it ever got to that it would be a sad life indeed. All that Hollywood hype—it's depressing, it's dangerous. I could never embrace it. I wish I could embrace it a bit more. I often question why I make movies because I hate showing them, I don't get enjoyment out of sitting with an audience, it takes me a couple years to look at something I've done—now the Pee-Wee movie is the only one I can enjoy." At this point, Burton not only did not want to look at his movies, he *genuinely* did not want to make them, either—at least not the one Warner Bros. now wanted, which was, predictably, a *Batman* sequel.

By this time, he and Lena had settled into a home in the Hollywood Hills and, in a typically Burtonian outburst of bohemian romanticism, turned the living room into an art studio where they could both work at sketching and painting. Already more than comfortably well-off after *Pee-Wee's Big Adventure* and *Beetlejuice,* Burton was now wealthy beyond his wildest dreams thanks to *Batman.* Had it suited his fancy, he might easily have stayed in his home studio with Lena and painted away for as long as he liked. However, the reality of the situation was that Burton was far from seriously burned out on his true medium—indeed, he was ready to tackle his most personal project yet.

Turning down Warner Bros.' requests for either a *Batman* or *Beetlejuice* sequel, he offered them an idea for a story he had already tried to interest his agents in, immediately after the success of *Pee-Wee's Big Adventure* in 1985. The screen idea was based on an image that had been lodged in his head for years—the image of a boy with scissors for hands. At the time he'd originally tried to sell the unique concept, he had yet to attain the clout *Beetlejuice* and *Batman* gave him within the film industry, and his idea had been met with a remarkable (but predictable) lack of enthusiasm by the business movers and shakers. It had been little more than that at first: an image, a childhood preoccupation. "They're an interesting invention, they cut through things. I mean, scissors are both simple and complicated. They're a very simple design. But I remember as a kid I could never figure out how they worked," Burton told the *Los Angeles Times.* That, and the notion it generated in Burton's mind, was the core of a very personal concept: the premise of a person who cannot touch anything without damaging it. "But with scissors, there's something in the theme of somebody not being able to touch that I love. I just wanted a character that—visually, there he is, internally, externally. It's a visual representation of what's inside. I've always felt, just for me, for some reason, it encompassed a lot about how I feel about things, I don't know if that makes sense. But there's something about it that rings true for me," Burton explained.

However, Burton's screen concept did not ring true for Warner Bros., who quickly passed on Burton's proposed $20 million project. In all honesty, Burton was delighted, and there's every reason to suspect that he deliberately pitched the idea in such a way that the studio would reject his next screen project offered per his contract with them. "I've been trying to get away from the Warner Bros. deal.

When you get into these deal situations, you become part of the 'family'—and we all know how screwed-up families are," Burton confided to *Newsday*.

At Twentieth Century-Fox, then production head Scott Rudin was considerably intrigued by Burton's new screen project. His interest was probably more in the idea of luring Warner Bros.' hottest director into a change of studios than it was in *Edward Scissorhands* (1990) on its own merits. Regardless, a remarkable deal was struck with the Fox studio where Burton and screenwriter Caroline Thompson were hired to turn the concept into a screenplay—a screenplay over which Fox would exercise no creative control whatsoever; and upon completion of which, Fox would have only a limited period of time in which to accept the project or the rights would revert to Burton.

To say the very least, this was an unusual approach in control-conscious Hollywood, and a clear testament to the strength of Tim Burton's perceived worth in the wake of *Batman*. Burton was extremely concerned that the new script be just exactly right. A good deal of his apparently secure future was actually riding on it. This was the first of his features to be created from whole cloth, from a story that originated with Burton. It was the next logical step, of course. The bid for genuine auteur status was certainly to be expected. Without a doubt, Burton had been involved with the scripting of his previous projects, but they had all at least come in with built-in structures. This was very different. But even more, *Edward Scissorhands* was essential to him on a much more personal level: "Every detail was important to Tim, because it was so personal," co-scripter Caroline Thompson commented late in the production.

The risk of Burton falling flat on his face was not inconsiderable. The movie easily would be his strangest work to date. It fell into no known screen category. Worse, everything Burton had touched so far had turned to gold and this fact, as might be expected, already had produced a degree of resentment both in Hollywood and in critical circles. There were certainly more than a few people out there who would have loved to see Tim Burton—or at least his success—taken down a peg or two. However, Scott Rudin's faith in the new wunderkind of Hollywood was not misplaced, and it was seconded by Twentieth Century-Fox's new studio chairman, Joe Roth. Fox didn't hesitate very long in approving the script Burton and Thompson had concocted. In fact, *Edward Scissorhands* was one of the first projects for which Roth gave the green light.

Burton's pet project, the one that would most clearly be his, was now under way—and this was just the beginning of his problems.

Often when a filmmaker comes away from an elaborate, costly, draining screen production, he will opt to undertake something smaller and simpler, with the idea that "smaller, simpler" will be easier, will be a holiday by comparison. Just as often, the supposed "vacation" turns out to be more grueling than the experience it was intended to counterbalance. (A notorious example was Ken Russell's choice to follow his horrific film, *The Devils* [1971], with a pleasant and innocent musical, *The Boy Friend* [1971]. Numerous stock players and technicians who had weathered the production of the former, never worked with the director again following the anything-but-pleasurable experience of the latter.) *Edward Scissorhands* was, in many ways, exactly that sort of experience, not in the least because the bottomless wallet Burton had access to on *Batman* simply was not there for the follow-up picture.

Burton was confined to an acceptable, but hardly staggering budget this time, necessitating a good deal of resourcefulness on his part and on that of production designer Bo Welch. There was no way to build the film's principal set of a suburban neighborhood, so it became necessary to adapt an already existing real suburbia for the setting. What Burton had in mind was the suburbia of his childhood, but that suburb was no longer new, the essence of the "planned community" Burton envisioned. In Burbank, the houses had been added onto, the spindly plantings of thirty years ago were now lush trees, and the whole sense of tract-house uniformity had been so altered, that any consideration of shooting in Burbank was out of the question. The solution was located about twenty miles north of Tampa, Florida—a newer housing development in the little town of Lutz (a side trip to the genuine 1960s Southgate Shopping Center in Lakeland, Florida, completed the look for the exteriors)—specifically, one cul-de-sac street called Tinwhistle Circle, still undergrown and sporting the meager efforts of the builders' casual landscaping attempts. The flat Florida landscape differed from Burbank, California, and the building styles of the 1940s and 1950s had been modified for more modern tastes, but, in spirit, this was the suburbia of Burton's imagining—almost.

The key element to unify the look of the neighborhood was Bo Welch's decision to repaint each of the houses in one of four colors—described by him in *Newsday* as "sea-foam green, dirty flesh, butter, and dirty blue." In part the idea was simply that painting them in these less-than-tasteful colors would enhance the newness, smooth away any sign of texture to the structures, and actually make them look more alike than a single color scheme would have done. And while the new decor certainly achieves this—especially when put up against the bright blue Florida skies filled with arresting cloudscapes—it added one other thematic dimension by subtly stressing the vague and somewhat pathetic suburban notion of a halfhearted attempt at individuality. Without a word being uttered, the colors clearly indicate the inhabitants' instinctual urge to want to be just a little bit different from each other, to express something of themselves, but within certain strict guidelines—almost as if being different is fine, so long as every fourth person is different in the same way.

Casting was something else again. Burton knew he wanted nineteen-year-old Winona Ryder in the film, having responded and related so well to this burgeoning talent on *Beetlejuice*. The feeling was mutual. "Tim talks my language, you know? Did you ever meet somebody you could just *talk* to? That's how I feel about Tim Burton. We have the same sensibility; we think the same things are funny," explained Ryder. Plus, Burton had it in mind that it would be a rather perverse kick to cast her against type by decking her out with blond-red hair and makind her a cheerleader—a characterization about as far removed from *Beetlejuice*'s Lydia Deetz as can be imagined. Beyond the joke level, though, he knew she could bring a sense of depth and gravity to the screen role.

The supporting players were relatively easy to cast as well, and no one other than Vincent Price even could have been considered for the role of the inventor who creates Edward. But what of Edward himself? An astonishing array of actors—some of them wildly unsuitable—were interested in the pivotal part. At one time or another, the range of intrigued hopefuls included Tom Hanks, Robert Downey Jr., Michael Jackson, and, most peculiarly of all, William Hurt, who, nearing forty, was certainly far too old for the title assignment. Twentieth Century-Fox had their own ideas. They wanted box-office magnet Tom Cruise. In fact, Cruise was actually announced for the part at one point. Burton has never openly stated that he was necessarily opposed to the idea of Cruise in the key role. Thankfully, the issue never came up since Cruise decided the character, as it stood, was not sufficiently macho for him! (One cannot but wonder if twenty-something Cruise understood the screenplay at all.)

Then Johnny Depp (born in 1962) came along. Depp's first theatrical film credit was a supporting role in Wes Craven's *A Nightmare on Elm Street* (1985), where he had the experience of being killed by Freddy Krueger, whose razor-gloved fingers might be said to be an horrific precursor to the main character in *Edward Scissorhands*. Also on the big screen, Depp had costarred with Rob Morrow in the puerile sex romp, *Private Resort* (1985), had a featured role in Oliver Stone's acclaimed Vietnam War study, *Platoon* (1986), and played the Elvis Presley–style lead in John Waters's eccentric satire, *Cry-Baby* (1990). However, Depp's principal claim to fame at the time lay in the Twentieth Century-Fox TV series, *21 Jump Street* (1987–90), or, more to the point, as the pinup boy the small screen series had turned him into. The actor was now anxious to shed the pretty-boy image derived from playing Tom Hanson, one of the show's young undercover police officers.

Nothing appealed more to Depp—who would become known for his daring and unorthodox screen choices—than the idea of portraying a screen character whose beauty is masked behind a pasty complexion, a mop of black hair, and numerous scars from constantly nicking himself with his own "hands." The fact that he was engaged to Winona Ryder at the time seems not to have entered the scenario at all. Burton admitted to having a passing familiarity with Depp from magazine covers, but claimed never to have seen a TV episode of *21 Jump Street,* and cast him solely on the merits of meeting and talking with the discontented young star.

Even with everything set and the location tended to, shooting was not without incident, simply because of the Florida climate. The Sunshine State can be miserably hot (something that is even more of a problem for people in makeup and costume—especially for makeup and costuming the likes of which Johnny Depp was dealing with) and the humidity almost unbearable. However, there are other environmental drawbacks in the locale, as well—namely, bugs, and very specifically, an annoying insect called a love bug (or rather love bugs, owing to the fact that they normally travel in hordes and travel two-by-two in conjugal bliss). These insects do not sting, nor, in fact, do they do much of anything, apart from committing mass suicide on the bumpers, grilles, and windscreens of oncoming traffic; but neither do they exactly belong en masse in front of a camera lens. They seem to have beleaguered the production on more than one occasion. "Do you know what's the number one reason people leave Florida? Bugs," opined co-producer Denise DiNovi when *Premiere* magazine visited the *Edward Scissorhands* set. With typical perversity, Burton was more philosophical about the annoying pests: "I love 'em. I dunno—bugs, man! They're all around us!"

Worse than bugs, heat, casting problems, locations, or anything else, though, was the burden this most personal of films placed on Tim Burton. The 105-minute *Edward Scissorhands* turned out to be something that almost made him long for the uncertainty of *Batman*. "It's harder because it's something I'm completely connected with. I feel more volatile. I feel myself in weirder moods. I'm more interiorized. Emotionally, it's harder, but it's more satisfying," he explained. No doubt. He also spoke of the movie as having elements of a personal catharsis. "I'm still too close to it. I'll know better in a few months just what I've exorcised," Burton informed *Newsday* at the time of the film's release.

One thing was clear from the onset—*Edward Scissorhands* was Burton's effort to resolve a great many conflicting emotions within himself. Knowing Burton's background, the immediate response to hearing that he was making a film about a misfit in suburbia was to assume that he was going to completely skewer and satirize its inhabitants. And that temptation may have been there, but the emotions dealt with in *Edward Scissorhands* are far more complex than that. The contempt and loathing for the artifice of suburbia that is evidenced to some degree in early films has here softened. His take on suburbia has become more sympathetic: "It's not a bad place. It's a weird place. It's a place where some people grow up and ask, 'Why are there resin grapes on the wall?' (and others don't). We're trying to walk the fine line of making it funny and strange without it being judgmental. It's a place where there's a lot of integrity."

Hearing Tim use the word "integrity" in connection with suburbia seems almost blasphemous, but it is also obvious that he is coming to terms with aspects of his childhood that he had long sublimated. Elsewhere Burton would comment, "I used to look at my house and say, 'Why is this hanging on the wall? This weird blob of wood that's been shellacked and has a clock in it?' You ask people, and it's not like other cultures, where they know why it's there. You'll ask people, and they won't remember."

TIM BURTON

Co-scripter Caroline Thompson also remarked, "His work has a real affection for neighborhood life. You'd never see it as condescension. And although he perpetuates this perception of himself as having been damaged, from my perspective it's just the opposite. I think he's escaped some fundamental damage that shuts most other people down." In many ways, Burton's career in general, and *Edward Scissorhands* in particular, substantiate her view. However, it would be a mistake to assume that Burton set out to create an outright valentine to suburbia and his youth. "What they do to Edward is more a comment on American behavior—or at least how people behave in Los Angeles. There's this immediate niceness that gets peeled away until you find out that maybe they don't like you as much as they pretend to and gradually they're not so nice to you," Burton also noted. "You assume the mask of suburbia for outward appearances, and yet no one knows what you really do," offered Burton at another time. (It is certainly no accident that while Bill Boggs, the father in the film, played by Alan Arkin, has a job and goes to work on a daily basis, no one ever hints at just exactly what it is that he does for a living.)

Of course, the most immediately striking thing about the title character is just how much Edward resembles Tim Burton; Edward very clearly *is* Burton's onscreen alter ego. However, Burton himself—and Caroline Thompson—both claim, not altogether convincingly, that Edward is *not* a portrait of Tim Burton. The flurry of publicity material that accompanied the film's making would carry a wide variety of viewpoints, including some rather inconsistent ones from Burton. Vincent Price flatly stated, "Tim is Edward." Caroline Thompson would insist that the character is more based on a dog she'd owned! At one point, Burton would say the character has much to do with Johnny Depp (an interesting concept, since the image, script, and project considerably predated Depp's involvement): "He's more that character than anything else he's done. There's a sadness about Johnny I just respond to—and I find it kind of funny."

Denise DiNovi, one of the project's producers, would come close to saying Edward is Tim without actually saying it: "In a way Edward really is the artist who does not fit into the world." In other places, Burton stresses his similarities to Edward: "There was a long period of time where I just hadn't been able to connect with anybody or have a relationship. Everybody goes through periods like that—the feeling that you can't connect, you can't touch." And yet again, he denies the self-portrait by saying, "That would be very pretentious of me. I couldn't have done it. I had to look at Edward and be able to laugh at him." However, Dianne Wiest (who plays Winona Ryder's on-camera mother in the movie) may have said it best in describing *not* Edward, but Burton: "I don't know anyone I've responded to in this way. People love him. I really love him. I would do *anything* for him. When I think of Tim Burton, it's a feeling, not a thought. I feel somehow there is so much pain and thankfully so much talent with which to express it. His is an absolutely unique and innocent point of view about the world." But at the same time, she also would say that she felt the character of Edward goes beyond Burton's own preoccupations to achieve a more universal status: "I think we're all Edward Scissorhands. Tim no more than the rest of us."

As if to throw it in the faces of his detractors who constantly complain that Burton is incapable of telling a story, Tim not only offers a very straightforward narrative with *Edward Scissorhands,* but goes one step further by presenting the film as a bedtime story being told by an old woman to her granddaughter. In essence, he is reinventing himself *as a storyteller* and the fascinating thing is that he turns out to be very good at it. What he and Caroline Thompson create in *Edward Scissorhand* is essentially a modern-day bedtime story, a suburban fairy tale, and quite possibly the most resonant myth of our time—as well as one of the best films ever made about adolescence and American life.

11 | SUBURBIA RESPLENDENT

But if you had regular hands then you'd be like everybody else.

TV AUDIENCE MEMBER
in *Edward Scissorhands* (1990)

EDWARD SCISSORHANDS IS A REMARKABLY STRIKING work from its first image—the Twentieth Century-Fox logo in chilly blue with snow falling on it and the first melancholy notes of what is perhaps Danny Elfman's finest score to date on the soundtrack. From this the film moves into a less abstract, but even more mysterious variation on the traveling-shot background opening of *Batman*. Here what is seen is identifiable: an arch, an old door, a strange statue, a flight of worn stone stairs, peculiar-looking factory/lab equipment, something like a mechanical man, marching mechanical men as part of a machine, more strange gizmos, a descent into the dark opening of one such machine, flashes of cookies—star, man, dog, heart-shaped, the same sort of cookies drifting downward past the camera—a pair of hands, a spiraling shot moving back from Vincent Price as the Inventor apparently lying on the floor with his eyes closed, darkness, snow, a long shot of a crumbling mansion on a hilltop. . . . Out of context, these ghostly, monochromatic blue images are all but incomprehensible, albeit tantalizingly so, until the film has been fully seen. Here, then, is a world of deep mystery—the point, of course, being that this environment of complexity is going to turn out to be born of the most prosaic thing imaginable: suburbia.

Soon the viewers find themselves in an oversized bedroom with an equally oversized fireplace. An old lady is tucking her granddaughter into bed. "Why is it snowing, Grandma?" asks the child. Finally, the grandmother agrees to tell her the long story: "I guess it would have to start with scissors. Well, there are all kinds of scissors and even once there was a man who had scissors for hands. . . ." She then tells her enraptured grandchild about the man-made Edward, whose creator died before he got to finish the man he invented. During this preamble, the camera glides out the window and up to the mansion itself. The camera then moves back to reveal just the side of Edward's face.

We soon see the neighborhood, offering us our first good look at the pastel houses, the carefully tended lawns, the treeless landscape, and the impossibly sanitary mien of this little world. In light of the fact that when Burton cross-references an old film, it is always his memory of that film, his *idea* of it that he uses, it is only to be expected that he would do the exact same thing in creating his suburban neighborhood. This is suburbia filtered through Tim's mind—almost a half-remembered dream of the abhorrent place.

Enter Peg Boggs (Dianne Wiest), the resident Avon Lady who, it turns out, has been prowling these neighborhood streets forever and has seemingly never made a sale, not even to her portly neighbor Helen (Conchata Ferrell) nor to an oversexed local, Joyce (Kathy Baker). So today the determined salesperson tries her luck at the crumbling old mansion on the hill at the end of the street. This house seems to be an outgrowth of Burton's childhood preoccupation with the mysteries of the cemetery near his own house—a place of abiding interest in an otherwise bland landscape; only here, he can give the mystery form and render the childhood imagination real to viewers.

The grounds inside the mansion's rusting Gothic entranceway are something else yet again—a perfectly manicured private expanse of marigolds, gerbera daisies, and lisianthus, all setting off wonderful topiary sculptures of fantastic animals and, as a kind of centerpiece, a gigantic depiction of a human hand. As she crosses the threshold to this strange and gloomy interior, which looks like a cross between an Antonio Gaudi building and Herman Rosse's sets for *Dracula* (1931), she finds a long-disused factory at its core. In an attic room of this seemingly deserted manse, she discovers a strange bed tucked away in an old fireplace, the walls around it a collage of magazine and tabloid newspaper cuttings, most related in some way to hands. At length, she spots someone—Edward—crouching in the shadows. She starts to back away after she notices the lethal-looking scissor blades that take the place of his hands.

When she asks him about his peculiar "hands," he explains that his creator has died before completing him. As the Avon saleslady studies him further, she notices scars on his face—obviously caused by his makeshift hands. She soon decides that he should come home with her.

Edward is captivated by his first glimpse of suburbia, but no more fascinated than the neighbors are by the arrival of this very odd-looking stranger in their neighbor's car. The local gossipmongers are soon in action, calling each other, trying to find out who this visitor might be. Nosy they are, but Burton takes pains to suggest in the movie that all of this is less *malicious* than simply a desire for anything that will break the interminable boredom that is inescapably the lot of those living here.

Edward is enchanted by his first look inside the Boggs home, unquestioningly taken with its blandness and tacky decor. What draws his attention is the display of family photographs and especially the pictures of daughter Kim (Winona Ryder), and he seems to fall in love with her image at first sight.

Many of the special touches in *Edward Scissorhands* are likely to go unnoticed on a first viewing. However, upon examination, it becomes apparent that very little here is without point. Kim's bedroom boasts a collection of snow globes, which are certainly related to the picture's snow imagery and are a tacit clue to one aspect of her personality. There is even a hint of her possible dissatisfaction with her world—a high-school pennant on the wall is partially covered in such a way that it reads simply, Bland. Her mirror, much like the space around Edward's bed in the big house, is surrounded by pictures cut from magazines and family photos. Obviously, there seems to be a connection between Edward and Kim before they even meet. Similarly, many things that appear to be only minor comedic touches are very deliberately designed to clarify Edward's character and his basic dilemma. Not only does he nick himself anytime he touches his face, but a tentative poke at Kim's water bed causes a leak. He genuinely cannot touch anything without the risk of damaging or even destroying it.

Peg's notion, of course, is to make Edward "normal," or, more correctly, to make him fit in. In her world, it is very important to fit in—to "assume the mask of suburbia." But while she is laboring away at this ill-conceived task, the neighbors are clustering about outside, speculating on her strange guest.

Dinner is a painful ordeal for Edward. Not only does he find it impossible to manipulate the silverware, but Bill Boggs (Alan Arkin) insists on engaging him in small talk to make him feel comfortable, which, naturally, seems to have just the opposite effect. Bill Boggs is a thoroughly nice, patient, but ultimately indecipherable man. "He's into lawn mowers. He likes thinking he's a dad. That's about it," Arkin told *Premiere* magazine, further elaborating that Bill and Peg "get along beautifully," but that it's merely a surface connection without a real relationship: "It's like people pretending to have a relationship. People are remembering how people are supposed to act. They're wondering how Robert Young would do it on television." No wonder that no one knows what Bill does for a living, and Bill himself is so utterly lost in his role of dad and trying to be the quintessence of normal that he rarely seems to listen to anything that is said. He bumbles along a path dictated by a set of preconceived notions of life that does not allow for the recognition of anything outside those notions.

The more outspoken (i.e., not yet socialized into things) and thoroughly real Kevin (Robert Oliveri), the Boggs's young son, is actually easier for Edward to deal with, despite his somewhat gruesome preoccupation with Edward's hands and his utterly thoughtless idea of taking Edward to show-and-tell at school!

While Peg works at making Edward feel at home and transforming him into something "normal," Edward turns his talents to quickly turning shrubs outside into a topiary Tyrannosaurus rex dinosaur, much to the delight of everyone. The moment, however, is spoiled when Esmeralda, the resident religious fanatic, accosts the Boggs family by marching into the yard and announcing about their guest, Edward: "The power of Satan is in him, I can feel it!" Peg and Bill do their best to smooth this over and restore the sense of normalcy and neighborhood solidarity, dismissing her as an aberration.

Farther into the film, Edward's memory is jogged by the sight of an electric can opener, and then unfolds the manner in which the Inventor originally came upon the idea of creating Edward. In a wonderful scene of the Inventor's factory in action, much of the imagery behind the opening credits is shown, and it's revealed that all that fantasticated machinery is doing nothing more than making cookies, much to the personal delight of the Inventor. (It is constructive to consider the similarities to Burton's previous film about Pee-Wee Herman, in that this is how Pee-Wee might have ended up in his old age.) Suddenly, the idea dawns on him that he might make a man from the parts around him. What is completely charming and utterly Burtonesque about this, is that it is both entirely visual—it explains everything satisfactorily on an emotional level, and explains *nothing* on a logical one—and is totally accepted at face value by nearly everyone who sees the movie.

Later, the Boggs's barbecue party is an amazingly on-target shorthand depiction of Burton's concept of how people are nice at first, but less so as the layers peel away. Everyone indeed *seems* nice, but there are strange undercurrents of something else in the backslapping "good ol' boy" fellowship of joking about Edward's hands. It suggests that Edward, no matter how obviously different, must be just like these suburbanites, and, if he isn't, then he must somehow be made to conform. While Peg seems to be the only person in her particular circle of friends with a motherly interest in Edward, the others, led by randy Joyce, view him with an idea toward sexual exotica. On the one hand, then Edward is cautiously accepted as being one of the boys (obviously, the men can't really conceive of anyone being anything else), while being accepted for his novelty value on the other. It's entirely a surface thing, with the "masks of suburbia" in this case being the masks of cordiality.

It is at this point in the proceedings that Burton introduces Kim Boggs—previously seen only in photographs that serve to fuel Edward's imaginary vision of romance. On the surface, the character is pretty prosaic and not at all in keeping with Edward's vision. That she is part of a shallow and less-than-attractive clique of a popular jock-and-cheerleader crowd is immediately apparent, as is the fact that these supposedly admirable kids are a lot less innocent than is casually assumed by the adults in the film.

There is nothing particularly appealing, either, about Kim's jock boyfriend, Jim (Anthony Michael Hall), a lumbering hulk who obviously thinks he owns Kim. According to Burton, Jim is "just like the guys you knew in high school. I was always horrified by guys like this because—*they always had girlfriends!* I think what it is is that these guys, because they look like football captains, the image of American-dream youth kind of thing, and yet they're scary and they're violent—I think girls respond to the image and then get bullied and frightened by them on a subconscious level." In many ways, Burton may be correct, but ultimately part of this idea is the one element in *Edward Scissorhands* that strikes a false note. There is little doubt that the portrait of Jim is pretty much on target, but the turnaround with Kim, when she rejects her vile boyfriend in favor of the sensitive Edward, is a little harder to accept. It plays a bit too much like an "everynerd fantasy"—that if only the pretty cheerleader could see the real person inside, she would certainly choose to be with him.

Not surprisingly, Kim's first encounter with Edward is a disaster, despite her dad trying to put things right between them. Kim's is the first voice of familial discontent concerning Edward. She is bothered that her mom brought him home and that she is allowing him to stay there. Clearly, integrating Edward into Kim's world is not going to be so easily accomplished.

Edward, however, is still the novelty hit of the neighborhood, happily creating fanciful topiaries for the residents. He finds his true métier, however, when he tries his "hand" at clipping a poodle, which leads to him designing elaborate cuts for all the neighbors' dogs, and then, at the behest of Joyce, for the women of the neighborhood, all of whom are soon bedecked in increasingly fanciful and fantasticated hairdos.

This newfound talent affords Edward a certain celebrity status, securing him a place on John Davidson's daytime TV talk show. At first glance, the sequence may seem an unnecessary digression. However, upon closer examination, it is central to the film and to the core of Burton's paradoxical views on the topic of being "different." In the first place, it is stylistically and thematically consistent that Kim should recognize that she has positive feelings for Edward in a manner not dissimilar to his own discovery of her. He fell in love with her picture; she realizes she loves him when she sees his image on TV, not in real life.

The point for Burton, though, comes when someone in Davidson's TV audience suggests (yet again!) that she knows a doctor who might be able to help Edward and make him like everyone else. And that is the crux of the matter and one of the most telling moments in Tim Burton's entire filmography: the suggestion that for all his creative abilities and his carefully crafted image of willful strangeness, Burton might rather be "like everyone else," and that this impossible desire is at the center of the vague melancholy that infuses all of his screen work. Burton would address this idea again in, of all places, *Batman Returns,* where he adds another layer to it, as we shall see.

Edward's celebrity status leads to the idea that he should open a beauty shop (although no one seems to consider the necessary cosmetology licensing laws). Turned down for a bank loan to start his business venture, Edward's dream is put on hold. Instead he falls into a scheme with Kim's boyfriend, Jim. Jim has seen how Edward can pick any lock and thus wants him to help Jim steal from his own father. Jim hopes to sell the stolen merchandise to buy a van and afford a place where Jim and Kim can have privacy. Preying on Edward's credulity, Jim convinces Edward to take part. The results are predictable: Edward gets caught and Jim lets him take the blame.

It develops that Edward knew all along that he had been put up to helping Jim rob his own house, only going along with the gambit because Kim had asked him to. Serious neighborhood discontent with Edward now takes root. Peg and Bill stubbornly remain loyal to Edward, even after, in a fit of mistaken jealousy (Kim has gone to break things off with Jim), Edward destroys the drapes and wallpaper in their house.

As the neighborhood situation worsens, the situation soon alters dramatically. Everyone in the Boggs household pretends that things are all right—everyone, that is, except Kim, who has come to love Edward and see his worth. The culmination of her new feelings come in the film's beautiful "Ice Dance," where Edward first makes "snow" by carving an ice sculpture of an angel, while Kim, entranced, dances through the falling shavings of ice. It is an almost heartbreakingly beautiful moment, perfectly depicted by a brilliant filmmaker—and his cast and composer—at the height of his powers. The only possible complaint is that it ends too soon, when this singular moment is interrupted by the arrival of Jim, whose sudden presence causes Edward to accidentally cut Kim. Venting his anger and jealousy on Edward, Jim calls him a freak that "can't touch anything without destroying it." Edward wanders off into a neighborhood that no longer considers him desirable.

Edward's own behavior does nothing to help at this point. The undercurrent of danger in the character has surfaced, and he stalks through the streets, hacking away at his topiaries as he goes, and snipping off his suburban clothing, revealing himself in the black leather outfit underneath. With the police after him and all that's happened, even the sympathetic Peg realizes that pretending things are fine isn't going to make it so.

Once Edward's anger passes, he returns to the Boggs home, where he meets Kim. She says, "Hold me." Raising his shearlike hands he realizes the danger in this and the impossibility of it all. The scene dissolves into the final flashback where it is explained why Edward was never finished. The Inventor had succumbed to a heart attack before he could attach a pair of perfect human hands onto his creation. Thereafter, the hands were pierced and broken by Edward's scissors, leaving him forever unfinished.

These sadly idyllic moments are soon shattered by Jim, who is out for revenge. Jim attacks Edward, who, in turn, slashes his arm. Edward then rushes back to the mansion with the police and the neighbors—now an angry mob—in pursuit. As the cops proceed up the hill to the mansion, Kim and, unfortunately, Jim, have gotten there first. Jim and Edward fight and in the melee, Edward runs him through, sending him falling out of a window to the ground below. To try to save Edward, Kim, who has now admitted she loves him, heads off the oncoming crowd. She convinces them that Edward and Jim have killed one another.

The film then reverts to the framing bedtime story, as the old lady tells her granddaughter that Kim never saw Edward again. Slowly removing her spectacles and seen in close-up for the first time, she reveals that she is Kim, many years later. The scene briefly shifts to Edward, unchanged, still tending his topiaries on the hill.

Absurdly, ridiculously, and unashamedly romantic, *Edward Scissorhands* is first and foremost a triumph of conviction over realism, of feelings over thought. There are gaps aplenty in the plot for those who want to look for them. However, almost no one, apart from some critics, seems to be inclined to bother about the gaffes, and who can blame them? Burton has fashioned the perfect modern-day fable, and he has done it on his own terms, which, more interestingly, others can relate to as well.

In his approach to this movie, Burton actually takes his quest for creating a separate world and a separate time further than he had dared even in *Batman*. *Batman* took place in a studio world. Its peculiarities with the time period— what might be called never-never time—were therefore less jarring than they might seem here. Timewise, *Edward Scissorhands* appears to be taking in several periods at once. The houses and decor are clearly 1960s-vintage, while the cars and many of the other trappings are more modern. The script also contains casual references to VCRs and CDs, which brings the film up-to-date with the time it was made, thus blending the eras. For that matter, the framing story itself would have to be set somewhere in the next century, yet it takes place in a far cozier and more old-fashioned surrounding than anything else in the film. Nonetheless, it fits in just as well as the rest. Burton deliberately seems to dare the viewer to attempt a literal reading of the movie, and, indeed, the film is so brilliant, so perfect in itself, that it defies any such reading on its own.

When the film was completed, Fox was pleased with what they saw, though not entirely certain how to best market it. Even more than *Beetlejuice*—at least *that* was clearly a comedy of sorts—*Edward Scissorhands* was impossible to pigeonhole. Its basic tone is certainly comic, but it never goes after big laughs, and has an ending that is at best bittersweet, and at worst tragic. It is a fantasy, yet it brings the illusion of reality to the fantasy by its offhand acceptance of those elements. One thing the studio was certain of—they did not want prerelease posters featuring Edward, for fear the public would think it was a horror film! As a result, the prerelease artwork features not Edward, but examples of his bizarre hairdos! After the film's release, they would offer for public consumption at least three different posters: two would feature Edward (in the shot that would be marketed on T-shirts) and would differ only in that one has a butterfly perched on his scissors, and the other poster featured Edward and Kim embracing.

Test screenings for the film were encouraging. *Edward Scissorhands* received far higher approval ratings than had either *Pee-Wee's Big Adventure* or *Beetlejuice*. Studio executive Joe Roth saw visions of having an *E.T.*-sized blockbuster on his hands, but wisely didn't aggressively push the film in that direction. "We have to let it find its place. We want to be careful not to hype the movie out of the universe," he reasoned.

The critics, on the other hand, had a literal reading in mind, it seemed, when they screened the film. As usual, Roger Ebert (*Chicago Sun-Times*) ended up being baffled by Burton's intentions, claiming that the central character was "strangely remote" and that the other characters in the picture are so "stylized and peculiar" that they make Edward into "another exhibit in the menagerie, instead of a commentary on it." Again, Ebert praises Burton's technique, damns his content, and is obviously starting to lose patience waiting for the Burton film where, in his view, content and technique are on an even footing. Philip Strick of *Sight and Sound* approached *Edward Scissorhands* with singular literal-mindedness, flat-out stating that the story takes place in the 1960s and pondering questions of why the Inventor gave his creation those hands to begin with (apparently, he missed the fact that those were the hands on the automaton from which Edward was made and they had originally served a function). One fully expects Strick to question next where Edward gets all that ice in the story line, which, thankfully, he doesn't. However, he does ultimately conclude that the film is "of little importance." Duane Byrge in the *Hollywood Reporter* found Burton's new, "one-joke" entry to be "a gummed-up supernatural yarn." He predicted it would only sell to hard-core Burton fans. *Beetlejuice* supporter Pauline Kael of *The New Yorker* backed away from *Edward Scissorhands,* saying, "It has no mystery: it's pre-interpreted. And Tim Burton is being too personal, too tenderly self-serving." In the *New York Times,* Janet Maslin was far more receptive, saying, "The film, if scratched with something far less sharp than Edward's fingers, reveals proudly adolescent lessons for us all."

Edward Scissorhands was not an *E. T.,* as the studio hoped, but it most certainly did prove to be a perfectly respectable hit that doubled its $20 million investment within a week, before going on to continued brisk box-office business—much of it in the form of repeat business. Whatever had been a fluke about the success of *Batman,* one thing clearly wasn't in question any longer. Tim Burton made movies that people saw more than once, regardless of whether they were action blockbusters or romantic fantasies.

While working on *Edward Scissorhands* with Vincent Price, Burton hit upon the idea of making a documentary on his hero, which he intended to call *Conversations with Vincent.* This intriguing little project was shot in black-and-white over a three-day period in the spring of 1991 at the Vincent Price Galleries in East Los Angeles. What was to have been a fairly straightforward question-and-answer documentary, however, ballooned into something more elaborate when Burton decided to bring his own critical faculties to bear on Price's entertainment work and what it had meant to him. This alteration required extensive revisions and the tracking-down of a good deal of archival footage—a problem that was magnified because its preassumed limited appeal caused the project to be shunted constantly into the background as Burton's feature-filmmaking took precedence. Reportedly, the most recent version of the work clocks in at about an hour, making it unwieldly for theatrical release, and to date it remains closed away and essentially unfinished.

12 | BATMAN ON BURTON'S TERMS

You're just jealous because I'm a genuine freak, and
you have to wear a mask!

DANNY DeVITO
as the Penguin in *Batman Returns* (1992)

EVEN BEFORE *EDWARD SCISSORHANDS,* WARNER BROS. had been anxious to get Tim Burton to helm a Batman sequel. At first, he flatly refused. During the production of *Edward Scissorhands* in 1990, however, he shifted ground. One day he might be doing it; the next, he was; then he wasn't; and so on. One trade-paper article reported (correctly) that Sam Hamm was writing a script for what was then called *Batman 2,* but that Burton was undecided about whether or not he would direct the project. He had reservations about his actual contributions to the success of the first *Batman,* which he tended to view as a success based more on its being a "cultural event" than from anything he had done. "I get pressure from studios and other people and agents to do it. And then my friends say, 'Don't do it, why would you want to do a sequel?' I don't take either side of the fence. I just need to finish this [*Edward Scissorhands*]. Otherwise, I'll make a decision based on being in a bad mood or something," Burton explained, adding that "doing sequels doesn't excite me. I've been lucky so far. While there are flaws [in my work], the reason people have generally had a good response to my work is that it feels fresher. . . . I don't consider myself an accomplished filmmaker. I have to do projects where I have something to offer."

Certainly when Tim read Hamm's script, he had something to offer—advice to get a new script. According to producer Denise DiNovi, the Hamm script was done just to see if Burton had any interest in the project, and as written, he did not.

Daniel Waters, who had written *Heathers* (1989), featuring Wynona Ryder, was next up at bat. He says that Burton virtually put it on a basis of "I dare you to make me make this movie." Whether for good or ill—opinion is still divided on that point—Waters took on the dare by writing a script to which Burton said yes, or at least to which he provisionally said yes. Before it was all over, Waters had produced no less that five drafts of the *Batman* follow-up. "I was going to be the first writer to give Tim Burton a great story—three acts, *bam, bam, bam*. But after the first couple weeks with Tim, you realize it's not going to happen. He just doesn't think like that. He operates on this abstract, associative level," commented Waters, adding, "It's not like I had a screaming fight with Tim. You learn to stop worrying and love Tim's weird synapses, the way he puts things together." Waters did, in any case, bring something to the script that had been missing in the original—a sense of humor about the whole thing. The first *Batman* had limited its humor to the Joker's one-liners. Waters's effort had the wit even to poke fun at the narrative blunder of Alfred's waltzing Vicki Vale into the Batcave and to take a few jabs at the vapid nature of Vicki's character in the bargain.

Once Waters was off the project, Burton next called in screenwriter Wesley Strick for (uncredited) rewrites. Most of these came in the form of hacking out large chunks of Waters's narrative, the most significant of which was to remove the character of Robin, who, in Waters's version, had been a gang leader in cahoots with the Penguin before turning against him and joining forces with Batman. Strick's main addition to the plot line was the Penguin's plan to kidnap the children of Gotham's rich set. Even that element would be eventually minimized. "Tim was really leery of spending a lot of screen time with kids in jeopardy," explained Strick. When in post-production Burton was asked about the film's plot by *Entertainment Weekly*'s Steve Daly, he quipped, "Haven't you heard? There is no plot." By the time of its release, many critics and quite a few viewers would agree.

The script, however, wasn't entirely the key to the expensive project. A financial deal that had put Burton on similar footing with the astronomical money Jack Nicholson had received on *Batman* certainly entered into the decision. So, too, did the fact that Warner Bros.' original plan to shoot the sequel on the still-standing Anton Furst *Batman* sets in London went by the wayside. Burton would be allowed to lens the film in Los Angeles with all-new sets designed by Bo Welch. Burton's reasoning on this was twofold. He wanted something fresh, and he did not want to shoot at Pinewood. Despite the fact that fresh sets would drive the production costs to $100 million (some say the production ended up costing as much as $120 million), the studio agreed. Warner Bros. president Terry Semel said, "We were very, very eager to have Tim direct the sequel. He was the first creative person to make sense of *Batman* and we felt he was the one who could take it to the next level."

The next level was considerably higher than Semel—or anyone else—thought at the time, since what that mostly would mean, would be that Burton wanted *no* compromises this time around. No pop songs by Prince to contend with. No interference from executive producer Jon Peters or anyone else. As Denise DiNovi explained, "He had graduated to a point where he wanted to make movies that are his movies. And this is one hundred percent Tim's movie." Granted. And this was a fact that Warner Bros. would come to regret greatly on a number of levels.

Burton clearly did not want to retread his original movie. Since Batman's background had been effectively covered in the first offering, he felt it was fine merely to introduce him—and, by extension, Alfred, of course—as a fully-formed character in *Batman Returns*. Among other things, this allowed the script room to explore the origins of two of its villains, Catwoman and the Penguin. Its third—more human—villain, Max Shreck (named for the star of F. W. Murnau's horror classic, *Nosferatu* [1922], but made up more to look like Rudolph Klein-Rogge in Fritz Lang's *Metropolis*) was left more or less without a background. This much was fine. Where Burton—or rather the studio—ran into difficulty was in the concept of the Penguin, which proved to be markedly different from the one presented in the comic books. Burton called the Penguin his "least favorite character" as offered in the comics and the 1960s TV series. To Burton, the Penguin was portrayed as "just a guy in a tuxedo." He wanted more.

Between himself and scripter Daniel Waters, Burton got more—a good deal more—than the studio really wanted. The Penguin would be given a completely fleshed-out background. He would be a horribly deformed and monstrous infant, abandoned by his parents and raised by actual penguins living in the sewers under Gotham's "old zoo." No one much objected to this concept. It was fanciful to the point of being bizarre, but, after all, the film was largely a fantasy anyway. However, the Penguin, as he finally emerged in the plot line, would be far more grotesque than anyone could have imagined. Worse, he would come equipped with an innuendo-laden sexual voracity that helped cause the film to flirt with losing its essential PG-13 rating. According to scripter Wesley Strick, a lot of this material came with the actor cast as the Penguin, who "didn't want to play a villain who was remotely lovable." The star would come up with the bit where the Penguin eats a raw fish, hacks out numerous jokes, and generally punches up all the less delicious aspects of the character.

Casting the Penguin was easy: the diminutive, stocky Danny DeVito. No one else even ran second. In fact, DeVito was thought so essential for the part that he claims he had read in a newspaper he was being considered for the role some eighteen months before he was even asked. Casting Catwoman was a far less cut-and-dried affair.

The Selina Kyle/Catwoman role in *Batman Returns* (1992) had originally gone to Annette Bening, but she had to bow out late in pre-production because she, having wed superstar Warren Beatty, became pregnant. This sudden news and change in plans threw Burton and Denise DiNovi off balance. "We were freaked out about it. When Tim called me with the news, we sat in silence on the phone for, like, three minutes," DiNovi later admitted. The only other possible choice in their minds was Michelle Pfeiffer, who, of course, ended up costarring in the feature.

However, she was far from the only choice in the mind of one other actress, Sean Young, who was determined that *she* should play the part herself. She was quite prepared to go to great lengths to get the part. She based her claim largely on the strength of her abortive involvement on *Batman,* where she had to be replaced by Kim Basinger at the last moment in the role of Vicki Vale. The problem was that, apparently, no one wanted her for Catwoman (for that matter, Jack Nicholson had advised against her for Vicki Vale). However, she was not equipped to take this dismissal lightly. She literally stormed the studio, dressed as catlike as possible, talked to producer DiNovi, cornered Warner Bros. executive Mark Canton in his office (apparently hoping to find Tim Burton there), and laid out her case before Canton and Michael Keaton (who was returning as the film's hero), who happened to be in a meeting with

Canton at the time. After her sales pitch, she departed, only to show a videotape of her antics later on TV's *The Joan Rivers Show*. Whether or not Sean
Young actually ever saw Burton (rumor has it that he hid from her on the
studio lot) is open to question, but she was certainly determined!

Despite having had four successful Hollywood pictures in a row, Tim
Burton was not a happy man in many ways. During—and certainly by the end
of—the *Batman Returns* shoot, the rumors that all was less than idyllic in his marriage to Lena Gieseke, were confirmed but not commented upon. Perhaps this
was why he thought the in-sync, out-of-sync relationship between Batman and
Catwoman depicted in the movie seemed, as he told one reporter, normal to him.
It may also account, to some degree, for the fact that one of the major differences
in tone between *Batman* and *Batman Returns* is that, where the hero of the former
is somber and thoughtful, the Batman of the latter film tends to be somber and
angry—and much of that anger would appear to be directed at himself.

There were other things, too, that seemed less than rosy for filmmaker Burton.

His relationship with Anton Furst had become very vague. The *Calendar*
section of the *Los Angeles Times,* in discussing the film's production design
noted, "The late Anton Furst, the Oscar-winning British designer of *Batman*
and a close friend of Burton's, was not part of the film's team due to Furst's
exclusive contract with Columbia [Pictures]." When asked (in *Premiere* magazine) about Furst's suicide (he killed himself in November 1991), Burton said,
"We were friends and I haven't been able to talk about it. It's still very painful
for me and hard to talk about. But we were friends, and—he was a delicate
person, and coming here just accelerated a process, really. And it was just painful
to see. See, I've been through it, and I resisted. I try not to listen to too much
praise, to be equally suspicious of praise as I am of criticism."

Burton further noted of the late Furst, "And then on the other side of it,
he was into his own thing, and in some ways for me, it was good—and this is
before his death—that he wasn't doing it, because for me to do this movie, I
needed it to feel fresh in a way. We tread a fine line here, and I like the sets,
actually, better. They're fresh and different." If the latter sounds a little callous, it
perhaps was. In the *Vanity Fair* article, "Tim Burton's Hollywood Nightmare,"
the account is a little different: "Among those whom Burton unceremoniously
cut off was Anton Furst, who had won an Oscar for his *Batman* sets and, in

1990, was under contract to Columbia Pictures to design and direct his own movies. Furst hoped that a loophole would be found that would allow him to work on *Batman Returns* (a Warner Bros. film). But Burton had no interest anyway. The sensitive, less-than-stable Furst was said to be bewildered when Burton stopped taking his calls. They never reconciled: Furst committed suicide a few months later."

At the same time as this, others recounted tales of Burton's inexplicable and cavalier dismissal of friends and co-workers. (This is the same period when Tim fired his long-standing agents to take a deal with powerhouse talent agent Michael Ovitz—or, more correctly, had Denise DiNovi do the face-to-face negotiations for him, as Burton is notorious for avoiding confrontations.) Yet, it is worth noting that, paradoxically, it would be Burton who, in a show of loyalty, would give Paul Reubens his first screen role (in *Batman Returns* as the Penguin's father), following the comedian's arrest for public indecency in 1991, when he was charged with "masterbating" (as the police report read) in a porno theatre in Sarasota, Florida.

In many respects, however, it must be admitted that Welch's sets proved to be superior to those used on the first film. They appear more spacious. Gotham City seems larger, and, more to the point, the sets seem genuinely Burtonesque. Furst's group had a greater tendency to favor browns, where Welch's entire look—at least on Burton's movie—is heavily centered on blue, and blue might be said to be Burton's signature color. Moreover, Welch's sets are more fanciful and less ominous than the ones in *Batman*, which may be a very good thing indeed, considering the harsher tone of the sequel.

When Tim Burton commented to the media that in *Batman Returns* he could "see a little bit of every movie I've made," he really wasn't kidding. In a lot of ways, the adventure epic is almost a grand compendium, a sort of summing-up of his creative achievements up to that time. Danny Elfman (whose music is also a first-rate blend of his previous work with new elements; the score often seems like a mixture of the first *Batman* score and the one for *Edward Scissorhands*) was quite correct in calling the film "operatic." It is certainly that, and for all the murk surrounding its production, it is one of Burton's most accomplished works so far. And, possibly it is even more revealing than the deliberately personal *Edward Scissorhands*.

All smiles for his 1976
Burbank (California) High School
graduation picture.
COURTESY OF SETH POPPEL
YEARBOOK ARCHIVES

Tim Burton—the rising young
A-list filmmaker makes a name
and look for himself.
COURTESY OF GAMMA LIAISON/
GEORGE ROSE © 1989

Hanging out with a friend in 1989. COURTESY OF SYGMA/T. O'NEILL

Testing out the Caped Crusader's Batmobile on the set of *Batman*. COURTESY OF SYGMA/T. O'NEILL

Tim Burton and friend, actress Lisa Marie, at the premiere of *Mars Attacks!* (1996) in Los Angeles.
COURTESY OF SYGMA/RONALD SIEMONEIT

Out on the town with constant companion, Lisa Marie. COURTESY OF CORBIS/MITCHELL GERBER

13 | DARK DAYS AND DARKER NIGHTS

Ah! The direct approach!
I admire that in a man with a mask.

DANNY DeVITO

as the Penguin in *Batman Returns* (1992)

As IF IT WERE A HOLDOVER FROM *EDWARD SCISSORHANDS,* *Batman Returns* opens with snow falling, in this case around a Warner Bros. logo, before the film plunges into an exquisitely designed, completely visual precredits sequence dealing with the origins of the Penguin, née Oswald Cobblepot, a (suggested, but not seen) monstrosity born into the ritzy Cobblepot family on a winter night. The fashionable Cobblepots (Paul Reubens and Diane Salinger) do what any respectable members of the haut monde would when faced with such a situation—take Baby for a walk and clandestinely dump him—Moses-like in a basket—into the drainage system that runs into the sewers under Gotham's old zoo. (Bizarrely, the whole Moses angle—the abandonment of the infant in a basket to float downstream, supposed Semitic overtones in DeVito's makeup, the plot to kidnap the firstborn of Gotham's rich and powerful, et cetera—was taken very seriously in some quarters, causing the film to be branded as having anti-Semitic overtones.)

In typical Tim Burton fashion, the credits (styled after those on the original film, with the delightful addition of having the word Batman unfold like a bat spreading its wings) are played over the infant Penguin's journey into the sewers, where the infant, eventually, is surrounded by a group of curious penguins. By this point, the film is five and a half minutes old and Burton has not made even a tiny false step, nor has he wasted a single moment. Everything counts and everything is so nearly perfect that it makes the viewer long to see what Burton might do with a completely dialogueless feature film.

Nothing could live up to this opening and *Batman Returns* doesn't quite, as the scene shifts to Christmas in downtown Gotham "thirty-three years later," where the annual lighting of the tree, in the film's demented version of Rockefeller Center, is taking place. The big news of the day, in fact, is the rumor of a creature with flipperlike hands existing in the sewers. High above all this, in the penthouse office atop Shreck's department store (with its bizarre, grinning-cat logo), Shreck (Christopher Walken), the Mayor (Michael Murphy), and several others, are discussing Shreck's proposed power plant for Gotham. Overhearing this is Shreck's personal secretary, Selina Kyle (Michelle Pfeiffer). The meeting soon breaks up for Shreck and the Mayor to make speeches at the event in the street below. The celebration in the streets is interrupted by mayhem launched by the derelict Penguin and his gang. Police Commissioner Gordon (Pat Hingle) signals a brooding Bruce Wayne (Michael Keaton) of the city's need for Batman. (Interestingly, Burton has commented that he has tended to rely less and less on storyboards for his films, but this sequence comprises shots that almost look like the literal depiction of storyboarding at its best.)

The sequences of carnage involving the Penguin's kidnapping of the mogul Shreck and Batman's intervention are undeniably brilliant, lucid action sequences, far more elaborate and accomplished than anything in *Batman,* and certainly more original. Nathan Stein, one of the members of the mime troupe, Mumm, used for the circus performers in the chaos-on-the-streets scene (he plays one of the Uncle Sam–on–stilts characters), said that Burton exhibited a genuine flair and feeling for the action interludes in this film. "He really goes for the action sequences, which is why my part got expanded, even though it got cut to like under twenty seconds! Eight weeks of work got cut way, way, way down."

The action scenes on *Batman Returns* were not without their peril, either. In the scene where the Batmobile topples the two Uncle Sam–on–stilts characters, Stein relates that the stunt people were firing live fireworks around them (one of which hit his partner in the finger): "There were some challenging moments up there. We were juggling fire. I mean, I had to stand juggling fire with my partner as the Batmobile comes whizzing by. I'm juggling *inches* from the fins of the car. Then the slats come out and cut the stilts from under us and we fall. That was really some of the most personally challenging, scary kind of work I've done, stuntwise. You always have to look out for yourself on those things, because any director who's thinking about a million things is not going to be thinking about your safety. We had some real scary moments and we had some real physical challenges. It was not a cakewalk."

Exciting stuff, but with Elfman's terrifying score (a blend of circus music and the *Dies Irae,* the Latin mass for the dead) on the soundtrack and the over-the-top imagery of skull-headed motorcyclists, gore-faced Uncle Sams, devil firebreathers destroying cute stuffed animals, et cetera, this *Batman Returns* sequence is way too intense for most children, and is the first of several elements in the film that caused a parental backlash upon release. It might have been worse. As it stands, one of the fights Burton lost with the ratings board of the motion-picture industry is a shot of firebreathers actually igniting fleeing Gothamites. This sequence had to be excised in order to secure the film's PG-13 rating. (Oddly, a shot of Batman blithely burning a firebreathing devil alive was not considered too strong for public consumption!) But, as Nathan Stein said, "Well, his films *are* dark."

As it develops, in the melee the Penguin kidnaps Shreck to secure his assistance in a bid for a kind of normalcy, or at least respect, for this underground criminal—and to find out who his parents were. To this end, the Penguin has spent years getting the goods on many of Shreck's nefarious dealings. Recognizing defeat—and with a plan of his own—Shreck concedes and their bargain is sealed.

Having set up this aspect of the plot, the film then turns its attention to the development of Selina Kyle and the events that will lead her to become Catwoman, a somewhat more serious and far-less-gruesomely-comedic business than that with the Penguin. Her character is easily the best defined in the film, and the one in which Burton and Waters clearly are most interested. A bright young woman caught in a world of men who value looks over intellect and who dismiss the concept of a woman with intellect in any case, Selina lives a lonesome existence built on fantasies of sitcom normality. ("Honey, I'm home!" she cheerfully announces upon entering her apartment, before remembering, "Oh, I forgot, I'm not married.") Her sole companions are her cat (of whose apparent sex life she's tolerantly jealous) and her answering machine.

The only complication in Selina's dull life occurs when she discovers Shreck's plot to drain off Gotham's electricity and then sell it back to the city! For her resourcefulness, Shreck shoves her through a window, to what is presumed to be her death, below. In one of *Batman Returns'* more fancifully, deliberately unclear moments, it is never made certain whether Selina is actually dead and is somehow brought back to life by the horde of cats that chew and nuzzle her seemingly lifeless form, or if she is saved when her fall is broken by the grinning-cat awnings she rips through on her way down. Whichever is the case, the scene, accompanied by Danny Elfman's weird Bartók-like rhythmic music, is unsettling in its sheer strangeness.

Recovering—or returning to life—Selena goes back to her apartment and goes berserk, tearing up her apartment. Suddenly she comes across a black plastic outfit that will become the genesis of her Catwoman suit.

Later, when the Catwoman is shown in all her glory, the first noticeable thing is that her suit—not to mention her needlelike claws—bears a remarkable resemblance to Edward Scissorhands—something that is obviously not coincidental. This is part and parcel of the extreme complexity of the movie as it fits into Tim Burton's work overall. While it is easy to point a finger at the Burton onscreen alter ego in all of his previous works, it is less so here, simply because *Batman Returns* is of such remarkable density that Burton is, in various ways, related not just to Catwoman, but also to Batman, the Penguin, and even Max Shreck (though Shreck comes across largely as a jab at Hollywood power-broker types in any allegorical reading). In some respects, *Batman Returns* is actually a very self-accusatory work, since the filmmaker is here depicting far more of his darker side—perhaps due to the turmoil in his personal and professional life—than he heretofore, or subsequently, dared.

In a particularly clever swipe at media manipulation and the credulity of human beings, the Penguin stages the most blatantly obvious event to introduce himself to the world. Having one of his henchmen kidnap the Mayor's baby during a speech, he then proceeds to "rescue" and return the infant in a matter of seconds. That anyone actually buys the lame offscreen encounter between kidnapper and Penguin is amazing. However, they do and the Penguin emerges as both hero and sympathetic media figure. His pleas for wanting to understand his origins interest Bruce Wayne, who, after all, has something of a fixation about parents. That Bruce "buys into" this ploy at first, is hardly surprising. Yet, the deeper resonance of the Penguin's bogus plea seems to extend to Tim Burton himself and the deep-seated resentment he obviously feels at the perceived shortcomings of his own childhood.

Under the guise of discovering who he is, the Penguin establishes himself in the Hall of Records where he assembles a list of names. Drawing a parallel between the Penguin and Bruce, this is played against Bruce's researching the possible connection between the Penguin and a villainous circus troupe whose members had included an "aquatic bird-boy." Bruce's motives, too, are open to debate and are pointedly questioned by others in the narrative. Again, the sense that Burton is getting at something deeper and more disturbing about himself is inescapable.

In a grotesque parody (nonetheless, drawing another parallel between the two) of Bruce's ritualistic visit to the site of his parents' slaying in *Batman,* the Penguin, with much ceremony and false piety, pays a visit to the graves of *his* parents, laying a rose for each in front of the tombstone. When a reporter notes that since his parents are dead, Oswald will never be able to settle the score with them, the Penguin agrees: "True. I was their number one son, and they treated me like number two, but it's human nature to fear the unusual. Perhaps when I held my Tiffany baby rattle with a shiny flipper, instead of five chubby digits, they freaked, but I forgive them." Taken in conjunction with Burton's background and his screen work overall, these lines of dialogue have the disturbing quality of pent-up hostility attempting to be sublimated by a gesture of magnanimous forgiveness. That the Penguin's bogus words are solely for the benefit of the media and his admirers, again suggests that Burton is both more and less than he lets on in his nonpublic persona. It is also telling that this fabricated personality is a smash hit with the public at large, who are captivated and charmed by the manner in which the Penguin presents himself to the world. Is Burton perhaps telling us something about his own private self?

Enter the Catwoman into the proceedings. She seems, at first, to be a vigilante of the night à la Batman himself, but proves to have her own agenda of nonfocused anger. One of the most surprising aspects of the critical reaction to *Batman Returns* would be the almost universal praise for Michelle Pfeiffer and her Catwoman. Pfeiffer certainly deserves the praise, but in reality Catwoman is the least focused character in a film where the plot and the motivations of the characters are almost invariably a sore spot with the critics.

When Catwoman reemerges as Selina, her hair is wilder, her glasses are gone, and there is no sense of anything but self-confidence. Understandably, Shreck may be appalled by her back-from-the-dead appearance, but Bruce is clearly fascinated by this new Selina. The obvious question that filmmaker Burton is here pondering is this: Has a mask been removed or has one been put on? The question—like many such in a movie bristling with characters who live entirely by role-playing—remains unanswered, perhaps simply because it is unanswerable with any degree of certainty. Blessedly, Burton seems to instinctively realize that he doesn't have the answers to these questions, and must settle for the not-inconsiderable achievement of at least posing the proper queries.

In a spectacularly outré sequence, Shreck escorts the new media darling to a "surprise," which turns out to be the campaign headquarters for Shreck's bid to have Oswald Cobblepot elected mayor of Gotham. The Penguin proves himself a not entirely tractable candidate, being more interested in attempting sexual relations with his female media advisor (Jan Hooks) than he is in adapting to her idea that he wear gloves. He takes an instant dislike to another advisor who makes sport of his appearance. He reacts by chomping down on his tormenter's proboscis with a resultant spray of blood, the residue of which allows the Penguin to play the remainder of the scene with blood dripping from his mouth. It is all perversely funny, but it is certainly humor at its darkest and most distasteful—almost worthy of moviemaker John Waters—and is one of the sequences that helped caused the parental backlash that dogged the release of *Batman Returns*.

Shreck's plan is to have the Penguin's gang launch a reign of terror on Gotham to undermine the Mayor's credibility and allow for a special election to name his replacement. The reign of terror is competent action material, amusingly and excitingly staged, but the point here is somewhat different. Since these sequences have an altogether unusual quality, they may be the only action scenes in cinema history designed to enrich characterization, which they do with a vengeance.

When Batman meets the Penguin for the first time, he asks the Penguin what he's really after. Their encounter is interrupted by Catwoman somersaulting into the scene with an opening, "Meow!" just before *her* handiwork pays off and the entire bottom floor of Shreck's building explodes. She vanishes in the explosion. The ever-lecherous Penguin announces, "I saw her first," and escapes, while Batman, spying Catwoman climbing a nearby building, takes off after this apparent new threat to the city.

The subsequent rooftop battle between Batman and Catwoman is an amazingly perverse take on the battle of the sexes, and the weirdest courtship (perhaps "mating ritual" would be more apt) imaginable. After attacking Batman and being soundly punched, Catwoman accusingly glares at him, leading to Batman apologizing. His reward is a kick in the crotch. Their love-hate relationship develops as each jockeys for power. Perhaps only two people wearing masks—of whatever kind, literal or figurative—*can* really connect in Burton's world. It is hardly surprising that such a connection would be both unusual and mutually destructive.

Further into the narrative, Bruce and Selina set a date for a dinner. Their encounter is a shrewd variation on the Batman-Catwoman one, with both inadvertently dropping veiled hints as to their other selves. They are openly appalled at the newspaper reports of the events of the night of their original, adversarial encounter. The interesting thing about this is the idea that super-heroes and villains alike are so concerned with their public images that bad—or at least inaccurate—press takes precedence over all other concerns.

When Bruce and Selina have their first date, it is here that Bruce explains that he had a girlfriend, but that she couldn't deal with what Selina calls his "duality." This examination of Bruce's personality is difficult not to associate with Burton's own marital problems at the time. Amusingly, the pair's subsequent attempts at lovemaking are thwarted by the wounds they inflicted on each other as their other selves!

In the course of *Batman Returns,* the Ice Princess (Cristi Conaway), who is to relight the Christmas tree in Gotham Plaza, is kidnapped by the Penguin. She proves to be one of his accomplices, who dies in the course of the villain's nefarious schemes. The ever-crafty Penguin makes it appear Batman was responsible for the young woman's death. This leads to more confusion in the see-sawing relationship between Batman and Catwoman.

Meanwhile, Batman's own troubles are far from over. Not only does it appear that he murdered the Ice Princess, but he soon learns that the Batmobile is no longer under his control, but is being manipulated by the Penguin. This state of affairs leads to the death of many innocent Gothamites at the "hands" of Batman, the apparently reckless driver.

As the movie progresses, the Penguin is ultimately thwarted in his bid to join the human race. It leads him to acknowledge, "I am not a human being! I am an animal!" The dastardly creature's rejection of his own humanity and the human race is really nothing more or less than an extremely dark variation on Edward Scissorhands returning to his private world when it seems that the real world has no place for him. That the Penguin's notion—kidnapping and murdering the firstborn children of Gotham's smart set—is, to say the least, more extreme and vengeful, is an intriguing comment on the less-than-cozy side of Tim Burton, which he has hinted—even warned—exists from his earliest screenwork.

The masked ball—a sequence that, in the pruned version of the *Batman Returns* script, makes dubious geographical sense, in that it is held in Shreck's department store, which we last saw blasted out of existence—is one of Burton's most accomplished pieces of filmmaking, especially as concerns the encounter between Bruce and Selina. Perhaps, because of the sexual tension inherent in the unconsummated nature of their relationship, this is the most successful onscreen depiction of an adult relationship that Burton has achieved to date. As the pair dances, Selina encourages Bruce to slip her away to a king-sized bed in the bedding department. When he questions whether this means they will have to remove their costumes, she replies she is fed up with "wearing masks." Before the duo can resolve the complexities of their alliance, the

Penguin literally crashes the party and takes Shreck hostage, back into the sewers with him.

Imprisoning Shreck, the Penguin explains his plan to lure the children of the city's most prominent citizens with circus performers, so he can bring them to his lair. The actual kidnapping of the youngsters is given fairly little screen time (as noted by scripter Wesley Strick, director Burton was never easy with the idea of the children being so imperiled). Within the plot line, the Penguin's crime is thwarted in its early stages by Batman.

Much like its screen predecessor, *Batman Returns* allots a generous amount of time—nearly twenty minutes—to its final act. However, the pacing here cannot be faulted (as in *Batman*). Some of the sequences to this segment, however, proved to be a nightmare of similar proportions, for different reasons, to crafting a coherent ending out of nothing on the original picture. "It was horrible. I don't think there was a day where somebody wasn't getting hooked up to some bizarre contraption. And our schedule was actually based on the penguins. Here you are juggling all this stuff, the biggest-name actors, the set, and everything is based on the fact that the molting season is coming," Burton told the *Los Angeles Times,* as concerns dealing with his bird-filled climax. With some fifty live penguins of two species, a raft of animatronic penguins, people in penguin suits, elaborate effects, and all the rest, it is little wonder that the climax to *Batman Returns* was something else again to get on film. Against all conceivable odds, though, Burton managed it.

As *Batman Returns* concludes, the Penguin and his forces are vanquished, while Shreck is eliminated. As for Batman and Catwoman, they have discovered anew that with their assumed identities peeled away, they cannot relate to one another on a normal level. As part of the climax, there is a strangely moving and even stately moment, as the giant emperor penguins emerge and, like pallbearers, move the body of their leader (the Penguin) into the waters of the lake while Batman looks on. This scene, brilliantly staged, exciting, and yet entirely character-driven, is the Wagnerian finale *Batman* strove for and missed. Burton did not miss a second time.

Unlike the somewhat tacked-on tag scene of the previous entry, *Batman Returns* concludes in this same somber tone, with Bruce being driven through the streets of a dark, wintry Gotham by Alfred. As they drive off into the night the camera moves up through the skyscrapers to reveal the Gotham skyline. The Batsymbol appears in the sky and Catwoman rises into the frame, looking at it for the fadeout.

When Warner Bros. screened the expensively mounted film Burton had made, they were immediately disturbed by its dark tone. The industry ratings board was even less pleased, and Burton would be fighting with them almost up to the movie's release date. On some points he was adamant, but in other cases he had to give in, since the studio was simply not going to release the picture with anything harsher than a PG-13 rating. (A PG-13 classification on *Batman Returns* was bad enough, as it would limit the age range of youngsters who would pay to see the movie.) Actually, the changes made to appease the censors would hardly matter. Granted, individual shots could be trimmed in most cases. (Some items, like the Penguin dripping black bile from his mouth and nose in his final scene, simply could not be cut, but would have had to be reshot—something Burton had left no time for, possibly deliberately.) But there was nothing that could alter the overall grim tone of *Batman Returns*.

When *Batman Returns* opened in June 1992, the notices were often surprisingly good. Kim Newman in *Sight and Sound* magazine concluded, "This is a rare follow-up that refines and extends the original, suggesting further possibilities to be explored, preferably by the same creative team." Gene Siskel of the *Chicago Tribune* weighed in favor of the movie: "This time the richness of the Batman movie is not in its production design, but rather in Burton's and screenwriter Daniel Waters' Freudian view of adult human behavior. If all this makes *Batman Returns* seem overly serious, well, that's an overstatement. But it should be a pleasure for nonadolescents to encounter a comic-book action picture in which the characters are more important than their gadgets." Kathleen Carroll of the *New York Daily News* was more guarded in her not-dissimilar, positive response, saying, "All in all, this Freudian-inspired freak show packs a strong punch, but its nasty tone is unsettling enough to make one wonder if the movie is appropriate for children." In many respects, hers seems to be the closest reviewers got to the central "problem" of the film—Burton had made a supposed children's picture that wasn't suitable for children.

Typically, Roger Ebert of the *Chicago Sun-Times* was baffled by the release in many ways: "The film is filled with possibilities, but they don't connect, and the final impression is of great art direction, haunted by a confusing story." In other words, Ebert was expressing the same basic complaint he had had about every Tim Burton picture. Owen Gleiberman of *Entertainment Weekly* called the film "exhaustingly inventive," going on to say that the picture had "too many competing characters, too many sets (every scene seems to unfold on a different surreal soundstage), too many ideas that don't go anywhere." *L.A. Weekly* called the film "comic-book Fellini," noting, "but it's the Fellini of *Satyricon,* of self-indulgence, in which director Tim Burton, whose dramatic imagination is out of whack with his visual imagination, externalizes the implicit madness of a millionaire who dresses up like a bat and lurks in the rafters of the city."

As with its predecessor, *Batman Returns* boasted a strong opening—grossing $96.7 million in ten days at the box office. However, it also quickly slumped. Second-week attendance dropped by 47 percent. Not only was the film not getting the repeat business associated with *Batman*—and with Tim Burton in general—something else was happening. *Variety* noted that the movie had opened wider (i.e., on more screens) than any film in history, meaning more people saw it in its first week than usual: "When more people go to see a movie at the beginning, more are badmouthing it if they don't like it, and it falls off faster." Even Warner Bros. admitted that this was happening. One studio executive complained, "It's too dark. It's not a lot of fun."

This, however, was only the beginning of the troubles for *Batman Returns.* The real problem arose when parental groups focused on the film. The violent and sometimes horrific parts of the movie were scaring small children, while their parents were appalled by the picture's frequent use of sexual innuendo. On the one hand, this raised the issue of parents who ignored the fact that the film was rated PG-13 ("Some material may be inappropriate for pre-teenagers"), but this reasonable question was countered by the fact that the film boasted a merchandising tie-in with McDonald's, which was promoting it by giving away *Batman Returns* toys in their child-oriented Happy Meal packages. McDonald's came in for more flack than the movie, especially when they tried to distance themselves from it by claiming that their commercials for the tie-in products were not meant to entice children to see the movie. No one was buying that one, but in all fairness, no one from McDonald's had seen the movie when they agreed to the promotion. Whether or not any of this hurt McDonald's is open to question, but it undeniably hurt *Batman Returns* and, to some degree, Burton's moviemaking career. Without a doubt, Warner Bros. was going to want a third Batman picture, but there was equally no doubt that they would prefer one *not* made by Tim Burton.

On a more personal level, performer Nathan Stein, who had been in *Batman Returns,* commenting to this author in February 1998 on the reaction of children to the film, said, "I made the mistake of taking my parents to the opening and it was sort of the opposite effect. I wished I hadn't brought *them*! I didn't think, by and large, whether it was dark or light mattered; I just didn't think—other than Catwoman, who was an absolute breath of fresh air—that the story or the experience was thrilling. I didn't find it thrilling, but then, I know the mechanics of making a movie. I think that Tim Burton—I really consider him a painter—as a director kind of lets the talent do what they want. I don't think he necessarily has a great actor's interpretation of a scene at all. I really think he has a painter's framing and a coloring of a scene. Working on the set, he was really very technical. He never had any colorful instructions for the actors. He would [give] instructions to his ADs [assistant directors] here and there, but pretty much everyone was on their own.

"He was the master puppeteer in many ways. Then again, I was involved in the action scenes, but I think he just pretty much lets the actors go once he casts the choices. Tim was just like, 'Oh, I like that idea. I think we want to expand your part.' There was more back then—there was a kind of innocence, there was kind of a much more naiveté about him. He wasn't really hardened. But *Batman Returns* was disheartening to see with my parents. I wish I could have seen it alone, because I could have been a little more sensitive to it."

Stein is careful to add another possible reason for the perception of the *Batman Returns* as so dark: "Who knows? When seen down the line, it may seem increasingly less dark. You've got to remember that you see it in relation to the headlines that hit you at the time and what seems dark one year, seems laughable the next. The headlines of the day do affect you when you go out for entertainment, because it's been said to you, in a sense, like entertainment. And

I think at the time it was really too dark because the Gulf War was right in your face still. That does play in your mind and you view the film in those contexts, and they can't know that when they go in to make the movie."

All that to one side, Stein's lasting impression of Tim Burton is what he calls a "snapshot": "We were auditioning for him over at the Warner Bros. lot over in Burbank. We did a bunch of tricks for him out on the lawn, and for some reason we had to go back one day to drop off some more stuff—some pictures or a video or something—and we went into his offices and there was a secretary in the outer office, and we said, 'Is Tim here? He wanted us to drop this video off,' and she said, 'Sure, but he's busy right now.' So we left her the tape, but then we were walking by his office door and it was open, and he was there at the desk and we leaned in and saw him—and he was just sitting behind the desk, absolutely still, almost like shell-shocked, with his sketchpad in front of him. This was in the throes of super pre-production, or right before production started. It was just the look of the artist and his sketchpad. Obviously his head was so full and it was like he was shell-shocked to the point of catatonia."

Considering the enormity of the undertaking before him, there is little wonder at Burton's unique work mode. Had he any idea what the reaction to *Batman Returns* would be, and what lay ahead, he may well have been even more overwhelmed by the creative challenges that lay ahead of him.

14 | BURTONLAND

The next time you get the urge to take over someone
else's holiday, I'd listen to her—she's the only one
who makes any sense around this insane asylum!

SANTA CLAUS
in *Tim Burton's The Nightmare Before Christmas,* 1993

BY THE TIME *BATMAN RETURNS* WAS IN PRODUCTION
in 1991, Tim Burton already was a name to reckon with—someone to compare to Steven Spielberg, only a more artistic, personal, and decidedly quirky
Spielberg. Tim had quickly passed from being just a director, to being acknowledged by the film industry as a *filmmaker* (with all that the name implies,
including projects he conceived, as opposed to ones for which he was hired).
Even Burton's detractors were quick to concede that there was nobody quite
like him in the Hollywood moviemaking community. He was, in fact, well on
his way to becoming an institution—with his own production company.
Writers and directors were now coming to him with their dream projects.
Studios—even Disney—were courting him for forthcoming releases. For a
time, there was even talk (which Burton invariably denied) of a Burton-themed
amusement park, Burtonland, that would have been something along the lines
of a singularly odd Disneyland. Tim Burton the artist was in very real danger of
being engulfed by Tim Burton the mogul.

There are, after all, only so many hours in a day, and yet, as Burton was finding, there are an amazing array of tempting projects to undertake—far more than any one man can successfully accomplish. As a result, it was inevitable that Burton would find himself in the position of delegating authority to others, in order that some of his ideas—and the ideas of others—that appealed to him would actually become reality. Setting aside his involvement in such projects as *Family Dog,* Burton's first such effort bore the slightly ironic title, *Tim Burton's The Nightmare Before Christmas* (1993), a concept dating back ten years, to his days at Disney. A few moviemakers have included their own names as part of the title of their final product (*Fellini's Satyricon* [1970], *Fellini's Roma* [1972], and *Ken Russell's ABC of British Music* [1986] come to mind); however, Burton has the distinction of being the first—and possibly the last—filmmaker to incorporate his name into the title of a film he did not himself make!

Burton concocted this Dr. Seuss–influenced project at a time when the Disney studio was giving him a free hand as a conceptual artist in the early 1980s. At the time, little of what Burton was creating was considered even marginally commercial, and an expensive, full-scale stop-animation feature such as he envisioned was completely out of the question. The very idea of making a film that was both a tribute to *and* an expansion of such seasonal TV fare from Burton's childhood as *Rudolph the Red-Nosed Reindeer* (1964), was unthinkable. Even when that less-elaborate TV film was made, stop-motion animation was considered a bit old hat. In the early 1980s—before its resurgence via MTV and specialists in the field like Aardman Animations (who made Peter Gabriel's landmark "Sledgehammer" video)—it was positively quaint. Burton knew this when he developed the idea and never seriously expected it to be made. However, it remained a cherished dream, and one that held particular appeal to him when his life seemed to be getting away from him. Ten years and four hit films later, it was another story. Now he knew he had the clout to make such a film, but there were two significant problems: Everything he had created at Disney still belonged to Disney, and he was committed to the gigantic undertaking of *Batman Returns* and couldn't direct the film himself. Moreover, very possibly he didn't want to. Burton has gone on record as not being especially fond of animation for its own sake, and the time and sheer tedium involved in making a stop-motion feature-length movie would be enough to daunt all but the most hard-core animation fanatic!

An early notion that he could perhaps just retrieve his story and concept from the studio fell through, as might be expected: "You signed your soul away in blood when you worked there. They owned your firstborn. I kind of gently said, 'Could I just have it back?'" Burton told *Premiere* magazine (November 1993). Disney clearly wasn't going for that. After all, Tim Burton was the hottest of the hot new filmmakers, and a Burton property was not something a studio was anxious to give away. Moreover, the minute he showed any interest in *The Nightmare Before Christmas,* Disney knew they had something that might well entice the one director every studio wanted, into working for them. It was quite a switch from the days a decade ago when they had grudgingly approved the bare-bones budget for *Frankenweenie.*

Suddenly Disney actively wanted Burton on their team. They were willing to finance his previously impractical and "un-Disney" idea. Fortunately, Burton took it all in stride, philosophically. He cared more that he won out in the end and that his dream picture would get made; he let go of any remaining resentment over his not-altogether-pleasant previous tenure with the studio. As such, he responded positively to the new regime headed up by Michael Eisner and Jeffrey Katzenberg; the latter, in particular, had become a staunch supporter of the filmmaker and his project. Plus, an alliance with Disney kept him from becoming too closely aligned to the sense of being part of the Warner "family." This was an idea to which he had always been resistant, owing to an innate distrust of being part of a "family" of any sort (an interesting attitude in light of the extended-family atmosphere of his virtual stock company of creative associates).

The question of a director for *Nightmare* was another matter, but one that was settled by one of the few lasting friendships he had formed in his early days at Disney. He had met Henry Selick when both were more or less just spinning their wheels at the studio in the early 1980s. "Henry was also working on a lot of projects there that never got made. He couldn't take it there anymore. So we struck up a friendship. A 'Where the hell are we?' sort of thing," Burton explained. In the intervening years, Selick had carved out a niche in stop-motion animation with work for MTV and short films like *Slow Bob in the Lower Dimensions* (1990).

Selick was a perfect choice to bring Burton's challenging idea to fruition. Not only did the two share a similar artistic sensibility ("We live on the same planet—if not the same neighborhood—in our sensibilities," noted Selick), but Selick had been familiar with the basic premise from its beginnings. (He had been one of the few people who had seen Burton's original drawings and character models executed by future Burton visual consultant Rick Heinrichs when the idea had been nixed ten years earlier.) The notion was both familiar and appealing to Selick, and, to top it off, Burton offered him a great measure of creative freedom, as well as his first chance at a feature film. Moreover, Burton freely admitted that Selick was the most brilliant animator working today, and even intimated that the man probably was actually better suited to make the venture than he. That Selick would be all but buried in the film's publicity was understandable, since what commercial-minded Disney wanted was a Tim Burton film.

If the degree of freedom Tim offered Selick was great, the level of creative input Tim handed over to composer Danny Elfman was even greater. Burton's original poem story for the film was dramatically dubious, boasting only three characters, and in need of fleshing-out. Since *Nightmare Before Christmas* was to be a musical, it was therefore decided that the songs should come first, meaning that Elfman would be largely responsible for the shape of the entire film.

Nightmare was a heavy responsibility for the composer—and the greatest chance the movies had yet afforded him. In the end, Elfman's songs and score were far and away the most eclectic of his career to date, reflecting nearly every aspect of his musical tastes—ranging from the Kurt Weill–influenced "This Is Halloween" to the Cab Calloway–inspired "Oogie Boogie's Song"—yet somehow remaining essentially Elfman's own very distinctive work. His impact on this project is incalculable. When the film gets to "Oogie Boogie's Song" and becomes a deliberate homage to the Max Fleischer cartoons of the 1930s (Elfman even includes a spoken break in the lyrics that is straight out of *The Old Man of the Mountain*)—an area already explored by Danny's brother Richard in 1980's *The Forbidden Zone*—the film occasionally seems to be more Elfman than Tim Burton! As Elfman told *Movieline*'s Stephen Rebello (November 1993), he had warned the Disney people at the onset, "You're not going to get a pop ballad out of this"—explaining, "*Nightmare* could never work by trying to squeeze it into that *Beauty and the Beast* framework—you know, a six-song, contemporary Broadway-ish Disney musical."

The collaborative effort between Burton and Elfman was perhaps their closest ever and quite possibly the most satisfying. "There was a period of time when we were all trying to figure out how to get started. None of us had done a musical. Tim sent me a whole series of color drawings of Jack Skellington, the sleigh, and the reindeer. The drawings really got me going," Elfman noted.

The arrangement that evolved from this was simple: Burton would bring Elfman a chunk of the story and tell it to him. "It became a clean, pure process of my beginning writing from the first song and working chronologically. I'd call Tim every three or four days, he'd come and we'd talk about where the story went next, he'd leave and I'd already be hearing the next song in my head. I started demoing them all up, singing them, until, eventually, we were really excited to be telling the whole story and fleshing out the characters in music," revealed Elfman in *Movieline* during post-production. In many respects, this resulted in the screenplay being as much Danny Elfman's work as that of the credited writer, Caroline Thompson, since the ten songs that effectively tell the film's plot line take up most of the seventy-five-minute film. The script that she finally fashioned was built around the songs that she noted were 80 percent complete before she even came onto the project to replace the original writer, Michael McDowell, who ended up credited with the "adaptation," even though Thompson says she never saw his script.

Pre-production on *Nightmare Before Christmas* was of paramount importance, since Burton would be involved with *Batman Returns* and pre-production on *Ed Wood* (1994) during much of its making. As such, he would be able only occasionally to visit the studio in San Francisco—a converted warehouse in the South Market District—where Selick and his crew would be making *Nightmare* in July 1991. To completely ensure that the resulting movie would bear Burton's distinctive signature, very little could be left to chance. That the soundtrack would be recorded first helped, since that would dictate a great deal of the film. The voice casting also played a key role in assuring a Burton tone to the proceedings, utilizing the talents of such Burton regulars as Catherine O'Hara, Glenn Shadix, Paul Reubens, and, of course, Danny Elfman (though, for reasons never made clear, Chris Sarandon was called in for the speaking voice of Jack Skellington).

Visually, what Tim relied on was Selick's ability to make a film that fully reflected his own vision—and in many ways, that's exactly what he got. Looked at in context, it is obvious that *Nightmare Before Christmas* is an offering that could only have been made in the wake of the Tim Burton pictures that preceded it. (For example, when Jack Skellington dresses up as Santa Claus, he even echoes Catwoman's sentiment upon donning *her* costume in *Batman Returns,* saying, "And I feel so much better!") The earlier films clearly inform its look throughout, perhaps nowhere as clearly as in the sections that take place in the "real world," which not only resemble the modelwork in *Edward Scissorhands,* but also that of *Frankenweenie* (and, by extension, that of Burton's own childhood), when Jack Skellington is blasted out of the sky into a neighborhood cemetery. The spirit of Burton, as defined by his earlier movies, is precisely what the designers drew on to make the film a Tim Burton picture as much as possible without his direct participation in its actual making. Ultimately, the film ends up feeling as much like an homage to Burton as a film *by* him, which is not necessarily inapt, since *Nightmare Before Christmas* can hardly be said to be a Tim Burton film in the literal sense.

The narrative of *Nightmare Before Christmas* is simple: Jack Skellington (the King of Halloween and most important citizen of Halloween Town) is tired of being the frightmeister. Thus, when he stumbles upon Christmas Town, he concludes he wants to take over *that* holiday instead. His efforts at becoming Santa Claus are nothing short of disastrous for many reasons—not the least of which being that werewolves, vampires, ghosts, ghouls, and zombies have pretty peculiar ideas of what constitutes acceptable children's toys. In the end, Jack realizes the error of trying to be something other than he is. If this all sounds like familiar Burton territory, that's probably because it *is*, and that's both the weakness of the film and, in a curious way, its strength.

There really is little new in *Nightmare*. Burton is simply restating the theme of the outsider trying to fit in, until he finally recognizes the impossibility of his obsessive quest. Truth to tell, Burton explored the theme far more satisfyingly in *Edward Scissorhands,* but there are several telling changes as Burton revisits this theme. They are changes that indicate a more pleasant, and healthier, acceptance of "being different" than the isolation to which Edward is doomed at the climax of *Edward Scissorhands*. This time the main character neither begins, nor ends up, alone. Rather, Skellington has a circle of friends, a respected place in his (admittedly peculiar) world, and a woman who loves him and can be with him. This is quite different from *Edward Scissorhands!* It is perhaps most significant that Jack Skellington's successful love interest, Sally, is a patchwork creature made by a mad scientist. Whatever Sally is, she is no perky cheerleader holdover of Burton's adolescent imagining, but a savvy, resourceful, and thoroughly *adult* companion. The irony, of course, is that Sally, a creation of total fantasy, is far more real than Edward's Kim Boggs could ever hope to be.

As a result of this new, evolved point of view in *Nightmare Before Christmas,* the film makes an interesting comparison to *Batman Returns* in its reflection of Burton himself. The anger that seeps through his Caped Crusader entry is nowhere to be found here. There is, instead, a sense of hopefulness and, more, a sense of coming to terms with himself and, more significantly, with his accomplishments.

As usual, it is impossible not to see a good bit of Burton in *Nightmare's* central figure. However, Danny Elfman's songs and Caroline Thompson's dialogue go a long way toward creating a vision of Burton that is, for once, articulate, letting the viewer more *into the mind* of the character of Jack Skellington and, by obvious extension, Tim Burton. It is not difficult, then, to imagine that the defiantly triumphant voice that runs through the song, "Poor Jack," is Burton's. Jack may have made a shambles of Christmas (just as many have suggested Burton did of *Batman*), but he is quick to note that he did the best he could, that it afforded him a fleeting satisfaction unlike anything he'd known, and that, if nothing else, he left behind him stories for those in his wake to tell. Jack's words are, of course, Elfman's not Burton's, and it's impossible to tell how much the moment owes to which artist. However, Burton tacitly endorses them by accepting them for the film, and, in many respects, the sentiment is borne out and elaborated upon in his own next project, *Ed Wood,* which is a richer exploration of Burton's evolving theme of the outsider.

Whatever its merits on a thematic basis and as part of Burton's *oeuvre,* there is no getting around the fact that *Nightmare Before Christmas* is a noteworthy technical achievement. Stop-motion films, in various forms, date back to the very beginning of the movies. The process of making an object—or a character—appear to move by exposing one frame of film at a time and carefully repositioning the object slightly, was a staple of the trick films of France's Georges

Mélies at the turn of the twentieth century. Various animators had experimented with the process throughout the intervening years, notably Willis O'Brien who made *The Lost World* (1925) and *King Kong* (1933), and his protégé Ray Harryhausen, whose screen works made up a good deal of Burton's childhood viewing. Burton himself had used this approach on his first film, *Vincent* (1982), and it was an essential ingredient, later in the 1980s, for the effects in both *Pee-Wee's Big Adventure* and *Beetlejuice. Nightmare,* however, was something far more elaborate and different. The whole idea was to take stop-motion animation to its absolute limit by aligning the time-honored techniques with the latest in computerized technology. The basic approach was the same, but new technological achievements allowed for a new sense of freedom as to what could and couldn't be done.

The basic stop-motion technique calls for everything except the moving figure to be nailed down very securely, thereby preventing any unwanted movement between exposures. This, of course, extends to the camera. As a result, stop-motion films are by necessity generally static in terms of camera movement. The advent of the motion-control camera—or "mocon" as it is familiarly called—allowed *Nightmare Before Christmas* to achieve a freedom of camera movement not previously available in stop-motion animation. The movement information for this device is controlled by computer, so that the camera actually can move during the shot. This allows the film to utilize such techniques as elaborate crane and tracking shots. In short, the mocon permitted *Nightmare Before Christmas* to look more like a "real" movie, by giving back to it standard filmmaking techniques that previously had been rendered impossible by stop-motion. The results were nothing less than amazing, and occasionally heart-stoppingly beautiful. Everywhere the film turned, there was something new and different to delight the eye and pique the imagination—something fresh and genuinely wonderful.

The Disney people knew they had something special and, to their credit, gave the film a full-scale launch, complete with a *"Making of"* book, merchandise tie-ins, and plenty of publicity.

Jeffrey Katzenberg, in particular, was very pleased with *Nightmare Before Christmas,* saying, "I think the film's breathtaking. Audiences walking into a movie theatre will have their socks knocked off. It's indescribable. No matter what you think the movie is going to be, you'll be surprised." Burton's *Nightmare* co-producer, Denise DiNovi, commented, "This is an opportunity for Disney to break out of the mold a little and surprise people." In his fore-word for the 1994 book about the making of the picture, an ecstatic Burton claimed, "It is more beautiful than I imagined it would be, thanks to Henry and his talented crew of artists, animators, and designers." For once, the hype was fully justified. There had never been a picture like it. And there may never be another.

Despite the free hand that Burton and his collaborators had been given on the $30 million production, the Disney studio was naturally concerned about just how this decidedly off-center movie would fare at the box office and with the public at large. In every press release concerning the film, the studio went out of its way to stress that this was "something a little different," while Katzenberg talked nonstop about the fact that its technical brilliance was matched by its "heart." Disney/Touchstone president David Hoberman, who clearly wanted to enjoy the prestige of *Nightmare* more than anything else, presented a philosophical attitude, telling *Premiere* magazine, "I hope it goes out and makes a fortune. If it does—great. If it doesn't, that doesn't negate the validity of the process."

Danny Elfman himself was a little nervous on two counts—he thought per-haps the "Oogie Boogie" number in *Nightmare* went a little too far and might even appear racist to viewers unfamiliar with the vintage Max Fleischer–Cab Calloway cartoons it salutes, and, even more, that Disney might interfere at the last moment. "Disney's been great. So far," he told *Movieline,* adding, "But I keep waiting for something to happen." In point of fact, something nearly did. The studio was very uncomfortable with the "Oogie Boogie" number and, at one point, Burton trimmed the number considerably, ending it when the camera dis-appeared into Oogie's mouth for a blackout. Ultimately, Burton chose to exercise his contractual advantage of having "final cut," and reinstated the scene, much to the chagrin of Katzenberg, according to *Entertainment Weekly.*

The critical reaction to *Nightmare Before Christmas* when it opened in October 1993 was mixed. *Newsday*'s Jack Matthews found that the technical accomplishment didn't "make up for its thin, gleefully morbid story or its for-gettable score," and felt that, while its wizardry would be appreciated by film students and scholars, it would be judged by its content in the real world, "and on that level it isn't much. It has a hero that isn't very likable, a dog who isn't very cute, music and songs by Danny Elfman that aren't very memorable, and, worst of all, a romance (Sally, one of the weakest heroines in fairy-tale history, digs Jack) that has little feeling." Owen Gleiberman in *Entertainment Weekly* was of much the same mind, calling Jack Skellington and the movie itself "a technical achievement in search of a soul," adding he'd never seen "a fantasy film that's at once so visually amazing and so emotionally dead." He continued: "In place of the inspired hellzapoppin slapstick of Burton's best movies (*Beetlejuice, Edward Scissorhands,* the first *Batman*), *Nightmare* provides a joyless frenzy of movement." The *St. Louis Post-Dispatch* echoed these sentiments, acknowledging the remarkable technique, while saying, "Unfortunately, it is not a very good movie." A year later, in his *Vanity Fair* article, "Tim Burton's Hollywood Nightmare," David Edelstein commented, "Burton pronounces himself thrilled with the results, and on one level he ought to be: its spindly denizens are magically fluid and creepy. But the plot is another fat lump of self-pity." Edelstein goes on to suggest that the film represents Burton's essentially one-note theme. "Here again is Burton's pet scenario: a sensitive soul attempts to 'present' himself and is miserably misperceived. . . . His films (and, for that matter, his interviews) had come down to making you understand how hard it is to be Tim Burton."

Surprisingly, *Nightmare Before Christmas* seems to have been the Burton film for which Roger Ebert of the *Chicago Sun-Times* had been waiting. "The movies can create entirely different worlds for us, but that is one of their rarest gifts. More often, directors go for realism, for worlds we can recognize. One of the many pleasures of *Tim Burton's The Nightmare Before Christmas* is that there is not a single recognizable landscape in it," he enthused. "Tim Burton, the director of *Beetlejuice, Edward Scissorhands* and the *Batman* movies, has been creating this world in his head for about ten years, ever since his mind began to stray while he was employed as a traditional animator on an unremarkable Disney project," Ebert continued, concluding that he "found the movie a feast for the eyes and the imagination." Interestingly, Ebert, who had been decrying Burton's lack of dramatic skills and story sense from the onset, never commented on those aspects of this entry.

Perhaps the reviewer who came the closest to "getting" *Nightmare Before Christmas* was Kim Newman in the British publication *Sight and Sound*. Newman deftly summed the film up: "The grotesques in Burton's films are harmless and usually pathetically lovelorn, save for those bloated freaks (Penguin, Joker, Oogie Boogie) whose malevolence keeps the plot boiling. If his slight distance means that *Nightmare* seems more like a film *about* rather than *by* Tim Burton, there are also signs that his collaborators, gaining the upper hand, have flattened out his tendency to all-over-the-show plotting and simplified his sometimes overfussy designs. . . . Although a fragile conceit, [it] is certainly more worthy of your time than any Disney 2-D cartoon since *Basil—The Great Mouse Detective,* and has a rich, inventive score by Danny Elfman (who also provides Jack's singing voice), which shows just how inadequate the trite pseudo-Broadway muzak of Menken, Ashman, and Rice has become."

This pro/con split among the reviewers (there was very little middle ground, and it often seemed to come down to nothing more than a question of taste, such as saying Elfman's score was "unmemorable" here and "brilliant" there, without much explanation from either camp) did not hurt the box office for *Tim Burton's The Nightmare Before Christmas.* Burton's unusual new screen project grossed $48,831,776 during its first sixteen weeks of domestic release, and then more than doubled its $30 million investment. If it never quite became the blockbuster hit for which the studio hoped, it was nonetheless hardly a disgrace financially. More expectedly, the film caught on quickly with cineastes and students of animation, leading to very healthy video sales, and a deluxe-edition laserdisc set that included a *"Making of"* supplement, along with *Frankenweenie* and, at long, long last, *Vincent.* All in all, no one had any reason to be in the least dissatisfied with *Nightmare.*

A far less satisfactory "collaboration" came in the form of *Cabin Boy* (1994), a project that was pitched to Burton by Adam Resnick and Chris Elliott. Both veterans of TV's *Late Night with David Letterman,* Resnick and Elliott had been the force behind Fox-TV's cult comedy series, *Get a Life* (1990–92), which had starred Elliott. Their original idea was that Burton would direct the film, with Elliott starring; the screenplay had been specifically written with Burton in mind. Upon hearing their pitch, however, Burton suggested that Resnick himself should direct the film, and that he and Denise DiNovi would produce it. This unexpected turnaround was as irresistible to Resnick and Elliott as it was ill advised. In reality, the material was not really the sort of thing Resnick was suited to—he and Elliott had very carefully tailored it (perhaps too carefully) to what they perceived as Burton's style and his unique gifts. In short, the screenplay really needed Burton's special touch to bring it to life, a touch that fledgling director Resnick just did not have.

That said, Disney/Touchstone's *Cabin Boy,* though a commercial and critical disaster, is not nearly as bad a film as its reputation suggests. Some of the sequences in this PG-13-rated effort are, in fact, blessed with a good deal of quirky charm, especially for the first two-thirds of its eighty-minute length. (The film loses its grip and sense of direction once it decides that a roll in the hay with Ann Magnuson turns Elliott's deliriously fey and prissy Nathaniel Mayweather into "a man.") The entire stretch of the film in which the ship, the *Filthy Whore,* traverses dangerous waters with mountainous icebergs on either side—a sequence clearly inspired by a similar one in Ray Harryhausen's *Jason and the Argonauts* (1964)—is, in fact, very well done. It only falls short in its final effect because of the inability of the CGI effects to truly capture the *feeling* of the old Harryhausen stop-motion effects it tries to recall. Still, the overall movie is a little like wax fruit—imitation Burton—despite utilizing the services of Burton costumer Colleen Atwood for its look and Danny Elfman's orchestrator (and Oingo Boingo guitarist), Steve Bartek, for its sound. (In addition, not to be overlooked are cameos by such diverse personalities as David Letterman and Ricki Lake.)

Would *Cabin Boy* have been a success with Burton at the helm? It seems doubtful. The screenplay, while not without its Burtonesque quality, tries too hard to present someone else's idea of "all the things Tim Burton does so well," and the results inevitably would seem more than a little like Burton directing a pastiche of his own work. Moreover, the film's sexuality is far too knowing—occasionally even leeringly so—to really fit into Burton's world (possibly one of the reasons why Burton turned it down as his own project in the first place). Had it been a Tim Burton production, *Cabin Boy* would have been a very curious departure indeed, and would have seemed like an appendage to his moviemaking career, rather than the not-uninteresting footnote that it is now.

At the same time, Burton was not in the best shape personally. He had spread himself thin. The negative backlash to *Batman Returns* had stung him badly. He was still shaken by Anton Furst's suicide. He had become overwhelmed by his status in Hollywood and the responsibility that went with it. His marriage to Lena, while still officially intact, was effectively over. And Tim Burton had fallen in love with someone else. Something was bound to give—and soon it did.

15 | BURTON ADRIFT AND ANCHORED

*I'll be interested to see if things become clearer or
not if I just spin out into complete abstract oblivion.*
                                        TIM BURTON, 1994

WHILE *NIGHTMARE BEFORE CHRISTMAS* WAS STILL
in production in 1991, Burton was spending the holiday season in New York. It
was there, on New Year's Eve, that his friend, screenwriter Jonathan Gems,
introduced him to twenty-something model and aspiring actress Lisa Marie
(née Lisa Marie Smith), whose waifish, haunted look had caught the attention
of photographers such as Robert Mapplethorpe and Bruce Weber, and secured
her a spot with designer maven Calvin Klein. At least, this is the most consistent and logical account of their meeting. One source pegs the encounter as
early as New Year's Eve, 1991, while another states that the two met in the fall
of 1992 at a party for Madonna. Whenever the meeting actually took place, the
connection between the two was immediate and intense. It is impossible not to
note that, just as Tim had been swept away by Lena Gieseke during his trying
days at the helm of *Batman* (1989), he was here in an equally high-charged
emotional state because of the pressures of having been turned into something
like a corporation, in Hollywood's view.

This, however, was to be no whirlwind romance ending in marriage in a month or so, as had been the case with Lena. "Tim wasn't looking for a girl-friend at the time, but they just fell for each other the first time they met," Jonathan Gems later told *Premiere* magazine. Maybe so, but Lisa Marie and Burton didn't immediately act upon their mutual attraction, apparently at the insistence of Lisa. The pair did not officially become an "item" until Valentine's Day. According to her, it was "an old-fashioned courting thing. Tim was really glad he waited. At the beginning he wasn't, but he realized it later."

In many ways, Lisa Marie almost seemed like a somewhat more savvy female version of Burton. She had a similar lost and haunted quality, and, like Burton, she had left home in her teens, albeit a little more adventurously. Burton only made it as far as his grandmother's when he found home life inimical to his taste. Lisa struck out for Manhattan and a career at the age of sixteen. "I had a feeling that I'd met her before, which is kind of weird because I don't have those kinds of feelings. Ever. . . . It's one of those things you kind of hope for in your life but you begin to think it's not possible, to have that kind of ultimate connection," Burton revealed in *Us* magazine. In one sense, it's perfectly understandable that Burton had a sense of having met Lisa Marie before. She bears a resemblance to *Nightmare Before Christmas*'s Sally—and not just physically. Just as Sally's Burtonian innocence seems tempered with a kind of practicality that is more grounded in reality than the object of her affection, so, too, does Lisa Marie vis-à-vis Burton. In this respect, it's almost as if Lisa Marie was the real-life embodiment of a character Burton dreamed existed.

"I think she saved his life," Jonathan Gems remarked in the *Premiere* article, a sentiment Lisa Marie echoed, adding that the lifesaving was a mutual thing. Her own career wasn't really going anywhere and she, too, had felt adrift until their meeting.

Ultimately, these assessments may well be right. Nowhere can one find a contradictory word about the positive effect of their union. Gems told *Premiere* in 1996, "Tim was very successful, very young, and he was sur-rounded by gold diggers. He just lost his faith in people. Then Lisa Marie comes along and she's like a child, very loving and generous and caring. And gradually, over the past few years, he has healed up to the point where he has lost his distrust of people." However, the beneficial nature of the alliance was neither instantaneous, nor immediately apparent. Burton was still living life inside what seemed to him an increasingly intense pressure cooker, and, after all, he was still married to Lena.

Burton's first move was to separate from Lena in early 1993, paving the way for his romance with Lisa Marie in earnest. And yet, his next step was more baffling to his intimates: He simply shut down and walked away from it all. This was certainly not entirely unprecedented in Burton's life. Indeed, it fits a long-established pattern—leaving home as a teenager, breaking off his relationship with Julie Hickson, his approach to dealing with Anton Furst. . . . As David Edelstein noted in his *Vanity Fair* article, "He's famous for ducking people." Certainly his history proved that much, but this was far more extreme. Burton left his production company with no one to guide it, cut off old friends and co-workers like Danny Elfman and Henry Selick, and simply, in Edelstein's words, just let it all "drift away," and—along with Lisa Marie—"became a nomad," throwing himself "into chaos." Burton's explanation to Edelstein was, "What I've tried to protect is a certain creative space."

Burton himself seems to have been a little perplexed by the reactions of his friends and co-workers. "I hide. I hid before. I don't return phone calls and nobody used to get on my case. They'd just go, 'That's our Tim, we love 'im, doesn't answer his phone calls.' Now it's like, 'Why the fuck don't you return our calls?'" he told Edelstein with alarming ingenuousness. What Burton failed to grasp, perhaps deliberately, was that it's a little different being this irresponsible artist when that's all you are. It's quite another thing when the responsibilities of heading up a production company with a great many people depending on you become involved. Numerous projects that needed his support—Selick's film of *James and the Giant Peach* (1996), for one thing, and several proposed things for Danny Elfman—were just allowed to fend for themselves in this period.

His old friends and co-workers found his behavior difficult to take in stride, and impossible to dismiss with the usual glib, "That's just Tim." What had once seemed nothing more than an endearing quirk was looking more and more like sheer self-indulgence. Making the situation just that much more intolerable was the fact that Burton never actually made his intentions known to anyone. There was no official shutting down of Tim Burton Productions. He simply stopped dealing with it and, to the best of his ability, avoided everyone and everything associated with the company. The move was a strange one, and, to some degree, Burton overcalculated just how far his persona of perplexed innocence would cover him and excuse his behavior.

One of Tim's oldest associates, Rick Heinrichs, told *Vanity Fair*'s David Edelstein, "Friendship isn't something that he needs or knows what to do with. Tim would go through periods where he'd try to be a friend, but it never seemed comfortable on him. And that's fine." Henry Selick was a little more terse on the topic, saying, "When you work with him and live with him you're going to get bloodied and hurt and bent out of shape." He then softened his tone a bit to concede that this is perhaps true of all artists. "He's a true artist. As much as breathing or eating or maybe more, he's committed to his movies." By 1996, when Burton had made great strides in mending fences with his old friends and associates, Selick could comment, "I think Lisa Marie has had a huge impact on his life. I've seen him eating vegetarian, he dresses better, and his personal hygiene has definitely seen a dramatic improvement."

Whether Burton's behavior at this time is understandable or even excusable is open to question, but it does appear that it was essential for Burton to get away from the whole business that his art had become, if only to regain his bearings.

Tim may have spent much of his so-called Hollywood hiatus not dealing with films, but he nonetheless never abandoned his creativity. That was never even a serious consideration, since Burton was, is, and probably always will be, a compulsive creator. During this time, he wrote and illustrated *The Melancholy Death of Oyster Boy and Other Stories* (1997), an odd little volume of mini stories in a vaguely Dr. Seuss style with his distinctive, Goreyesque drawings accompanying them, and spent months dabbling in still photography with Lisa Marie.

In 1992 a friend had taken Burton to meet the artist William Wegman, where Burton encountered the artist using the specially constructed Polaroid 20"x 24" Land camera. (There are five such cameras in existence.) This huge and hugely cumbersome piece of photographic equipment redefines the idea of impedimenta, weighing in at a whopping 235 pounds—not exactly the sort of thing one carries along for the family snapshot album, unless, of course, one happens to be a wealthy filmmaker who can afford the use of the camera, the film, and something like a small film crew to cart the thing around.

Burton was immediately fascinated with the idea of being able to instantly produce twenty- by twenty-four-inch color photographs, and almost equally intrigued by the basic impracticality of the camera itself. "It's such a ridiculous, absurd-looking thing, like a Dr. Seuss camera. Also, there's a certain problematic funkiness to this medium that intrigues me. The camera's heavy, and you can't move it around easily. You need a cameraman and a crew, so it's sort of like making a movie, only without the studio executives hanging over your shoulder," Burton told *Harper's Bazaar* (September 1994). One of the keys to Burton's interest in the medium probably lies in that last phrase.

Considering the nature of many of the photographs executed during these months—images showing Lisa Marie with nails driven into her head or made up to resemble a bleeding corpse or covered in spiders—it is unlikely that any studio executive would have allowed Burton, even at his most powerful, to have so completely indulged his imagination. Burton himself knew that he was skirting unusually dangerous territory, that the resulting photographs would very likely be perceived as an example of violence toward women. He was quick to point out to *Harper's Bazaar*'s Ralph Rugoff that he was responding to "what I understand about the modeling world and how people are treated and used there." At the same time, other photographs—called "Dioramas at the Museum of Unnatural History"—were of a more playful nature, featuring surrealistic still lifes and strange landscapes. When Rugoff commented to Burton about the way the photos seemed to cross the line between the natural and the man-made, Burton explained, "As I get older, the line between what's real and what's not gets more and more blurred."

Another key factor in this new creative endeavor was, of course, Lisa Marie. One of the things that obviously endeared her to Burton was that she could be a participant in his work, something that never seemed to have been possible with Lena. Possibly, it was simply the fact that Burton and Lena were two artists almost in competition, while Lisa Marie's artistry more readily complemented Burton's own ideas. Moreover, Lisa Marie was a good bit like a Tim Burton character come to life—she appears to have enjoyed "dressing up" and playing out roles, much as such Burton characters as Pee-Wee Herman, Lydia Deetz, Batman, Catwoman, and Jack Skellington do. In her, he found not only love, but a playmate and an active and willing participant in the creation of his art.

The photographs from these sessions finally resulted in a one-man show at Thomas Solomon's Garage, an avant-garde Los Angeles art gallery. Criticism of the showing tended to be typical of the sort usually afforded celebrities who step outside of their perceived realms; i.e., Burton's work was essentially viewed as that of a talented dilettante. It did not help that he had—with typical Burton quirkiness—chosen such an outrageous medium to bring his vision to life, since his choices made the whole affair seem a little bit like a stunt.

As we shall see, much the same fate would greet *The Melancholy Death of Oyster Boy*. Burton had had enough trouble being taken seriously as a film-maker without expecting to take the rest of the art world by storm in the bargain! However, the importance of the experiences lay more in the fact that these projects allowed him to keep on creating—still the ultimate subversive, and therapeutic, act in his mind—while getting away from the world of the movies and its pressures and, more importantly, his status as a burgeoning movie mogul.

It is, of course, an oversimplification (and overdramatization) of the events to say that Burton turned his back on Hollywood and the movies for two years. He was never completely out of touch. He was around for the finish of *Nightmare Before Christmas* during this time, as well as its premiere, and he got behind the film in a promotional sense. Similarly, he had projects in the works. He was just not pursuing his career in a wholly active manner, preferring to go at it easily and make his next move count.

For a time Burton was attached to Columbia's *Mary Reilly* (1996), the studio's revisionist version of *Dr. Jekyll and Mr. Hyde,* which was ultimately filmed by Stephen Frears. At no point does this seem to have been a key project so far as Burton himself was concerned. The film itself was a none-too-successful attempt to repeat the success of Francis Ford Coppola's *Bram Stoker's Dracula* (1992), but the script was not as good, and it's unlikely that Burton's visual sense would have been sufficient to take on the film and put it over. For Burton, it was mostly a bargaining chip to get to make the film he really wanted to make— the film that would bring him back to the movies and earn him the best reviews of his career, the film with which, in many ways, Burton would come to his creative—and possibly personal—maturity: *Ed Wood* (1994).

16 | ED WOOD IN HOLLYWOOD

Pull de strings! Pull de strings!
Dance to dat for which you were created!

BELA LUGOSI
in *Glen or Glenda* (1952)

EDWARD D. WOOD JR. (AS HE INVARIABLY BILLED himself) has gained the reputation—not entirely fairly—of being the worst filmmaker of all time; after all, he wrote, produced, and directed the worst film ever, *Plan 9 from Outer Space* (1959). But as any first-year film student can tell you, *Plan 9 from Outer Space,* for all its bad acting, loopy dialogue, illogical plotting, and cardboard cheesiness is far, far from being the worst movie of all time. It just happens—through circumstance—to be the best-known bad film. It is also perhaps the best-loved such film and that's a factor that cannot be overlooked.

Ed Wood was born in Poughkeepsie, New York, in 1924, and fell in love with the movies at an early age. He also became enamored with something else—women's clothing. Not everyone would immediately think that these two loves could somehow be fused into one obsession. However, then, not everyone—in fact, hardly anyone—was like Ed Wood, who, if nothing else, was probably the most blindly optimistic filmmaker that ever lived. That positive outlook got him started making 8mm films even before his teens, and later brought him to Hollywood (after serving in the Marines—supposedly with women's underwear beneath his battle dress—in World War Two). He came to the West Coast in pursuit of his ultimate dream—to be a real motion-picture director. The astonishing thing about all this is simply that Wood did indeed achieve that quest, albeit in the most bizarre manner imaginable.

Ed Wood was, in many respects, the ultimate auteur—he quite literally did it all, from writing to directing to acting to making props to building (if the term can be applied here) "sets." This was not so much a mark of Ed's versatility and independence as it was done out of sheer necessity. (No Hollywood studio would even consider letting him work on a film, let alone actually make one.) As a result, there is a kind of idiot nakedness about an Ed Wood picture, in that there really is no one else on whom the credit—or blame—can be bestowed. Even if there were, it seems unlikely that anyone else would want it. The probability of a Pauline Kael coming to the forefront and announcing that the co-writer of Wood's *Bride of the Monster* (1955), Alex Gordon, was the true guiding force behind the film, à la her famous claims for Herman J. Mankiewicz on *Citizen Kane* (1941), is not great.

What is most amazing about the films of Ed Wood is not how bad they are, but that they were ever made at all. Wood's first screen efforts were a few short films. (The first, *Streets of Laredo* [1948], was never properly finished, though former Wood actress Dolores Fuller and her husband, Philip Chamberlin, have recently restored and completed it to the degree that such was possible.) Wood came into his own with the mesmerizing *Glen or Glenda* (1952), which he made for schlockmeister George Weiss, supposedly to cash in on Christine Jorgensen's then famous story of her sex-change operation. In Wood's hands, however, the idea quickly mutated into his own, frequently incoherent, apology for transvestitism, since most of the black-and-white film concentrates on Glen (played by Wood himself, under the sobriquet of "Daniel Davis") and his dilemma concerning his penchant for dressing up as "Glenda," especially as it relates to his engagement to Barbara (Dolores Fuller), who lives in complete innocence of Glen's unusual and potentially disconcerting habit.

In a burst of amazing luck, Wood managed—for $1,000 of Weiss's money—to coerce the aging, morphine-addicted, and down-on-his-luck horror star, Bela Lugosi, to appear in the project, playing God, or at least an all-powerful being, who controls the actions of the film's characters (along with stock footage of buffalo stampedes and other seemingly unrelated events) by crying,

"Pull de strings! Pull de strings! Dance to dat for which you were made!" At other points in *Glen or Glenda*, Lugosi merely ponders the question of sexual identity—"And what are little boys made of? Is it snakes and snails and puppy dogs' tails? Or is it brassieres! And corsets!"—reaching no clear conclusion. One thing, however, is obvious: This is not simply another bad movie; this is a *resplendently* bad movie! It has a vision, a theme, and absolutely no clue what to do about either of them. It also marked the first of three Wood feature films with Lugosi.

The relationship between Wood and Lugosi was a curious one. It was partly commercial, since an Ed Wood picture with Lugosi, no matter how low the fortunes of this veteran horror-film star had sunk, was infinitely easier to get financed and distributed than an Ed Wood picture without the Hungarian-born, has-been actor. Moreover, Wood, for whom nothing was as important as getting his movies made, was quite willing to cash in on Lugosi a full three years after his death by parlaying a few minutes of film featuring the actor into a starring role (with the aid of the most ludicrous "double" in the history of cinema). Yet for all that, Wood was very supportive of Bela and offered him work—and more importantly, a sense of purpose and self-worth—at a time when no one else in Hollywood would. There is no denying that Wood genuinely cared for the revered horror star of his youth and did as well by him as his meager budgets and dubious talents would allow.

Of course, the parallels between Tim Burton and Ed Wood are immediately striking: the youthful efforts at making films, a cavalier lack of concern for the niceties of logical storytelling, a worshipful relationship with a beloved horror icon from childhood, the love of dressing up and being another person. This parallel extends even to the amusingly confessional aspect of the artist who will do anything—including steamrolling friends and longtime associates—to get his movie vision out into the world. Even though she does not play the character in the film, there may even be a touch of Lisa Marie in Burton's vision of the all-understanding Kathy Wood, who believed in and stuck with Ed to the bitter end, after his original love, Dolores Fuller, had had enough of Ed's lifestyle. Moreover, Burton admired anyone who made anything—and even more, a person who did so against all odds. It was easy for Burton to see that he easily could have suffered a fate similar to that of Ed Wood. Thus, in 'ms inevitable that Ed Wood would become the subject of a

ion picture.

...owever, *Ed Wood* was not a project that originated with Burton
.. all. This is perhaps odd, since *Bride of the Monster* and *Plan 9 from Outer Space*
were television staples during those years when Burton was escaping into any
horror film that came his way, and he certainly knew them. Screenwriters Scott
Alexander and Larry Karaszewski had cooked up the idea after reading
Rudolph Grey's anecdotal Wood biography, *Nightmare of Ecstasy*, a collection of
often contradictory—and frequently hilarious—reminiscences of Wood's collaborators and friends. Known for their screenplays for *Problem Child* (1990) and
Problem Child 2 (1992), comedic works that had been branded as among the
worst of all time, the pair thought it would be a natural if two of the "worst"
screenwriters of all time wrote a movie about the supposed worst director of all
time. The cycle was made complete by the duo peddling it to director Michael
Lehman, whose film *Hudson Hawk* (1991) was also a strong contender for
inclusion in the pantheon of all-time worsts!

With this idea in mind, they took the project to Burton, much as Adam
Resnick and Chris Elliott had done with *Cabin Boy*, only this time Burton
immediately wanted to make the film himself. The parallels to his own life and
the chance it offered him to do something different and speak out on so many
of the things he believed in, were simply irresistible to him. What of the original director, Michael Lehman? The popular theory at the time was that Burton
effectively "muscled" him out of the film project, giving him executive-producer
status as a consolation prize. However, this supposed bit of ruthlessness appears
totally unfounded, according to both co-producer Denise DiNovi and Lehman
himself, who told *Premiere* magazine (October 1994), "When we presented *Ed
Wood* to Denise and Tim, we really didn't have a game plan. Tim read the treatment and flipped. He said he really wanted to do the movie and I was committed to *Airheads* [1994]."

An immediate problem arose. Burton wanted to make the film in black-and-
white and Columbia Pictures was utterly resistant to the idea, claiming that it was
impossible to sell a black-and-white film in foreign markets. Their solution was
that Burton shoot his film on color stock and have black-and-white prints struck
for the domestic marketplace, but allowing the studio to hawk the film overseas

in color. This may sound like a reasonable compromise, but it isn't. There is an entirely different art to black-and-white cinematography, as well as to makeup, costuming, and nearly every other design aspect of such a film. Besides, color turned into black-and-white simply isn't the same. Not only is the lighting wrong, but the images pick up unwanted contrast and the effect is far from desirable; or, as Burton phrased it flatly in *Premiere,* "It looks like shit." Burton, therefore, dug his heels in, and Columbia vetoed the project, which, so far as Burton was concerned, canceled his already lukewarm desire to make *Mary Reilly.*

Jeffrey Katzenberg at Disney, on the other hand, had no such reservations about *Ed Wood.* If Tim Burton wanted to make it in black-and-white, then Disney would allow him to do so. Burton had gotten on well with Katzenberg on *Nightmare Before Christmas* and was plainly delighted by his decision. Whether or not the Disney people on the whole wanted *Ed Wood* per se as much as they wanted Burton to commit to a long-term working arrangement with them (which he never did) is open to question.

Despite his somewhat erratic recent behavior, Burton was still the hottest property around the Hollywood scene. (He would soon be eclipsed, to a degree, by the new whiz kid on the film-industry block, Quentin Tarantino, with his film *Pulp Fiction,* released the same year as *Ed Wood.* Nevertheless, Tarantino quickly proved to have less staying power than Burton.) Moreover, Tim might still be amenable to, yes, a theme park—a notion that had never quite died, despite Burton's own apparent lack of interest in the idea. The possibility of signing Burton—even at the expense of letting him make a commercially dubious, personal film, made just that much more suspect by being in black-and-white—was not something the studio was passing up. For his part, Burton's attraction to Disney did not have much to do with the studio itself (despite his pleasant relationship with them on *Nightmare Before Christmas* and later, *Ed Wood*). Burton seems, not unreasonably, to have harbored a degree of skepticism where Disney was concerned in light of his early years with them. He was drawn to Disney because of the presence of studio honcho Katzenberg. (Ironically, Katzenberg's defection to Warner Bros. would prompt Burton to follow him and sign with his old studio. This not only lost for Disney the services of Tim Burton, but also left them with holdovers like Adam Resnick and Henry Selick, whom they had taken on primarily in order to court Burton.)

That, however, was all in the future. The making of *Ed Wood* was the concern of the moment and Burton seems to have been intent on one thing in particular: This would be a film unlike any he had ever made. In this he was only partly successful, which was neither wholly undesirable (who wants a Tim Burton picture that isn't like a Tim Burton picture?), nor unexpected (could Burton make a film that was not clearly his?). But there are things about *Ed Wood* that are clearly, consciously, deliberately different.

Of course, the most immediately noticeable difference between *Ed Wood* and Burton's earlier films is the lack of a Danny Elfman musical score. The movie was made during their highly publicized, yet never fully explained, rift. The situation seems comparable to Burton's failure to tell Anton Furst that he didn't want him to do the sets for *Batman Returns*. It's difficult not to conclude that he simply didn't want Elfman to do the score and, avoiding confrontation, just started avoiding him and not returning his calls. There would even be a certain amount of logic to Burton wanting to make a film without an Elfman score, especially coming after *Nightmare Before Christmas,* where Elfman's imprint was on the finished product nearly as much as Burton's.

At the time, moreover, there was also the theory afoot in the film business that Elfman's scores were now such an essential part of the films that Burton couldn't make a picture without him. With *Ed Wood,* Burton not only proved that he could make a film without an Elfman score, but that he, too, knew something about soundtracks and the effective use of music. Despite its score by Howard Shore (a reasonable, even expected choice, since Burton has often expressed admiration for the films of David Cronenberg, for whose work Shore generally provides the music), a good deal of the music in the film is actually recycled from the *Ed Wood* movies themselves.

Back in the 1950s, Wood, of course, had no money for original scores and had to rely on library music—and usually from the least impressive film-music libraries—for his movies. That Burton could take this trite, hackneyed music and use it effectively is remarkable in itself. That he could take the stupefyingly vapid "Love Theme" from *Glen or Glenda* (1953) and apply it to scenes involving Ed's relationship with Kathy (most notably on their first date) and make the scenes moving in the process is nothing short of miraculous. So Burton did indeed prove something by eschewing an Elfman score on the film, but it's also possible that one of the things he proved was that no one's music suited Wood's life better than the music Wood applied to his own movies.

Ed Wood also differs from the Burton pictures that precede it in a key thematic sense, one that can be seen as a logical outgrowth of *Nightmare Before Christmas*. In that film, as previously noted, Burton finally offered the image of his misunderstood protagonist as capable of achieving something more than the magnificently brooding isolation of the two versions of *Batman* and *Edward Scissorhands*. Fitting in at last was not just a fantasy as it had been for Lydia in *Beetlejuice*. Here, Burton's hero is constantly supported by—and in turn supports—an extended family, despite the fact that its members are soundly denounced by the film's Dolores Fuller as "the usual gang of dope addicts and misfits." Here, Burton's alter ego is finally afforded a bittersweet "happy ending" with the woman he loves (Ed isn't condemned to making ice sculptures from afar in tribute to the great love of his life as was Edward Scissorhands). The irony, of course, is that Burton found this resolution in a "real life" story and had to play a bit fast and loose with the facts to bring it to fruition. Whatever it took, *Ed Wood* marks the first Tim Burton film in which there isn't so much as a hint of self-pity. Self-realization, yes, but self-pity—not at all.

Another intriguing and telling difference lies in the fact that *Ed Wood* is the first Burton movie deliberately made for adults. It's his bid for an adult film and his only R-rated film to date. The R-rating stems almost entirely from the hilarious, if historically questionable, outbursts of profanity from Bela Lugosi's character and, of course, the actor's drug use. The tough rating certainly has nothing to do with the title character's sex life and his penchant for angora sweaters and slit skirts. Actually, for a film featuring a main character who gets his kicks out of dressing up like a woman and a cast of characters living on the remotest and most bohemian fringes of society, *Ed Wood* is almost remarkably sexless. The closest the film ever gets to sexuality lies in Lugosi's aging adolescent preoccupation with the cleavage of TV horror hostess Vampira. ("I think she's a honey! Look at dose jugs!")

Within *Ed Wood,* the subject and the two women in his life are almost alarmingly chaste in their interrelationships. Even when making an adult film, Burton seems curiously uncomfortable when it comes to sex. To some degree, this was probably a conscious decision, since Burton and star Johnny Depp, the former star of TV's *21 Jump Street* (1987–90), wanted to keep all of Ed's cross-dressing away from any suggestion of campiness. (Considering Depp would be sharing screen time with Bill Murray playing the over-the-top, mincing, transsexual wannabe, "Bunny" Breckenridge, Johnny was rarely in little danger of himself seeming overly campy.) Yet the film's overall rejection of the sexual element is certainly in keeping with everything Burton has done.

Bringing the characters of *Ed Wood* to life was not in itself an easy task. One thing Burton knew from the onset was that he was not especially interested in historical accuracy for its own sake, especially where the characters were concerned. Frankly, he didn't think it was possible to nail down a "definitive" portrait of any of the movie's characters, since the contradictory nature of the accounts in *Nightmare of Ecstasy* clearly attested that there really was no such thing as a reliable, "true" story here in the chronicle of Ed Wood, filmmaker. Tim told *Premiere* (October 1994), "It says more about the nature of memory and how we all perceive things. It reminds me of my own memory, which is somewhat revisionist and foggy. I can definitely relate to that kind of denial and reinvention." As a result, he and Alexander and Karaszewski opted for the characterizations that most appealed to them and had the most dramatic—or comedic—validity.

Though critics sometimes would compare Depp's portrayal of Ed Wood to Jon Lovitz's transparent pathological liar from TV's *Saturday Night Live,* the real inspiration for the approach, according to Depp, came from Burton's advice that he study the manic enthusiasm of the Andy Hardy character Mickey Rooney immortalized in the old MGM movie series. Before it was over, Depp says, his on-camera character included bits of Ronald Reagan, Casey Kasem, and the Wizard of Oz, in addition to Andy Hardy. In short, every professional enthusiast Depp and Burton could think of, came into the development of the almost insanely optimistic Ed Wood. This could have easily made the character obnoxious beyond belief, but Depp filtered it through a kind of innocence that suggested nothing more than a sharpster who has become smitten with his own spiel. For the other, more outré, aspect of the onscreen director, Depp had to learn how to wear and move in women's clothing, giving him, he said, new respect for women. He added, "The same goes for transvestites." According to Michael Pye in the Virgin Airways publication, *Hot Air* (January–March, 1995), Depp even "took a kind of correspondence course from Miss Vera's Academy—a New York school for boys who want to be girls."

Trickier by far was the more multilayered role of Bela Lugosi. The character of Wood himself was open to far freer interpretation on the screen, since, apart from starring in *Glen or Glenda,* he was not a character much known to the public at large. Thus, audiences would have no preconceived expectations as to how Ed should appear onscreen. In contrast, the legendary star of *Dracula* (1931), *The Black Cat* (1934), and *The Raven* (1935) was another matter. Everyone has a notion of what Lugosi should be like. What neither Burton, nor actor Martin Landau (cast as the horror star) wanted, was the Lugosi of a hundred bad impressionists. Landau had been Burton's first, and only, choice for the role. According to the veteran actor, still best-known for his 1966–69 stint on TV's *Mission: Impossible,* Burton even told him, "If you don't do it I may not do the movie because I don't know who else could do it." Tim's reasoning to Landau was simple—and tied to his own personalized response to the material: "Because you've worked with the best directors in major movies and wonderful performances, and you've worked with terrible directors in awful movies, as Lugosi has, and you've worked with everybody, you have a presence. That because of all that, you have an intensity that is needed. You can be theatrical and real."

Landau still wasn't entirely sold on *Ed Wood* unless the makeup could be made to work. He told makeup artist Rick Baker he wanted mobility in his face and a minimal makeup job: "I don't want it to look like makeup, which it fortunately doesn't, where you say, 'There's Martin Landau with a lot of makeup on.' I mean, you're dead." Even with the makeup, Landau had some trouble at first achieving the Lugosi style. "My face is much more expressive than Lugosi's. I mean, it does more. My eyes open wide when I get emotional. His close down. I'm like a piano when I smile. I got eighty-eight teeth. You don't see any teeth in his mouth. It's like a black hole. His mouth curls up oddly. He holds his head differently than I do. So I had to learn his face, literally learn it muscularly, so that I wouldn't have to think about it."

To this end, Landau watched twenty-five Lugosi movies ranging from the actor's great days in the 1930s to such time-wasting nonsense as the film that immediately preceded Lugosi's stint on Wood's *Glen or Glenda, Bela Lugosi Meets a Brooklyn Gorilla* (1952). Landau recalls, "Lugosi is a mad scientist who was taking little animals and turning them into big animals. So a little monkey [turns] into a gorilla, who happened to be a man in a gorilla suit. And all of this nonsense is going on, and he was still damn good." From these things, and attuning himself to Burton's style and direction, Landau crafted the role of a lifetime, a truly worthy Oscar-winning performance. So completely did Landau become Lugosi onscreen that in the movie itself, it was possible for Burton to cut from footage of Lugosi's classic *White Zombie* (1932) being shown on television, to Landau, and keep the illusion intact. At no point does Landau seem to be himself or anyone but Bela Lugosi.

Since the focus of the new film, from Burton's standpoint, was the relationship between Wood and Lugosi, the other roles were somewhat easier to cast, with Bill Murray's outrageous "Bunny" Breckenridge stealing the show. Others were only slightly less remarkable. Burton alumnus Jeffrey Jones made a nearly perfect screen Criswell, the blatantly and impossibly bogus "psychic," who specialized in the most preposterous prophecies imaginable. (Criswell once "predicted" that the city of Denver would turn into Jell-O, an event that, as of this writing, seems not to have occurred.) Wrestler George "The Animal" Steele stepped into the screen role of the hefty former wrestler ("The Super Swedish Angel"). He also used Wood stock-company regular Tor Johnson—a huge man, notorious for breaking toilet seats by his sheer bulk, with an equally huge appetite and sweet sense of humor. Patricia Arquette was a suitably sweet Kathy Wood, while Lisa Marie made for a visually striking and amusingly dry-witted Vampira (née Maila Nurmi). Martin Landau's daughter, Juliet, was perfection itself as the extremely peculiar Loretta King, the girl who became the heroine of *Bride of the Monster* because Wood thought (somewhat incorrectly) that she could finance the film. Sarah Jessica Parker stood in for Dolores Fuller in *Ed Wood,* capturing all of the actress's early gaucherie, a lot of her intelligence, but, in one of the film's few false notes, none of her sweetness and very real devotion to Wood.

What Tim wanted first and foremost was a film that did not, in any sense, make fun of its subject. "What is talent and what is not talent? My movies could just as easily dive-bomb. I know that better than anyone," he told David Edelstein of *Vanity Fair.* "It seems like such a fine line between what's perceived as bad or good. It should be an individual call, but there's this collective need to dub something the worst. Those films are just kind of unique. It's disturbing to me, when you go to screenings and people are laughing at someone who's putting his soul out there. It's scary that people respond that way," he explained to Gary Indiana in the *Village Voice,* further detailing his take on the act of creativity: "There's a weird power when you're making something. Any kind of creation is exhilarating, it's exciting. You get very singular in how you're thinking, it's like a drug. You do get delusional." Explaining much of what he connected with in Wood, Burton remarked about Wood's personal correspondence, "They raise that question of optimism or denial, or both. Perverse optimism and a healthy dose of denial. It's fascinating, the question of how you delude yourself, and how everyone sees everything differently. . . . This whole business of going to a theatre to laugh at Ed Wood's movies. They are funny, but you rarely hear people talk about why they're funny." Burton understood why the movies were funny and knew how to get that across without once appearing to take a condescending approach to his subject. In essence, he was creating a valentine to Wood—honoring him for simply having created something. This was his theme and the key to his project.

17 | VISIONS WORTH FIGHTING FOR

Here in dis forsaken jungle hell,
I have proven dat I am all right!

BELA LUGOSI
in *Bride of the Monster* (1955)

THE BIOGRAPHICAL FILM—OR BIOPIC AS IT IS FAMILIARLY
called—is perhaps the trickiest, most maligned, and most misunderstood genre
in movies. Granted, there have been many truly dreadful biographical films, but
there have also been a great many truly dreadful musicals, comedies, horror
films, et cetera. The biopic comes in for a special kind of abuse, however, since
it is subject to scrutiny on the basis of historical accuracy in a way that most
films are not.

There are essentially three approaches to the biopic. The most common of
these (and, by far, the least satisfactory) is the "historical overview," which
attempts to present a solid, sober, schoolbook rendering of a person's life, such as
the Paul Muni–William Dieterle movies from Warner Bros. in the 1930s (*The
Story of Louis Pasteur* [1936], *The Life of Émile Zola* [1937], *Juarez* [1939])—movies
that have a tendency to look as though they were designed around a fourth-
grade teacher's idea of history. Then there is the "historical episode" approach—
a more satisfactory tack that centers on a key point or defining time in its
subject's life. The biopics of George Arliss (*Disraeli* [1929], *Alexander Hamilton*

[1931], *Voltaire* [1933], *The House of Rothschild* [1934]) are the most famous of these, though the list would also have to include such historical romps as William Dieterle's *Madame DuBarry* (1934) and James Whale's *The Great Garrick* (1937). These entries are generally designed to function as snapshots of their subjects, to give a sense of the persons being portrayed without being a kind of cinematic history lesson. The third and most complex type of biopic is an outgrowth of this second form, the psychological portrait of the subject, where a key event (or series of events) is used to delve more deeply into the subject's mind. This more interpretive approach—which was pioneered by French filmmaker Abel Gance with works as wide-ranging as *Napoleon* (1927) and *Beethoven* (1936), and taken to new levels by British director Ken Russell with his composer biopics *Song of Summer* (1968), *The Music Lovers* (1970), *Mahler* (1974), and *Lisztomania* (1975)— is at once the most satisfying, personal, and controversial form of the genre. Not surprisingly, this is the approach taken by Tim Burton in *Ed Wood*.

Any film of this sort immediately invites questions of historical accuracy, especially when it recounts events recent enough to involve persons who are still alive and apt to take issue with what is depicted on the screen. Not only is *Ed Wood* not an exception, it is a particularly problematic example of this difficulty. As previously noted, the very source for the film, *Nightmare of Ecstasy,* consists of wildly conflicting accounts of the real-life figures and events involved. In at least one respect, this was a plus, since it didn't lock Burton and his writers into a strict story line—something that inherently appealed to Tim and his lack of interest in traditional notions of narrative. ("It's like a given now. Why even mention it anymore?" asked Burton of writer John Clark in his "The Wood, the Bad, and the Ugly" for *Premiere* [October 1994].) In essence, this allowed them to "Burtonize" the episodic events of Wood's life, centering on the period from 1952 to 1959, thereby creating a film that was as much about its director as its subject. Dramatically, the approach was certainly valid, but it was one that obviously wouldn't please everybody, as evidenced by the objections of several of the survivors of those days and, in the case of Lugosi, his son.

One of the principal criticisms of *Ed Wood* was the depiction of Lugosi as a man who may not have mastered English properly, but who most certainly *did* master all the swear words. This is a major point of contention and contradiction. Several accounts of people involved in Hollywood during Lugosi's life there have Lugosi swearing like a sailor. In contrast, others—notably Dolores Fuller (who told this author that *none* of them used language like that in the 1950s) and Bela Lugosi Jr.—claim that he never used words like the ones attributed to him in the script.

Ironically, while Lugosi's outspoken vulgarity is played up in *Ed Wood,* the director's own swearing is minimized at Burton's urging. This is doubly strange, in that Tim, as evidenced in numerous interviews, is no stranger to strong language! An examination of the way curse words are used in the film, though, reveals that Lugosi may well have used such language in the company of other men, but would never have done so in front of a woman or a child, which we never see him doing. Certainly, there is a large body of evidence from people who worked on Lugosi's film sets to support that view. In many respects, the truth on this point—or lack thereof—is of secondary importance to how well it works in the film, and there's no denying that it works very well. It actually helps to make Lugosi a full and more endearing character.

If any person in *Ed Wood* has cause for complaint, it is Dolores Fuller as she is played by Sarah Jessica Parker (and presumably as directed by Burton). The real Dolores Fuller is a lively, savvy, humorous woman, while Parker's performance presents her as a kind of sitcom moron for the first part of the film and a rather judgmental and not wholly pleasant character in her later scenes. Parker seems to have patterned much of her offscreen portrayal of Dolores on Fuller's underrehearsed and rushed performances in the actual Ed Wood films, which is not only inaccurate but unfair. Also, Fuller was by no means the hanger-on depicted in *Ed Wood,* but something of a show-business veteran who had made her screen debut as a background extra at the age of twelve in Frank Capra's *It Happened One Night* [1934]. During her years with Ed, she had regular TV jobs on *Queen for a Day* and *The Dinah Shore Show.*

Fully aware of the raw amateurishness of those performances in her past, Dolores Fuller nonetheless still objects to Sarah Jessica Parker's constant, tactless references to her on-camera as the worst actress of all time (all of which are completely out of keeping with Burton's general approach to the material and characters). In March 1998, Fuller told this author, "I said to her, 'You know, Sarah, if I'd had a director like Tim Burton instead of Ed Wood, maybe I'd have been a great actress, too.' But I didn't have those advantages of a great director and a big budget and rehearsals and more than one take, because Eddie always used war surplus and short ends [of film stock] for his movies."

It also didn't help that, unlike, say, Lisa Marie, who took the real-life Maila Nurmi out to lunch and shopping, to get to know her *Ed Wood* character, or Patricia Arquette, who spent a good deal of time with Kathy Wood, Sarah Jessica Parker apparently never contacted Dolores Fuller. Both Fuller and her husband, Philip Chamberlin, feel that Parker used the excuse of portraying "the worst actress who ever lived" to explain away her less-than-praised performance (which apparently was seriously truncated in post-production). "You see, I'm still doing pictures and I'm getting *great* reviews," Fuller noted. At the same time, neither she nor Chamberlin have anything but praise for Burton and *Ed Wood,* despite its "dramatic liberties." Fuller, in fact, said, "I think Tim Burton's fabulous. I'm a huge fan."

Whatever reservations one may have about individual aspects of the film's historical accuracy, the finished product as a whole is an unqualified success. In many respects, *Ed Wood* is a virtual compendium of the Burton movies that precede it. Any attempt to understand Burton's films and what those entries tell us about Burton and how he has grown as an artist—and, by extension, as a human being—must place this amazing work near the top of the list.

The opening of *Ed Wood* is both typically Burton—the altered studio logo followed by the mood-setting model work—and a delightful reworking of Wood's own style. Re-creating the "old Willows place" from *Bride of the Monster* in miniature, Burton's camera dollies in on it and on through the window with the kind of ultrastylishness and technical panache (not to mention sense of humor) about which Wood could only dream.

Using all the stock 1950s horror-film elements—overdramatic music complete with theremin, nonstop thunder and lightning—Burton tracks in on a coffin from which rises no less a personage than Criswell (Jeffrey Jones), whose real-life show also presented him in such a morbidly theatrical manner. Criswell proceeds to inform moviegoers of what they are about to see in a speech largely reworked from his introduction to *Plan 9 from Outer Space:* "[The following is] based on the secret testimony of the miserable souls who survived this terrible ordeal. . . . Can your heart stand the shocking facts of the true story of Edward D. Wood Jr?" This opening to *Ed Wood* is every inch the work of fans of his and utterly charming on that level, yet it remains essentially and unmistakably Burton's.

Much the same could be said of *Ed Wood*'s credit sequence—a kind of compendium of Ed Wood's films—as the camera prowls through a graveyard finding the principle actors' names on the tombstones, coming to a swamp complete with giant octopus that is attacked by irresistibly hokey flying saucers, ascending into the night sky with the saucers, following them to the HOLLYWOOD sign, and then pulling back across a model of Los Angeles. The camera tracks past the towers on the Pantages Theatre and, in a remarkably seamless transition, cranes down onto a much-less-grand theatre where a nervous Ed Wood paces the sidewalk under the marquee for his play, *The Casual Company*.

Here Burton gives us all the elements of an Ed Wood picture in an almost Buñuelian surreal manner (linking image to image without concern for "logical" content, much the way Luis Buñuel structured *The Phantom of Liberty* [1974]). Yet Tim ends up establishing a visual coherence that ultimately affords *Ed Wood* a cyclical form by beginning as it will end. Similarly, it's Ed Wood filtered through a Tim Burton perspective. The swampy graveyard is certainly appropriately Woodian, but the headstones look far more like those in *Frankenweenie* than anything else. What Burton has done, in effect, is fuse himself with his subject. In making *Ed Wood,* Burton virtually becomes Ed Wood— an Ed Wood with the one thing the genuine article lacked: talent.

Ed himself is sketched on-camera with remarkable economy—the nervous young playwright outside the theatre where his first play is being presented. The onscreen Ed then cannot resist standing in the wings, transfixed by and mouthing his own inane dialogue as the actors deliver their lines in a leaky theatre where they outnumber the audience. From the onset, Burton makes clear one of the key elements that must be understood about Wood—the man honestly believes what he's doing is good. Almost no one else may "get it," but Wood rarely questions his own talent (when he does, it's only for a moment) and the validity of his work, in a way that Burton finds not merely charmingly naive, but positively heroic. That Tim conveys this so that the viewer feels the same thing is one of the principal achievements of *Ed Wood*.

This is both underscored and elaborated upon in the film when Wood's acting troupe is next shown waiting in a bar for the early-morning papers that will carry the reviews for their stage efforts. The mood and look is that of the theater greats of the 1920s and 1930s sitting around Sardi's or the Algonquin Hotel, awaiting the verdict on a *The Front Page* or *Rain*. The reality is that the theater folk depicted here are an enthusiastically untalented writer-director, an aging, heavily made-up, caricaturish homosexual, a pair of very bad actors, and an undirected leading lady who gamely struggles with an impossible role. These hopefuls are waiting on a single review that wasn't even penned by the critic whose name appears on the publication's byline! The review, of course, is devastating—or would be to anyone but Ed, who manages to isolate some good from the criticism. This is real-life, pure Wood, and again, pure Burton. The distance between the scorn heaped on the play-within-the-movie, *The Casual Company,* and that which Burton actually experienced on *Pee-Wee's Big Adventure* (1985) is not so great. Burton knows this, identifies with this, and conveys the same to us in a few bold strokes.

Burton is also quick to establish the fact that Ed is enthusiastic about his own work not just in an egocentric way, but excited about the creative process in general and the things behind it. It is Ed's enthusiastic outlook and his constant creativity that captivates Burton, so it comes as no surprise that these charming vignettes lead directly to Ed, working at a movie studio in the greens department (which supervises the trees, lawns, flowers, etc., used on film sets), discovering that schlockmeister George Weiss (played by Mike Starr) is producing a biopic on transsexual Christine Jorgensen—a subject that is, of course, right up his alley (something that girlfriend Dolores can't quite understand at first).

The degree to which Ed is obsessed with getting his chance to make the Jorgensen story is both amusing and telling. It fazes him not at all that the film is no longer about Christine Jorgensen per se; though, in fact, this may well have better suited Ed's purpose. The buoyant Wood completely overlooks the fact that Weiss is little more than a good-natured vulgarian, whose only interest in filmmaking lies in turning a quick buck on an exploitative title, as well as the fact that Screen Classics is something less than a major studio, or even a reputable independent. Ed is willing to let Weiss in on his great secret to prove just why he is peculiarly in sync with this screen material: "I like to dress in women's clothing. . . . I know what it's like to live with a secret and worry what people are gonna think of it." That this daring confessional doesn't work on Weiss is only a temporary setback.

Nursing his wounds, Ed chances upon the improbable spectacle of an irritable, has-been Bela Lugosi trying out a coffin for another bus-and-truck *Dracula* stage tour. Ed immediately strikes up a friendship with Bela and offers to take Lugosi home.

Here the film, strictly speaking, strays into artistic license. In reality, Lugosi, at this time, lived in a shabby apartment and was still married to his fourth wife, Lillian. In *Ed Wood,* however, the long-out-of-work Lugosi lives in a tract house in suburbia, Lillian has already left him (his fifth wife, Hope, is never mentioned at all), and he complains that the world does not give "two fucks" for Bela. This last could probably be a typical bit of Lugosi self-dramatization, but the other changes made for the movie's narrative are more telling. Moving Lugosi to suburbia (he might be living in the *Edward Scissorhands* neighborhood, from the looks of it) is a typically Burtonesque device, detailing the director's unyielding fascination with the idea of that which lurks, or might lurk, behind the walls of those uninspired and uninspiring houses. Here, instead of a desperate effort at bland conformity, he shows us the cluttered, almost gothic, domain of the faded movie star, surrounded by a career's worth of memorabilia (almost a suburban *Sunset Boulevard*). The more reasonable expectation of finding the Boggs family from *Edward Scissorhands* is replaced with the surprise of an old, ill, morphine-addicted actor and his distinctive home life. For Burton, that is part of the fascination of suburbia—the unexpected behind the mask. The change is insignificant as concerns the portrayal of Lugosi, but something else again in terms of Burton. Tim has converted Lugosi into part of his own unique world and worldview.

The business of cutting out Lugosi's wives in the story line of *Ed Wood* is in keeping with one of the primary attractions of the Alexander-Karaszewski screenplay. The on-camera relationship between Lugosi and Wood parallels, in Burton's mind, his own relationship with Vincent Price. The relationships *are* parallel—Price's participation made *Vincent* a viable project, and Burton loved the veteran horror star, designing a role especially for him in *Edward Scissorhands.* (However, it is worth remembering that Price, though out of work at the time, had not fallen on bad luck, and Burton can in no way be viewed as his "savior" just because he offered him the role of the inventor in *Edward Scissorhands.*)

Removing Lugosi's wives—and minimizing Wood's own relationships in the scenario—keeps the focus on Ed's ties to the old actor and was quite deliberate, as Dolores Fuller made clear in discussing the making of *Ed Wood* with this author.

At the film's premiere in September 1994, Dolores Fuller made a beeline for scenarists Scott Alexander and Larry Karaszewski, "and I said, 'How could you write the story about Ed Wood when I know more about him than anyone alive?'" Their answer was simple: They had been afraid her input might too much alter the script that Burton had already acquired and liked. "It would have been a deeper love story, because we really loved each other," Fuller explained in 1998. "And it would have been a working team of how we strived to find backers together, and how I worked so hard to support us, and looking for locations, and talking the cops into loaning us their cop cars and their sirens, and going to the fire department. You know, I was helping him con these guys! Flirting with them and everything—getting them to loan me their fire trucks! We were a team!" Exactly, and this element is exactly what Burton would not have wanted, because it would have shifted the center of the movie away from the Lugosi-Wood association.

The meeting with Lugosi—an occurrence that, within the film at least, seems to impress no one but Ed—mysteriously prompts Ed to suggest pitching himself to Weiss, hoping to make the movie more sellable with a star in it. Amazingly, the idea works and, within the movie, Ed is given four days to knock out a script. Much like his on-camera mentor, George Weiss, Ed has taken to selling something he doesn't even own as yet. Due to his financial straits, Lugosi is in no position to refuse the part, though he wonders what kind of movie it is in which he has become involved. The result, of course, is *Glen or Glenda*. According to Dolores Fuller, Ed broke the news of his transvestism to her when he began production on the film, though Fuller seems to have taken the revelation somewhat better in real life than as depicted on the screen.

The scenes re-creating the shooting of *Glen or Glenda* are remarkably faithful to the final cut of the original picture. It deftly nails down the Ed Wood approach to filmmaking in the sequence where Wood and his crew make their first shot and Ed immediately is ready to move on to the next setup. When asked if he doesn't want a protection shot, his baffled response is that the shot was perfect! This blissfully assured—some might say delusional—attitude pretty much sums up Wood's actual filmmaking style.

The in-studio sequence within *Ed Wood* affords Martin Landau some of his choicest—and most controversial—material. This is especially true in the bit where Landau's Lugosi explodes about his former screen rival, Boris Karloff. He screams that the Britisher "does not deserve to smell my shit." Lugosi may not have actually said that in life. He may not even have said anything like it, but it does effectively sum up his apparent take on his old costar and rival. As such, almost any true Lugosi fan cannot but get a feeling of satisfaction from the moment.

Offsetting this deliciously comic moment in *Ed Wood* is Lugosi's immediate transformation back into the consummate professional. He turns into his old self before our eyes, launching into a take. He delivers Wood's inane dialogue with all the considerable mastery at his disposal. It is a truly magical screen bit, perfectly capturing the essence of the legendary Bela Lugosi and his inability to give anything less than 100 percent on the screen.

This is where Ed's relationship with Dolores starts to disintegrate, as she objects to his now fairly open cross-dressing, which on the set (within the movie) is accepted without question. This is very much at odds with Dolores Fuller's recounting of her time with Ed in the 1950s. Fuller was very much attached to Lugosi, whom she used to have over for dinner and who delighted in telling her six-year-old son wonderful stories. It is more than unlikely that she would have ever denigrated Lugosi as one of "a bunch of weirdos." Timewise, this doesn't fit well, either, since Dolores would stick with Ed for another three years, but it works to bring the story into line at a tractable length by telescoping events.

When the film-within-the-film comes out, Ed is not in the least deterred by the reaction to it. He proudly takes his cans of film to Warner Bros. by way of a résumé, where the producer who screens it, at first thinks the movie is an elaborate practical joke. Finding out that it isn't, he forthrightly informs Ed that it's the worst picture he's ever seen. This assessment might be daunting to normal mortals, but rather than taking this as a sign of defeat, Ed simply tells the executive that his next effort will be better. Ed seems genuinely baffled when he finds himself talking into a dead phone! It's funny and it's touching, but, as presented by Burton, it's something more: It's heroic.

His "next one" turns out—according to *Ed Wood*—to be *Bride of the Monster,* a film that was, in Ed's estimation, going to make Dolores Fuller a star by teaming her in a horror excursion with Lugosi. Actually, the idea was better than it might sound. The script, while full of the expected Woodisms, was both a workable affair and one that either shrewdly or by happy accident managed to combine an old-fashioned mad-doctor horror film with 1950s science-fiction elements. While it may not have made Dolores a star in actuality, it clearly could have been a good little film that advanced the careers of everyone involved. What happened was considerably different, of course.

While trying to find backers for his film, Ed meets Criswell, who confesses to Ed that he's not a psychic and that people only listen to his deliberately screwy predictions because he looks the part. Criswell soon becomes part of Wood's inner circle.

When Ed chances upon the presumably well-heeled aspiring actress Loretta King (Juliet Landau), he chats her up as a potential investor, attempting to entice her with the small role of a file clerk in *Bride of the Monster.* Unfortunately, Loretta is clever enough to realize that the only part of substance is the one Ed has written for Dolores. Since the film as a whole is the thing in Ed's mind, he hands over Dolores's key role to Loretta and in exchange, he thinks, Loretta will bankroll the project.

The interesting thing about all this is that here is a situation in the script that presents Ed—and by implication, Burton—in a far worse light than the reality of the events. In actuality, Ed *did* think Loretta King had money—or rather Ed and Dolores did —and she was handed the role in consideration of the money she put into the film. However, it does not appear that this was done behind Dolores's back, but was a joint decision that was typical of the numerous sacrifices Fuller willingly made in real life for Ed's sake.

What *is* curious in *Ed Wood* is the decision to make Ed's determination to make the movie—to create his art *at any cost*— look more self-centered than it was. As he had in *Edward Scissorhands,* Burton deliberately calls attention to the less attractive side of the obsessive artist (and, by extension, to his own less attractive side) by constantly underscoring the idea that this lovable, lost character was also potentially dangerous. The movie plays this fairly mammoth betrayal for laughs, but it nonetheless paints a darker picture of its biographical subject.

Afterward, it's impossible to see Wood as quite the innocent the earlier portions of the film suggest. That Ed turns out to be an amazingly inept hustler—only Ed could mistake an offer of a $300 investment for a $60,000 one—takes off a little of the edge, but not much.

The filming of *Bride of the Monster* in *Ed Wood* is, if anything, an even better depiction of the screwy world of independent filmmaking than the scene with *Glen or Glenda* had been. The re-creation of the sets and scenes from the 1955 film are truly remarkable, though not, in all cases, exact duplicates.

When the money runs out and it turns out that the remaining $57,700 expected from Loretta King is not forthcoming, the production has to shut down and the search begins anew for backers. Ed finds a new money man and readily agrees to the man's terms in exchange for the needed cash.

The legendary story of Wood and his cohorts stealing a rubber octopus used in Republic Pictures' *Wake of the Red Witch* (1948) is faithfully re-created—minus the fact that one of the tentacles was torn off in the process—paving the way for *Ed Wood*'s most amusing and touching scene involving Lugosi. The sequence is a night shoot in Griffith Park (without permits, of course) and the temperature and hour are telling on the veteran horror star, who finds it necessary to dose himself with morphine before tackling the dialogue. Gamely wading into the water with the octopus, Lugosi goes through his paces despite the cold and the malfunctioning monster. As a result of these unpleasant working conditions, Lugosi has a moment of revelation, realizing how far he has fallen, and, heartbreakingly, that it is largely his own fault.

The production-plagued moment has its effect on Ed, too, who quickly writes a new scene—one of the few pieces of genuinely good writing Ed ever did in real life—especially for his luckless hero. It is a speech that captures a miniature portrait of Lugosi at the end of his career and life. Again, Landau reflects the true magic of the real Lugosi when he re-creates this scene, bringing to it all the intensity at his command. Completely devoid of even a hint of comedy, it is one of the most remarkable moments in the movie. Even Dolores Fuller and Philip Chamberlin admit that here, at least, Landau *is* Lugosi.

The completion of *Bride of the Monster* signals the moment for Dolores to call it a day with Ed. The veracity of her departure as depicted in *Ed Wood* is open to debate, but again, it brings the film down to a workable structure. The finishing of the *Bride of the Monster* also poses another problem, in that it leaves everyone at sea with no sign of a new project.

With nothing to anchor him, Lugosi sinks deeper and deeper into depression and poverty, threatening suicide—before finally taking the step of checking into the state hospital for a drug cure. Here the film takes on a curiously modern tone with Lugosi briefly becoming a media sensation on notoriety alone. The anachronistic quality of all this is likely intentional, since it makes *Ed Wood* more intellectually accessible to a modern audience. Then, too, it is fully in keeping with Tim Burton's penchant for jumbling up time frames to create his own "anytime," and also makes the parallels with his own life more pronounced.

It is while Lugosi is in the hospital that Ed meets Kathy (Patricia Arquette), a sweetly naive girl, who is virtually the opposite of the film's Dolores Fuller. Here is where it seems obvious that Burton is using the two key relationships in Ed's life to mirror his own. Dolores roughly fills the role of Lena Gieseke, and Kathy stands in for Lisa Marie. Ed's ultrainnocent courtship of Kathy, with the two doing nothing more than talking, undoubtedly draws from the beginnings of Burton's relationship with Lisa Marie. Innocence is the keyword here.

Unfortunately, within *Ed Wood*, all is not going nearly so well now for Lugosi, who is released from the hospital well before his cure is completed, when his insurance runs out. Trying to give his friend a sense of purpose, Ed shoots unconnected footage of him that will ultimately form the core of the actor's appearance in *Plan 9 from Outer Space*. Historically, *Ed Wood* here plays significantly fast and loose with the facts: Lugosi *did* complete the cure, he almost immediately remarried upon his release, and he found film work in Reginald LeBorg's *The Black Sleep* (1956). However, the compressing of real-life events and the resultant deletions are necessary to the thrust of Burton's movie.

Later in *Ed Wood,* the Bela Lugosi character dies. It is at this juncture that Burton's narrative leads straight into its most extended single section, the making of the infamous *Plan 9 from Outer Space*. Though this final part of the film—making up nearly thirty minutes of *Ed Wood*'s running time—is bereft of Landau's engaging Lugosi, it makes up for the loss by virtue of the sheer verve with which the events are presented. Here, the film needs to take very few liberties with the material, since there are few stories about filmmaking that are as blessed with so many nearly unbelievable events as that of *Plan 9*. The story of how Ed actually got the film financed by the Baptist Church of Beverly Hills, after he convinced them that his script and the minimal footage of Lugosi would make enough profits for them to finance a series of religious epics, is true. That part of the price for their backing, so far as the church was concerned, involved having the cast and crew baptized into the faith is true. That the baptism was held in a swimming pool is also true.

The baptism scenes are hysterical, with the cast piously seated in the church, arguing about whether or not a hired chiropractor looks sufficiently like the late Bela Lugosi to play his double on-camera. The newcomer holds his baptismal robe over his face like a cape. This "convinces" some of the troupe that he is okay for the part. Again, scenes like this in *Ed Wood* depict the heroic lengths that Ed went to get his movies made.

The making of the film-within-the-film is presented in a series of bizarre vignettes that fully evoke the insanity of the enterprise. When the church demands that the movie be retitled to avoid the word "graverobbers"—anathema to the church–financial backers—it is ground Burton himself had been over in real life, on *Beetlejuice,* where the studio preferred the title *House Ghosts* (and even Burton's joking suggestion that the film be called *Scared Sheetless*), to its original one.

As in the other depictions on-camera of Ed Wood's filmmaking, Burton captures the essence of the movie that is being made. However, here he makes it an even more direct statement on the process of creation, with Ed constantly enthused over what he's making, in open defiance of the church representatives who insist on pointing out the production's more glaring errors. Driven to the end of his tether by their interference, Ed flees the set nearly in tears (much as Burton himself had done in England while making *Batman*). A chance encounter with filmmaker Orson Welles (played by Vincent D'Onofrio) inspires Wood to complete his "epic" his own way.

As if to reward Ed for his determination, Tim Burton makes the grandest gesture of his moviemaking career by giving the director something he never had in real life—a grand premiere of the "ultimate Ed Wood picture," *Plan 9 from Outer Space,* at the prestigious Pantages Theatre in Hollywood, in front of an enthusiastic and appreciative packed house. (In one of *Ed Wood*'s few noticeable economies in its relatively slight $18 million budget, the audience shots here are clearly from the same shoot as those used during Lugosi's disastrous television appearance earlier in the story line.) The premiere never happened, of course, but here Burton exercises perfectly valid dramatic license to make right for Ed in art, that which was never made right in life.

This gesture is Burton's ultimate statement on the heroism and validity of the act of creation—presented completely without condescension or judgment. His camera lovingly passes by the creators of *Plan 9* as they watch their efforts unfold on the screen in delight. It doesn't matter in the least that the film these people are taking pride in hardly qualifies as "good" in any objective sense. It doesn't even matter if they have deluded themselves. All that matters to director Burton is that they went out and *did something,* which is more than can be said for most of the people who enjoy feeling superior to Ed and his cohorts and their work. It is a beautiful celebration of the act of creation for its own sake, and one of the finest moments in any Burton movie. Possibly, it is simply one of the finest moments in film.

Burton wisely chooses to end *Ed Wood* with the premiere of *Plan 9* and Ed's decision that he and Kathy drive to Las Vegas and get married. (According to Dolores Fuller, Ed and Kathy never actually married, though they lived together for many years.) Ed's subsequent real-life descent into alcoholism and ever-more-demeaning jobs on the fringe of the creative world would have been nothing but a downer in *Ed Wood,* and would undermine the picture's theme. In any case, we know what lies in store for Ed, and ending the narrative here, with Ed blithely optimistic, carries an especially moving resonance.

Ed Wood was Burton's biggest gamble to date. Even though it boasted a very hip sensibility and a cast of stars with a strong following, it was far afield from anything he had done previously on-camera in terms of content. While it was thematically consistent and a conscious outgrowth of the themes found in the films that had preceded it, it *did* tell a strange and unique story about people many of Burton's admirers probably neither knew, nor cared about. Besides, conventional wisdom in Hollywood has it that the "youth market" has no patience with black-and-white movies. However, artistically, it paid off.

The reviews for *Ed Wood* were generally favorable. Once again, Roger Ebert (*Chicago Sun-Times*) came down on Burton's side, saying, "What Burton has made is a film which celebrates Wood more than it mocks him, and which celebrates, too, the spirit of the 1950s exploitation films." In *Entertainment Weekly*, Owen Gleiberman was equally enthusiastic: "In a feat of creative alchemy, Burton has tapped into something rich and poignant." Stuart Klawans in *The Nation* added to the praise by noting, "The unembarrassed warmth of *Ed Wood* emanates first of all from the director, Tim Burton, who has always sided with the misfits and weirdos. . . . Now, thanks to Tim Burton, only a hypocrite viewer will be able to look down on Ed Wood or deny a brotherly resemblance." In *Newsday*, Jack Matthews observed, "Though its tone is relentlessly tongue-in-cheek, Burton and his marvelous cast . . . never mock or belittle their subject."

People magazine's Ralph Novak found *Ed Wood* to be "a sweet, self-contained piece of work that aspires to nothing more than a cheesy integrity worthy of the master." *Newsweek* joined in, calling Burton's latest offering "sweet, sad and very funny," saying that the film "is a valentine to the tenacious spirit of an artist who will do anything to see his vision realized on the screen." The *Los Angeles Times'* Kenneth Turan said it was "thoroughly entertaining," adding, "*Ed Wood* is a fantasy for the terminally disaffected, proof for those who want it that an absence of convention and even talent need not be a bar to happiness or immortality." And Peter Travers in *Rolling Stone* enthused, "Burton has fashioned a celebration not of bad movies but of what it takes to get an uncompromised vision on the screen."

One of the rare voices of dissent on *Ed Wood*, however, came from the powerful *Time* critic, Richard Corliss, who found the film "dishwatery" and lacking in "the cartoon zest and outsider ache of *Beetlejuice, Edward Scissorhands*, or *Batman Returns*." The irony is that what Corliss seems to be missing in *Ed Wood* is the one thing most critics had grown tired of in Burton's work—the thread of self-pity.

Unfortunately, all the good reviews in the world cannot guarantee a film's success, especially without a hard push from the studio. Before the film opened, Frank Scheck commented in the *Hollywood Reporter* (September 23, 1994), "Finding an audience for this intensely personal and quirky project will be no mean feat." Indeed. The problem was that Burton had signed with Warner Bros. by the time the film came out, and Disney, no longer enticed by the prospect of annexing Burton to their studio, were not much interested in finding that special audience. Their interest had primarily been Burton, not *Ed Wood,* and the $18 million investment in the film was not in itself sufficient inducement for them to spend the time and money necessary to properly promote the feature. Industry observers agreed that *Ed Wood* was a specialized project that required a certain approach, and that the last thing it needed was for the studio to dump the film on the market in wide release, which is exactly what Disney did. *Ed Wood* was a movie that needed desperately to *build* an audience, and it was never given a chance in that regard. Moreover, there were reports from all over the United States that suggested the prints being shipped out were not of the highest standard or uniformity. Some were said to be "soft" in focus and soundtrack problems were noted elsewhere.

Burton took to the interview trail to plug *Ed Wood.* He and Martin Landau even headed up a special Bela Lugosi birthday salute on Ted Turner's cable superstation TNT (October 20, 1994). However, their efforts were not enough to build the anticipation necessary to put *Ed Wood* over to the public at large. Burton had a major critical success on his hands, but not one that was destined to do well at the box office. In its first seven weeks, *Ed Wood* grossed only $5,543,950. Even when Martin Landau won his well-deserved Oscar for his performance as Bela Lugosi, *Ed Wood* was still not guaranteed good box-office receipts.

Sometimes it seems that what it takes to get an uncompromised vision on the screen can also keep that vision from being seen. Fortunately, a film is a living thing and its reputation and popularity changes with the passing of time. One day *Ed Wood,* quite possibly the best film Burton has made so far, may find the broader audience it has always deserved.

18 | A *PLAN 9* OF HIS OWN

I just wanted to go back and do those kind of movies that I like seeing.

TIM BURTON, 1996

DESPITE THE CRITICAL RECEPTION AFFORDED *ED WOOD*, its lackluster box office (under $6 million in domestic release) did not put Tim Burton on top of the world, nor at the top of the heap where "hot" filmmakers were concerned. At the time, he was clearly eclipsed by Quentin Tarantino, whose flashier *Pulp Fiction* (1994) was not only doing big business, but garnering even better reviews than *Ed Wood* and knocking *Ed Wood* out of the number one position on many critics' "ten best" lists for the year.

Despite the modest showing of *Ed Wood,* Warner Bros. was certainly delighted to have Burton back in their fold. The prestige factor of Burton's film was enough to compensate for its commercial failure. In fact, as some studio executives saw it, that failure might even make Burton a little more tractable to studio methodology. At the same time, the studio was more than a little pleased that Burton was *not* at the helm of the new Batman opus, *Batman Forever* (1995), even if Burton's replacement (Joel Schumacher) supposedly caused Michael Keaton to drop out of the series. Burton was well aware of this and equally aware that his producer status on the film—while lucrative— was little more than an effort to keep his connection with the movie franchise in the minds of Burton fans. The last thing Warner Bros. wanted was another *Batman Returns* (1992).

Batman Returns, they did not get. Undoubtedly the decision to put Joel Schumacher in charge of the film was based on the fact that, while he was known for a certain visual stylishness (albeit a sort of faceless, generic stylishness), he did not have a reputation for any great thematic depth. Moreover, as a world-class pop-culture vulture and trend-follower, he would not object to the injection of pop songs into the proceedings (and the attendant merchandising tie-in album, of course), as Burton had done on the previous films. In other words, Schumacher would give them a *Batman* picture that was all flash and action, little thought, and wouldn't upset anyone; i.e., it would reinstate the status quo of the mindless summer action blockbuster. To a great degree, that is exactly what Schumacher gave them—a big, hollow glitter ball of a movie.

When *Batman Forever* was released, much of the critical opinion was that it was a welcome relief from the Burton entries, which, to a great degree, meant little more than that its lack of a real point was more in keeping with the critic's idea of what a comic-book movie ought to be. "The third installment of the *Batman* series, based on characters created by Bob Kane and published by DC comics, is the best to date," enthused *Boxoffice*'s Christine James, who went on to comment that "the big star is the jaw-dropping visual splendor." Less delighted overall was the *San Francisco Chronicle*'s Mick LaSalle, who found it typical of summertime big films, but noted that Schumacher "submerges his own style and essentially creates a Tim Burton *Batman* movie—minus the usual touches of the fey and grotesque, which we can easily do without." (One does wonder just what Schumacher's "own style" is supposed to be, unless it's merely design over substance.)

Roger Ebert of the *Chicago Sun-Times* cited the film for its fetishistic approach, noting that the new onscreen Batman (Val Kilmer) "would be a sensation in any leather bar," but found that Schumacher "makes a generally successful effort to lighten the material," and that "the film is great bubble gum for the eyes" and wouldn't have the same negative impact on children as its predecessor. What is interesting about this assessment is that it neatly sidesteps several issues, not the least of which is that a good deal of the furor over *Batman Returns* was generated by the film's sexual innuendo and there's no shortage of that in *Batman Forever,* along with a great deal of homosexual undercurrent. Ebert himself remarks on the on-camera relationship between Bruce Wayne

(Val Kilmer) and the newly introduced Robin (Chris O'Donnell), commenting on a sequence where the "subtexts" are "so deep you have to wade through them." Apparently, the general consensus was that sexual innuendo is fine *if* it's done with a knowing wink and a heavy dose of camp—so long as it doesn't visibly disturb the children. Youngsters may have been openly upset by *Batman Returns*, but it's hard not to wonder about the untold psychological impact of a film with a heroine (Nicole Kidman) who wonders whether she might stand a better chance romantically with Batman if she brandished a whip.

From Warner Bros.' standpoint, the big questions were popularity *and* lack of negative response. On that score, Schumacher's entry, whatever its merits or defects, delivered the goods. Its $333 million worldwide gross easily eclipsed *Batman Returns'* $280 million. In fact, *Batman Forever* was a kind of danger signal for Burton. It could have easily threatened to turn him into something not dissimilar to his original position at Disney: a conceptual artist, a man whose ideas were fine, but whose vision was too complex and bleak. It was not an enticing image.

More central to Tim's work were his producing chores on Henry Selick's *James and the Giant Peach* (1996), the combination live-action and animation film of Roald Dahl's children's story. It was an outgrowth of Burton and Selick's collaboration on *Nightmare Before Christmas*. Burton's active participation in this screen project was certainly greater than it had been on *Batman Forever*. However, the movie was still more Selick than Burton, and therein lay its central problem.

While fully able to translate and even expand upon Burton's ideas in *Nightmare Before Christmas*, Selick seems here too literal-minded and not altogether comfortable with directing the picture's live-action sequences. The nonanimated characters are rather unappealing and the presentation of James's (Paul Terry) villainous aunts, Spiker (Joanna Lumley) and Sponge (Miriam Margolyes), is not only grotesque, but their makeup and acting are better suited to a tacky children's TV special than to a $38 million feature. Moreover, the movie is badly in need of a Danny Elfman score. The shapeless Randy Newman songs that adorn the entry are too much pop-basic to lend real distinction. In fact, Roger Ebert's review in the *Chicago Sun-Times* of the film mentions the tunes as an afterthought ("Oh, and there are some songs"). Even those who did not care for Elfman's *Nightmare* songs, certainly noted their presence!

Even so, *James and the Giant Peach,* released by Walt Disney Pictures in April 1996, was—and is—a dazzling technical achievement and some critics preferred it to *Nightmare Before Christmas. People* magazine rated it as "a far livelier entertainment" and felt its adventures were far more engaging than the plot of *Nightmare Before Christmas,* the story of which they tagged as nothing more than "a skeleton coping with depression." Roger Ebert also admired the film's technical side and creativity, as well as its gleeful violence in disposing of James's parents by having them "gobbled up by a giant rhinoceros" right off the bat. To the appreciative Ebert, the ploy seemed like a deliberate parody of the standard Disney setup of an orphaned or somehow abandoned child making his own way in the world. What *James and the Giant Peach* has is creative verve and technical panache. What it does *not* have is much of a heart. Regardless of how one feels about Burton's continued self-examination—or self-pity—in *Nightmare Before Christmas,* it was clearly about something, clearly made by (and about) someone with statements to make. *James and the Giant Peach* was just as clearly a mostly uninvolved translation of Dahl's story to the screen. While it is clearly made by a genuine admirer of the source material, it lacks truly personal drive.

Perhaps the most important aspect of Burton's involvement as a producer on *James and the Giant Peach* lies in the evidence it provides that he was indeed now trying to make amends for his past treatment of friends and associates. It is as if he had learned the lessons of friendship he had espoused in *Ed Wood.* On a creative level, *James and the Giant Peach* paved the way for his reunion with Danny Elfman, whose contribution to Burton's next film project would be virtually essential. "In a nonspecific way, I would call what happened between the two of us a family feud. We had worked together for ten years and on six films together, and we had a creative blowout," Elfman told *Fangoria* magazine. Their reteaming could not have come at a better time, since perhaps no one but Elfman could possibly tap into Burton's vision on this project.

Just what Burton had in mind for a new film—presumably one that would recapture his box-office popularity—was not quite the most expected or promising screen concept. When he finished *Ed Wood,* Burton seems to have had no exact movie projects of his own in mind. There was talk of him finally finishing up his 1991 documentary, *Conversations with Vincent,* but nothing came of that, while the most hotly rumored project was a Catwoman spin-off from *Batman Returns.* That idea made sense in that Catwoman was the *one* ingredient everyone agreed was good about *Batman Returns,* regardless of how they felt about the movie as a whole. However, Burton, not necessarily known for doing the most expected or logical thing in the film industry, had another idea.

In 1962 the Topps Company (the major manufacturer and distributor of bubblegum trading cards) had issued a set of fifty-five cards under the title of *Mars Attacks!* The collectible in question was notorious for being startlingly graphic—and somewhat tasteless in choices of images—in its depiction of a Martian invasion of Earth. The cards were spawned when cards depicting the American Civil War had proved tremendously popular with consumers, owing in great part to the gory carnage of that set's battle scenes. Topps reasoned that an even more grisly card set might sell better still. The resulting cards proved to be everything the company wanted and a little bit more—so much more, in fact, that they had to be withdrawn from the market, due to the complaints of outraged parents. One especially unsettling image showed a pet dog being gruesomely burned to death. This, of course, made the cards rare and peculiarly valuable. A complete set in excellent condition now sells for around $2,000!

Screenwriter Jonathan Gems brought *Mars Attacks!* (and their companion set, *Dinosaurs Attack!*) to Burton's attention in 1994 and was surprised when shortly afterward the director announced his desire that the two of them turn it into a feature film. The appeal of the cards' history to Burton is immediately obvious—the public reaction to them had been almost identical to that of his own *Batman Returns.* In fact, one of the scenes that had to be cut from Burton's movie to secure its PG-13 rating involved characters being incinerated, much like the infamous card of the burning dog. But to base a film on a series of bubblegum cards? This was hardly the most promising concept imaginable, and not one that would occur to most people. However, there was yet another, possibly less obvious, attraction for Burton: The cards themselves really didn't tell a story as such. What could appeal more to a filmmaker who was constantly attacked by critics for being unable—or unwilling—to tell a coherent story?

The delicious irony of these two aspects of the new film project was not lost on Burton. Add in Burton's natural fondness for kitschy pop culture and the fact that trading cards were a big item in his childhood; with this in mind, the idea that *Mars Attacks!* was solid material for a Tim Burton film seems less dubious and more inevitable. Moreover, the material offered the possibility of creating what would at least *look like* an action blockbuster. There is a peculiar sense of Burton now giving the studio the kind of dumbed-down "big" picture they desired, yet doing it in a defiant manner that drew on his earlier, more "difficult" work and deliberately played on his lack of concern for narrative.

Jonathan Gems told *Fangoria* magazine (January 1997) that he wrote the screenplay for *Mars Attacks!* thinking it would "amuse Tim, but I didn't think he'd actually make a movie out of it because it was so freaky." Freaky it was, but Burton had never been bothered much by the bizarre. Then, too, *Mars Attacks!* had the obvious potential of being at once clearly the work of Tim Burton, and, at the same time, a real departure from his earlier work. In many respects, it takes off in a completely new direction, which suggests that *Ed Wood* was actually the culmination of a phase or period in what will one day make up Burton's filmography. The departure is apparent from the very onset: *Mars Attacks!* is the first Burton film where the title is not the name of its central character, for the very good reason that it is the first Burton film that isn't about a central character. Instead, it is about an event.

In fact, *Mars Attacks!* is coolly detached from most of the characters. The only marginally likable characters are the young and none-too-bright doughnut maker Richie Norris (Lukas Haas), his impossibly dotty grandmother (Sylvia Sidney), ex–prize fighter Byron Williams (Jim Brown), his estranged, long-suffering wife, Louise (Pam Grier), airheaded "New Ager" Barbara Land (Annette Bening), Taffy Dale (Natalie Portman), the disaffected daughter of the president, and, of course, pop singer Tom Jones (himself). Everyone else is just so much meat-on-the-hoof for the invading Martians—and they are usually pompous and phony and fully deserving of their spectacular demises. In this regard, the film has a much harder edge than any of Burton's earlier work. *Batman Returns* may have seethed with anger, but it was visceral and emotional. On the contrary, *Mars Attacks!* is amused and cynical. For all its very deliberate silliness, it is less the work of an innocent than it is that of a sophisticate, as if Burton here chooses to reveal yet another layer of himself.

It is not therefore surprising that *Mars Attacks!* called for a different production designer than Bo Welch, and a cinematographer very different from Stefan Czapsky (of *Edward Scissorhands*). The film needed a different look, a different feel, which is precisely what designer Wynn Thomas and cinematographer Peter Suschitzky brought to the project. The choice of Suschitzky was an especially good one and not in the least surprising. Burton is a self-admitted admirer of the films of David Cronenberg, with whose films Suschitzky is most closely associated, and for whom the cinematographer has created some of the hardest-edged, most highly polished, and distinctively objective imagery of all time. (*Mars Attacks!* contains several things that could be likened to Cronenberg, and, in fact, includes two references to Cronenberg's movies. The red surgical smocks the aliens sport reflect the ones used in Cronenberg's *Dead Ringers* [1988], and the name of the bus line that deposits Lisa Marie outside the White House, Starline Tours, recalls the name of the luxury apartment setting, Starliner Towers in Cronenberg's *They Came from Within* [1975].) In addition, Suschitzky had evidenced the ability to create kitschy pop images that were unusual in their heavy color saturation on his two assignments for Ken Russell, *Lisztomania* (1975) and *Valentino* (1977). This unique look was at once playful (somewhat like the pop art vibrancy of *Pee-Wee's Big Adventure*) and strangely menacing in its heavier colors. It was perfect for the vision of *Mars Attacks!*, which in terms of hues looks more like *Lisztomania* than it does either a Burton or a Cronenberg film, and adds just the right substance to the film.

Thomas Wynn's production design was again more sophisticated than that of Burton's past productions. The awe-inspiring "War Room" in which much of the latter part of the movie takes place is a worthy successor to the one in Stanley Kubrick's classic *Dr. Strangelove* (1964), from which it clearly draws its inspiration, while such original creations as the "Kennedy Room"—a secret room in the White House specifically designed for clandestine meetings of the amatory variety—deftly blend the sophisticated with the impossibly tacky.

The designs for *Mars Attacks!* are still in keeping with Tim's intriguing creation of a sense of a time outside a specific period. *Mars Attacks!* seems to be taking place in the present day, yet it also has resonant echoes of the 1960s running throughout it. The set for Sarah Jessica Parker's talk show, for example, would not be out of place in a similar all-star extravaganza from nearly thirty years earlier, *Casino Royale* (1967). This is less surprising when taking into account Burton's stated intent to draw upon the sprawling all-star "disaster" pictures from his youth. "*Mars Attacks!* is like those old movies; this is just that kind of genre that has been around for a while and seems to fit with it," Burton explained in *Starlog* magazine (January 1997). What he wanted to create was an amazing hybrid—an amalgam of traditional blockbuster filmmaking (hence his decision to shoot his first wide-screen movie) in the modern sense, *and* in an older sense, with a deliberately cheesy 1950s science-fiction premise that pokes fun at itself and at the whole concept of such movies. In most respects, that's pretty much what he got.

The major obstacle to success in the project Burton envisioned lay in the special-effects work. Without question, Burton sought the look and feel of an old-fashioned Ray Harryhausen film—mixing live action with stop-motion animation for his invading Martians. It seemed natural as an extension of *Nightmare Before Christmas* and *James and the Giant Peach.* However, on the scale necessary for *Mars Attacks!,* it proved far too costly and far too time-consuming, raising the projected budget of the film to $120 million, according to co-producer Larry Franco. While Warner Bros. was interested in Burton's spectacular project, they were not willing to go to such extreme lengths, especially considering the fact that the astronomical budgets allotted to his *Batman* pictures had ended up going considerably over the estimated amounts.

The attempts at re-creating the Harryhausen stop-motion look on *Cabin Boy* with computer-generated images had been disappointing, so Burton was not inclined to go this route. But Larry Franco had more experience with CGI effects, having just completed *Jumanji* (1995), starring Robin Williams. He knew something about the approach that Burton didn't. As he told *Fangoria,* "If you stop at some point and don't smooth out computer animation, it pretty much looks like stop-motion." Burton was sold. "We were able to create something that's not truly three-dimensional, but *seems* three-dimensional, and has the feeling of that old stop-motion," he told *Starlog* magazine. The procedure also drove the film's budget down to the still-lofty figure of $78 million, which, in the final analysis, was agreeable to Warner Bros. (In a stroke of luck, the film's production coincided with the demolition of a "futuristic" 1950s hotel—a towering structure with a top level that resembled a flying saucer—in Las Vegas, affording Burton an impossibly spectacular effect for no real money.)

Even at $78 million, the sort of all-star cast Burton needed for *Mars Attacks!* to work could have proved a financial stumbling block if the big-name players—many of whom had worked with Burton previously—had not agreed to take salary cuts in order to be a part of the enterprise. The major problem that was encountered lay in finding an actor of sufficient stature and natural authority to play United States President James Dale. The original choice was Warren Beatty. However, Beatty recently had alienated Warner Bros. with his own film project, *Love Affair* (1994), by—as the studio saw it—being altogether too much of a perfectionist, according to *Time* magazine. Paul Newman was also a contender, but vetoed the project over personal concerns about the movie's outright gleeful violence. Burton opted to approach Jack Nicholson, offering him either the role of the president, or that of the shifty Las Vegas developer, Art Land.

Not certain that the much-in-demand Nicholson would want either part, Burton was surprised—and delighted—when the powerhouse Oscar winner decided he wanted to play both parts. Nicholson, however, does not appear to have been one of the stars willing to take a pay cut. The *Time* magazine piece on his casting notes that the actor made close to $50 million on *Batman* and, quoting an unnamed source, that for *Mars Attacks!* Nicholson "wanted the world." Presumably, as with *Batman,* this was largely in the form of a share of the box-office gross and a piece of the merchandising action. In any event, Nicholson was worth the expense, since he anchored the movie in his role as the president.

The rest of the cast clearly reflected Burton's own tastes. Along with such expected big names as Glenn Close, Annette Bening, Pierce Brosnan, Martin Short, Natalie Portman, Christina Applegate, and Michael J. Fox, he brought in people with whom he had worked before in star capacities: Danny DeVito (the Penguin from *Batman Returns*), Sarah Jessica Parker (Dolores Fuller from *Ed Wood*), Sylvia Sidney (Juno from *Beetlejuice*). These name players were joined with lesser Burton luminaries for supporting bits: O-Lan Jones (Esmeralda from *Edward Scissorhands*), Joseph Maher (the neighbor from *Frankenweenie*), Rance Howard ("Old Man" McCoy from *Ed Wood*). In addition, he topped these names off with more cultish figures, usually veterans of movies from Burton's youth: Pam Grier, Jim Brown, Rod Steiger, Joe Don Baker, and Tom Jones. And, of course, there was a role for Burton's romantic interest, Lisa Marie. Ironically, it was she who walked away with nearly all the good notices for *Mars Attacks!* for her bit as a Martian in disguise. All in all, as *Mars Attacks!* took shape, it was proving to be at once huge and, typically, personal and quirky.

For a time, Burton brought in Scott Alexander and Larry Karaszewski to help smooth out, punch up, and bring the screenplay into sharper focus. Ultimately, though, only Jonathan Gems received writing credit (despite the fact that Tim himself had a great deal to do with the script). Perhaps the duo should have been kept on, because as it evolved, *Mars Attacks!* had script trouble that was not entirely compensated for by Burton's style and injections of visual humor. It's almost impossible not to *want* to like a movie that goes out of its way to fly in the face of nearly every idea of good filmmaking and current notions of good taste. (Gems even has remarked, "Doing this film always seemed so politically incorrect.") It's even harder not to want to see a filmmaker, who so obviously is pulling a fast one on the studio by only "appearing" to be delivering the sort of film they want, get away with it. Artistically, Burton succeeded part of the time; commercially, the studio was happier with *Batman Returns*.

19 | CHAOS, MASS DESTRUCTION, AND TOM JONES

An advanced civilization is by definition not barbaric.
PIERCE BROSNAN
as Dr. Donald Kessler in *Mars Attacks!* (1996)

PERHAPS THE WORD THAT BEST DESCRIBES *MARS ATTACKS!*
is "cheeky," and its cheekiness is apparent from the moment that a flying saucer invades the very Warner Bros. logo that precedes the film's opening. This hint is quickly followed by one of the movie's most celebrated images—that of a herd of burning cattle stampeding down a country road—an image taken from the original trading cards, but enlarged upon in its cheerful gruesomeness by having characters mistake the smell that precedes them for a barbecue! It's at once striking, absurd, grand, almost surreal, and disgustingly funny, which pretty much sums up all the ingredients that are best about the production.

If the precredit sequence is alarmingly good, the credits themselves are a remarkable fusion of the grandiose with the cheesy. They are backed by one of returning composer Danny Elfman's most deliciously over-the-top soundtrack pieces—an eerie, science-fictionish opening leading into a marchlike rhythm recalling English composer Gustav Holst's "Mars, the Bringer of War," all incorporating the use of a theremin and topped off with a spectacular Elfmanesque, wordless choral part. Visually, the scenes of the Martian ships amassing their forces is absolutely giddy in its snowballing complexity, size, and scope. It is truly breathtaking, yet the whole point is kept beautifully in focus by having the saucers themselves look exactly like what the real-life Ed Wood might have produced if he'd had the money and the know-how. The point is wonderfully clear here—Burton is making the ultimate 1950s sci–fi picture with everything that implies, but with a savviness the makers of those earlier films never imagined.

Very nearly as good, and equally smart in another sense, is the film's depiction of how all this is being dealt with in Washington. Burton places all the stock characters from such films in one room (in this case, the Oval Office)—the concerned president, the representatives of the military, and the pipe-smoking, all-knowing scientist. And then, since this is the latter half of the 1990s, Burton throws in just the right twists. Instead of one general, we have two. There's the traditional warmongering General Decker (Rod Steiger), who would be at home in any 1950s sci–fi film, and wants to keep the news of the Martian ships from the public, while simultaneously blasting the visitors out of the sky. However, he is offset by the moderate, but equally pompous, modern General Casey (Paul Winfield), who is less sure that a fleet of ships surrounding the earth is necessarily hostile (think Colin Powell).

In addition, there is the now ubiquitous presidential advisor, Jerry Ross (Martin Short), a smarmy sort of hanger-on, whose job, it appears, is to tell the president how to think. President Dale (Jack Nicholson) himself doesn't seem to have any genuine opinion on the matter and relies solely on the input he receives from these people, ultimately opting to agree with the more moderate view of General Casey; the logic of Dr. Kessler's (Pierce Brosnan) assertion that "an advanced civilization is by definition not barbaric"; and, most of all, Jerry Ross's concept that the people "are gonna love" visitors from Mars. In the mindset of the 1990s, after all, an invasion from Mars isn't so much an international emergency as it is a chance for effective public relations—given the right spin. President Dale may not have a clue what he thinks about the whole thing, but he knows what he wants in the spin department, quickly ordering a folksy television speech—"statesmanlike, historical, and yet warm, neighborly—that will mean all things to all people." The line between politics and entertainment is simply obliterated. Dale sounds more like a writer pitching a script to a studio in easily identifiable clichés, than he seems to be projecting the image of "the leader of the free world." It's apt; it's funny; it sets the tone for the film: These people fully deserve everything they get.

This theme is deftly underscored by the follow-up scene of Nancy Reaganlike first lady Marsha Dale (Glenn Close) busying herself with the "responsibilities" of her "office"—in this case choosing materials to redo the Roosevelt Room in the White House and posing for the casual publicity photo, while deftly shoving her decorator (Joseph Maher) out of the frame. Everything the first lady says and does is affected, pompous, and conscious of an image so transparently phony that it's hard to believe she buys her own act, let alone that anyone else does. As the film progresses, it is clear that the same phoniness is at the heart of most of the film's characters: The image is all, and image always is accepted over reality. Indeed, the first lady's daughter, Taffy (Natalie Portman) is the only wholly rational character—the only character who sees the absurdity of everything that surrounds her—in this section of the film. It is hardly accidental that the Burton character Taffy most resembles is Lydia Deetz, on whom she is clearly patterned, even to a hint of the morbid in her black-canopied bed. By extension, she also functions as one of the two characters in the film most closely related to Burton himself.

Within *Mars Attacks!* the action takes place primarily in Washington, D.C., Las Vegas, and Perkinsville, Kansas (with a brief interlude in New York City). In each of the settings there is a group of characters, largely unlikable and/or deluded and deluding. There are also one or two characters in each of the locales who are likable and can see through the nonsense that surrounds them. Conceptually, this works, but the script isn't able to place the diverse stories on equal footing. This defect becomes obvious the moment the film shifts to Las Vegas. Although the gambling capital's sections of the movie are among its more colorful parts—especially in the film's latter half—they are also among its least interesting. The entire plot involving ex-prizefighter Byron Williams and his attempts to better himself and reconcile with his estranged wife in Washington is unaffecting and approached on far too serious a level. Burton must have thought that casting 1970s blaxploitation film icons Jim Brown and Pam Grier in these roles would somehow justify it. He must have anticipated that their presence would be funny enough in itself, but it isn't. Moreover, Tim takes their relationship too seriously during the remainder of the film. Only when they—at separate points in the narrative—make sport of their established action-character screen images, do their scenes start to come to life.

The other side of the coin in *Mars Attacks!* is the too-broadly-sketched characters of Art and Barbara Land. Nicholson's dual presence as President Dale and the land-dealing sharpie Art Land seems designed to hint that the president and the barefaced huckster are pretty much interchangeable. The idea isn't bad, but again, the script doesn't do it justice. Nicholson himself is obviously having a fine time playing Art Land. However, this character isn't given anything terribly funny to do or say, and he mostly comes across as more vile than funny. Annette Bening's Barbara Land is at least sweet in a wholly ditsy manner, but here again, the film errs by being unable to mix her sweetness with much in the way of humor. As a result, she quickly becomes tiresome, or, at best, just never registers at all.

Burton is on surer footing on-camera with his New York characters—Jason Stone (Michael J. Fox) and Nathalie Lake (Sarah Jessica Parker)—a pair of media celebrities. He represents so-called "hard news," and she represents the world of fluff with her talk show, *Today in Fashion*. However, the demarcation between these two worlds of fact and fancy has blurred, so that it's hard to tell which is the more vacuous. Both are observed with a degree of wit (including an in-joke—Nathalie seems to have inherited one of Bela Lugosi's chihuahuas from *Ed Wood!*). Burton and screenwriter Gems clearly are able to nail their characters' narcissistic self-absorption with vicious precision. The central problem with these characters is that once they've been deftly skewered, the movie has no place to go with them. (It certainly doesn't help that a fine comic actor like Michael J. Fox isn't given anything funny to do onscreen.) Fortunately, both characters are fairly tangential to the plot, posing less of a problem than the Las Vegas segment of the film.

After setting up these characters and their situations, Burton holds off introducing the last—and in some ways, most important—personalities until after President Dale commences his "fireside chat." In his talk he equates such earth-shattering events as his own graduation from Princeton, the day Marsha accepted his marriage proposal, and the birth of Taffy, with the news that the earth is surrounded by Martian spaceships. What is truly frightening about this unconscious egotism is not just that it is fully believable, but that such a speech would, in all likelihood, be accepted by the media and the public without a quiver. And that's pretty much how the characters in the film take the speech, including the newly introduced Richie Norris (Lukas Haas), a sweet, but stupid kid who works at a doughnut shop in Perkinsville, Kansas. Not surprisingly, the only voice of dissent comes from Taffy, who, upon hearing her father announce the existence of intelligent life in the galaxy, comments, "Glad they got it somewhere." Indeed, there does seem to be a shortage of it on the Earth depicted in this movie. That the world of *Mars Attacks!* just happens to be awfully like the one we inhabit is no cause for comfort.

Perhaps the most singularly bizarre angle in *Mars Attacks!* is the presentation of Richie Norris's family—a ragingly patriotic, militia-minded, gun-toting clan, who inhabit a small trailer in rather too great a number. Richie's father, Glenn (Joe Don Baker), is the ultimate good old boy, a goal to which his older son, Billy Glenn (Jack Black), might aspire if his two brain cells ever met. The mother, Sue Ann (O-Lan Jones), seems to exist solely for purposes of sitting around and eating (though complaining about what she eats). The most appealing of this appalling collection of humanity is the visiting Grandma Norris (Sylvia Sidney), an outspoken, frequently out-of-it, apparently senile old lady. She has flashes of wit and sometimes, even in her amazing dottiness, a degree of perception that others in the story line, who are supposedly rational, definitely lack. So positively and warmly does filmmaker Burton respond to her presence that it's impossible not to wonder if there aren't traces here of the grandmother Tim went to live with as a teenager in Grandma Norris. Whatever the case, Grandma Norris is one of the film's most successful—and oddly human—characters.

The Richie character, of course, is the other side of Burton himself. Where Taffy represents his more detached, more amusedly cynical self, Richie is clearly Burton the innocent. (Lukas Haas, as presented in the screen role, actually bears an uncanny resemblance to Burton in his high-school photographs.) As with most of Burton's onscreen alter egos, Richie is largely thought of as less important than anyone else around him. In this case, Richie is aberrant in his sweet, quizzical nature. (As played by Lukas Haas, you just *know* that Richie does wonder why there are resin grapes on the table and a paint-by-numbers horse on the wall, but you also know that he gave up asking long ago, realizing that the reward for such curiosity would likely be a slap.) He is subjected to constant belittling comparison with his much-admired oafish brother. The only person in his family to recognize his worth is his grandmother—even if she has a hard time remembering who he is. Interestingly, there is little suggestion of self-pity in this particular characterization, indicating that perhaps Burton, like Richie, is reconciled to being misunderstood and doesn't care that much about fitting in anymore. Unlike most previous Burton movie characters, there is no trace of envy in Richie.

One of the more peculiar aspects of *Mars Attacks!* is the length of time the 105-minute movie devotes to setup alone. The picture has run nearly a half hour before we even see a Martian. This could have been disastrous were it not for the fact that the creatures are well worth the wait, especially the first one. (It appears worldwide on all televisions by jamming and taking over all signals, in time-honored sci-fi tradition.) The creature apparently has the earthly sense of kitsch (perhaps he knows his audience) to present himself much in the same manner that Ed Wood introduced Criswell in the opening of *Plan 9 from Outer Space*. That this giant-brained grotesquerie doesn't say much other than "Ack ack gack," hardly matters. Science, of course, will translate this for us in one of those typically "educational" moments that exist in most vintage science-fiction movies. The point is that the Martians are a sight to behold—one that justifies the buildup, and fully warrants Marsha Dale's adamant, "I'm not going to have that thing in my house!"

Even having at long last introduced one of his wonderfully awful Martians, Burton holds off having them *do* anything for a considerable period, while the world reacts, the largely incoherent message is translated, peaceful intentions are assured, and a grand welcome is prepared for the visitors. Of course, we know that in 1950s science fiction, Martians are *never* peaceful, that pipe-smoking intellectuals are invariably wrong in their assumption of the greater degree of civilization of any alien life-forms. Besides all this, the movie is called *Mars Attacks!*, which would seem to guarantee carnage of some sort. And yet the buildup to the first such instance of an actual attack is fairly measured once the

Martians have been introduced. As with the delayed introduction of the Martians themselves, this attack sequence is well worth waiting for.

Given the film's take on humankind, it comes as no surprise that the Martian welcome is approached by the main characters less as an historical moment than as a media event. Everything is judged on the basis of "How will this play on television?" and "How will I look on camera?" The humans' sense of proportion is self-centered and whacked-out. This is immediately apparent when a singularly smug and self-satisfied General Casey, on his way to the meeting place, take a personal call from his wife and boasts of his accomplishments in the military by simply being quiet and unobtrusive. Jason Stone preens in the reflection of the camera lens, while Nathalie Lake enthuses to her dog that the gathered crowd have "all come to see you." Once the alien ship lands and Casey greets the Martian ambassador, the event is judged at the White House solely on how well the general handled himself. In the human world of *Mars Attacks!*, image is everything.

To the Martians, however, image is nothing, and no sooner has the ambassador supposedly said, "We come in peace" (who knows how accurately the Rube Goldberg-looking language translator actually works?), than someone in the crowd releases a dove, which the ambassador promptly incinerates before turning his ray gun on Casey. The attack has begun and director Burton at once pulls out all the stops. The carnage is gleefully doled out by red and green ray-gun-toting Martians, leaving piles of cheerfully Day-Glo red and green (depending on which ray got them) skeletons in their wake. The effects and the images are breathtaking, but the real point of the sequence is the sheer manic delight taken in the destruction, and its grisliness being played for laughs. The high point occurs when Nathalie and Jason crawl toward each other in the fracas and join hands. Nathalie soon finds herself holding on to a disembodied hand that has broken away from a bright green skeleton! As if to top this off, the appendage is quickly appropriated by her chihuahua.

The truly remarkable thing about all this is that none of the mass destruction or "sick" humor of these and many subsequent scenes in *Mars Attacks!* seems to have bothered anyone watching the onscreen action. Of course, Burton and screenwriter Gems were very careful in establishing characters that no viewer could possibly object to seeing reduced to joyfully Christmas-colored skeletons.

(It is hard not to actually *relish* the image of the ultramacho Billy Glenn Norris being zapped as he unceremoniously turns coward and surrenders as soon as his gun falls apart on him.)

Indeed, what seems to have troubled critics of *Mars Attacks!* far more was the utter lack of motivation for the alien attack. Burton actually relished this aspect of his film. "We know not of their ways. That's part of what I liked about it. Everybody categorizes everything; everybody thinks they know so much. There are so many experts, but what does anybody *really* know? Not too much," Tim told *Starlog*. That's an interesting, and not inapt, explanation, but it might just as easily be said that it really doesn't matter why the Martians attack. It's enough that they do and their lack of any real reason for going on the offensive is in itself a sly send-up of the studio blockbuster mentality. By not offering so much as a lip-service explanation to the main plot premise, Burton neatly sums up the whole lowest-common-denominator approach that marks so much of today's film-studio thinking—a concept that *Mars Attacks!* actually deals with more fully in its conclusion.

Given the apparently retarded state of most of mankind presented in *Mars Attacks!,* it is hardly surprising that President Dale and his advisors are perfectly willing to think that this rampant destruction must be the result of a misunderstanding on the part of the Martians. (Taffy wryly suggests that doves might mean war to them.) Possibly, such image-oriented types simply cannot conceive that the Martians could willfully do anything so brazenly horrible—at least where everyone can see it. As a result, overtures of peace over this presumed "cultural misunderstanding" are immediately sent to the Martians, who, quite frankly, view the whole situation as a great joke. As more and more details of the Martian way of life are revealed to the viewer, it becomes obvious that what they mostly resemble are irresponsible, mean-spirited, porn-crazed adolescents with too much technology on their hands. This comment on our own society is an unsettlingly close-to-home observation that escaped critical notice.

It comes as no surprise to us, then, that the Martian ambassador's formal apology and stated desire to address Congress is nothing more than a setup for more carnage. In a scene designed to warm the heart of anyone who isn't a politician, the ambassador utters only a few words before drawing his ray gun and, with the help of his attendants, completely disintegrates Congress. While everyone else reacts with the horror expected of them, Taffy merely decides, "Guess it wasn't the dove." But the best line and moment is given to Grandma Norris, who clearly mirrors our own degree of wish fulfillment in response to the event. "They blew up Congress!" she cries in delight, before dissolving into laughter. It is perhaps the most cheerfully subversive moment in a movie full of such moments.

With this development, even the president has to admit that the Martians are somewhat inimical to good fellowship and promises to "take charge" of the situation, while, of course, trying to put the best face possible on the whole fiasco. His assurances of how things are under control quickly degenerates into something remarkably like a campaign speech, promising that schools will remain open and garbage will be picked up. Dale's actual strategy for dealing with the crisis is somewhat more vague, but nonetheless authoritative, which seems to be all that can be expected in a world where leaders have been replaced by images.

This paves the way for the movie's most critically acclaimed sequence. A Martian, disguised as a blonde bombshell (Lisa Marie)—or more correctly, as a kind of adolescent fantasy of a sexy woman—attempts to assassinate the president and the first lady by first getting to the childishly sex-obsessed Jerry Ross, the advisor to the chief executive. Though it is a relatively short segment in the final release print (Lisa Marie's performance takes up slightly less than six minutes of screen time), filmmaker Burton allowed an unprecedented amount of time for its (pre-) production development—three months. After all, it was Lisa Marie's scene.

To ensure that the sequence would be as near "perfect" as possible, Tim called in special movement choreographer Dan Kamin, who had worked with Robert Downey Jr. on *Chaplin* (1992) and Johnny Depp on *Benny & Joon* (1993). Kamin understood the priorities of the scene, as he recently told this author: "It was important to both of them. In certain ways, the film was built around that sequence. It's kind of the centerpiece of the film." And a fine centerpiece is what resulted. "The precision of the performance was the direct result of the fact that time was allowed for her to do this kind of preparation and create the nonverbal physical character," Kamin explained. Basing his concept of the Martians looking "sort of like skulls crossed with snakes," Kamin thought that a reptilian approach was the best way to go, and an idea that took him and Lisa Marie to the zoo for inspiration!

"We actually found a specific kind of lizard that we used as our model. It's called a basilisk. Tim and Lisa were interested in the creature having a rather frightening quality, and reptiles are rather frightening to most people. And one of the things that's frightening is how still they are. Stillness is not natural to people—we're always fidgeting—but reptiles remain real, real still when they're stalking, and then that tongue flicks out and gets the fly, or the snake darts at the prey. This gave us an image for our creature, because our creature had to not only be a sexy woman, but had to have underneath the native qualities of the Martian creatures," revealed Kamin. However, the lizard model wasn't sufficient unto itself, as he elaborated: "I was interested in the idea that a creature with that big of a head and that little of a body would have trouble moving its head in Earth's gravity, and that implies a certain way of moving the head. So we worked on isolating the head movement—like the body had to catch up with it."

In every sense, the Lisa Marie sequence works beautifully in *Mars Attacks!* and justifies the time devoted to it, both from the standpoint of its importance to the film and as a deliberate showcase for Lisa Marie, who is nothing short of brilliant in her execution of the otherworldly part. Again, this section of the movie harkens back to another big-budget extravaganza, with part of the action shot through an aquarium, in the manner of the "Look of Love" segment of *Casino Royale* (1967). However, the whole scene's real import to the plot and the approach of *Mars Attacks!* lies in its amusing depiction of the convoluted creativity employed by the Martians in carrying out their deadly plans. With all the amazingly powerful technology imaginable at the aliens' disposal, surely these invaders could very easily have merely incinerated the White House and everyone in it. Yet, they decide on this unnecessarily circuitous route. Why? Because—as Burton has said—"We know not of their ways." Possibly, but more likely it's simply that this reflects the overall tone of giddy destruction—the Martians take delight in just how inventively elaborate they can be in setting about their sinister work. (There's a charming lack of point to nearly everything the Martians do—even their experiments on earthly organisms. What possible logical reason could there be for keeping Kessler's disembodied head alive on their spacecraft? What scientific validity can be found in grafting Nathalie Lake's head onto her chihuahua and vice versa?) For the Martians, science has as much to do with the joy of how the thing is accomplished as it does with the end result. This rationale is precisely what should be expected of Martians coming from the mind of the moviemaker who presented us with Paul Reubens's magnificently complicated breakfast-making contraption in his debut feature, *Pee-Wee's Big Adventure* (1985).

The failure of the alien woman's plan—the creature is destroyed by Secret Service men when its attention is diverted by a parakeet—prompts the now infuriated Martians to the point of launching their full-scale attack, and the film erupts into full-blown, delighted destruction. As with every invasion from outer space since such motion pictures began, the Martians are predisposed toward blasting famous landmarks out of existence, which is possibly a statement on our own collective desire to see the status quo reduced to a smoldering heap of rubble. Burton's Martians are a little different, in that they have more specific notions of just *how* these things are done. Unlike the flying saucer in *Earth versus the Flying Saucers* (1956), Burton's boys are not content to merely destroy the Washington Monument. Instead, they cruise around it, aiming its fall this way and that until they can be certain of crushing a hapless troop of Cub Scouts in the process! With the movie now in high gear, the chaos mounts to a fever pitch, with Marsha Dale offed by a falling chandelier and the president driven into hiding.

Las Vegas is under attack next, with the Martians committing the ultimate cultural blasphemy by wiping out Tom Jones's band and backup singers, right in the middle of a performance of his trademark number, "It's Not Unusual." Here, the Las Vegas section of *Mars Attacks!* finally sprints to life, with Jones proving himself an agreeable on-camera ham with a nice sense of humor about himself. Meanwhile, the Martians happily obliterate everyone in their path, while announcing (via the language translator they seem to have looted somewhere along the way), "Don't run. We are your friends."

In rapid succession, the space invaders incinerate the French government (with the Eiffel Tower collapsing in the background), prove resistant to a nuclear warhead, pose for snapshots in front of the Taj Mahal as it is obliterated, literally bowl over the giant heads on Easter Island, and deface Mount Rushmore with their own images. While all this is going on, the Martian ambassador is overdosing on pop culture by watching TV while his minions destroy the earth. His entire mien is neatly summed up when the alien flips channels to *The Dukes of Hazzard* and laughs hysterically at this bucolic slapstick fare. It is Burton's unique vision of rampant chaos as he happily sets up late-twentieth-century culture to be knocked down with a comic vengeance.

As *Mars Attacks!* hurtles to its finale, the unstoppable Martians are well on their way to the destruction of the entire world, that is, until pop culture arrives to save the day—in two forms. By far the most creatively amazing of these is the use of the music of country singer–yodeler Slim Whitman. The idea that Whitman's vocal "yammering" would cause the Martians' heads to explode may not be terribly original. The concept itself is borrowed from the abysmal *Attack of the Killer Tomatoes* (1980), in which the intentionally ghastly song, "Puberty Blues," defeats the rampaging vegetation.

In contrast, Burton's use of Slim Whitman's version of "Indian Love Call" is quite another matter. In the first place, the mere idea of the Martians gleefully engaged in the pointless exercise of destroying an old folks' home is perverse enough, not to mention the fascination of a mentality that would think to drag a huge piece of electronic equipment through the home's corridors for the simple purpose of doing in one little old lady! Actually, it is this kind of overly elaborate, personalized destruction that is the space force's undoing. In particular, the attack on Grandma Norris causes her headphones to be unplugged, filling the room with the "dulcet" tones of Whitman yodeling for all he's worth, thus causing the Martians to expire in gooey agony.

What sets this segment apart (beyond style, polish, and wit) from its source inspiration lies in Tim Burton's canny use of a genuine bottom-of-the-barrel iconic figure, Slim Whitman. It would be impossible to find anything more distinctly Burtonian. In the film director's terms, it seems, the geek shall inherit the earth—after, of course, saving it! The more hip are almost destroyed by their good taste. When Tom Jones, in disgust, turns off the radio broadcasting Whitman's music, his life is in peril.

The bizarre solution to saving the Earth, alas, arrives too late to help the president and what remains of his team. General Decker is reduced to the size of a bug—still spouting gung-ho patriotic clichés—and summarily stepped on. Dale makes an impassioned speech to the Martians, moving the ambassador to tears and a hearty handclasp. Unfortunately, the handshake is nothing but another intergalactic practical joke involving a detachable, snakelike arm that skewers the president and raises the Martian flag from his corpse.

The other aspect of pop culture that helps save the day in *Mars Attacks!* is when Byron Williams allows Tom Jones and Barbara Land to escape the invasion unharmed by tackling the Martians in a fistfight. This scene nicely cashes in on Jim Brown's 1970s status as an action hero in blaxploitation film—and permits the character, in the movie's final moments, to be reconciled with another 1970s black icon, Pam Grier. Again, according to Burton, it is the most bizarre, almost surreal aspects of popular culture that come out winners. Whether this resolution is conscious or instinctive on Burton's part is impossible to determine. However, special movement choreographer Dan Kamin relates an interesting story concerning Burton's very real love for the sort of pop-culture films that are reflected in *Mars Attacks!,* as well as his resistance to more sophisticated forms of expression. While working with Lisa Marie on the movie, Kamin screened Ettore Scola's *Le Bal* (1982) for her, thinking that its wholly visual, dialogueless approach to characterization might be helpful in her understanding of the sort of role she was doing. "Tim came in and just couldn't bear to watch it, just hated it. It was just too, I guess, self-consciously artistic for him," Kamin revealed, making it clear that Burton's taste for the more "popular" is certainly genuine.

The eventual defeat of the Martians in *Mars Attacks!,* in fact, seems, in Burton's view, to leave the world open to a new civilization based firmly on the most kitschy artifacts of pop culture. In a very peculiar ceremony on the steps of what little remains of the Capitol building, a mariachi band gamely copes with "The Star-Spangled Banner." The first daughter Taffy (who has inherited the presidency by descent) hands out medals to Grandma Norris. Richie, who makes an incomprehensible speech about rebuilding the world using teepees instead of houses, leaves the movie to end with Tom Jones in the wilderness launching into "It's Not Unusual." As *Mars Attacks!* concludes, not only have the invading forces of evil been destroyed, but so also have the pretentious, the vain, and the pompous on Earth. What is left is the eccentric at the forefront and the pop culture reigns supreme. In short, in what appears to be Tim Burton's most calculatedly impersonal movie, he destroys most of Earth to turn it over to people like himself and those he can relate to, on his own pop-cultural level!

20 | ANATOMY OF A DISASTER

Some things are just weird in life.

TIM BURTON, 1996

WHEN WARNER BROS. EXECUTIVES SAW WHAT THEY were getting with *Mars Attacks!*, they were very happy with the movie Tim Burton had given them. Here—at least on the surface, which was all that really mattered in their eyes—was a Burton extravaganza as they had envisioned it. It was big. It was full of stars. It wasn't dark or troubling or angry. It was just what they had in mind when they thought of a fun movie, a blockbuster entertainment. Unfortunately, where audiences and most critics were concerned, it just was not fun enough.

Despite Burton's own joke that *Mars Attacks!* was a reasonable choice for a Christmas release since it was about invaders from a red planet who fire green ray guns, the entry would clearly have been better served as one of the carefree entries so typical of summer releases. Whatever else *Mars Attacks!* was or wasn't, it simply was *not* Christmas release material. It wasn't in the least sentimental (in fact, a more antonymic word would be hard to find for such a collection of deliberately joyous scenes of destruction, mayhem, and death) and it had no seasonal tie-in whatsoever. To judge by the film's rather arbitrary use of time frames establishing when the action is taking place, it appears that the original idea was that *Mars Attacks!* was intended as a warm-weather offering. However, Burton had not had a film of his own on the big screen for more than two years, and no one seriously contemplated holding up this ultraexpensive project for several months. Well-timed or not, *Mars Attacks!* was Warners' big Christmas release for 1996 and that was that.

Another factor that played against Burton's film at the box office was the release of Roland Emmerich's *Independence Day* earlier that year, in the summer. Though the two films, both of which had PG-13 ratings, were developed without any connection whatsoever (in fact, *Mars Attacks!* was in the works prior to *Independence Day*), they had remarkably similar plots. And *Independence Day,* starring Will Smith and Tommy Lee Jones, had been a huge hit, grossing $306,124,059 in its first week of release. *Independence Day* proved to be a genuine brain-dead blockbuster of the finest kind: noisy, pointless, illogical, filled with explosions, and immensely popular. It was also—apart from the ubiquitous one-liners that macho leading men invariably direct at bad guys, whether from outer space or not—played in dead earnest. Within a few months of each other, then, the public was presented with two very similar, yet almost exactly reversed, films about aliens attacking and trying to destroy the earth. Burton's and the studio's timing could not have been worse, and everyone involved with *Mars Attacks!* knew it and tried to put the best face possible on it.

On cable TV's TNT network show, *Rough Cut,* Tim Burton was asked if he thought of the 145-minute *Independence Day* as a competitor. "No, not really, because the impulse for me to do this movie was going back to more of those animated Ray Harryhausen movies, where you had 3-D animation characters involved, the old B-movies—the big-brain movies, they're called." Asked about the inevitable comparison of the two epics, scriptwriter Jonathan Gems told *Fangoria,* "If you were to compare the two, I would say that the best correlation would be the two films that came out in 1964 about the nuclear bomb. *Independence Day* (also known as *ID4*) is more like a movie called *Fail-Safe* and *Mars Attacks!* is like *Dr. Strangelove*. Both had similar story points, but their tones were completely different. The same is true here. In our film we take a very illogical approach to the reasoning for what's happening in the movie—which in that sense is similar to *ID4,* which was also totally illogical. In our case, though, it was intentional, while in *ID4,* it wasn't."

Gems's point has validity, but it was also wishful thinking to compare *Mars Attacks!* to *Dr. Strangelove,* even though the comparison was well-taken (and seconded by numerous critics). Worse, Gems's response completely sidesteps a key issue: *Dr. Strangelove* was the first of those two 1960s films to reach movie screens and was the clear winner at the box office, possibly for that very reason. In its soul, *Mars Attacks!* may have been *Dr. Strangelove,* but at the box office it performed more like *Fail-Safe.* Just how much negative impact *Independence Day* had on *Mars Attacks!* can only be guessed. Certainly, Burton's entry didn't start out auspiciously, generating a scant $9,384,000 on its opening weekend on nearly 2,000 movie screens—before reviews and word of mouth could have an effect on it. Perhaps viewers were already overdosed on movies about alien invaders from *Independence Day,* or perhaps the market for this particular film was never really there; *Mars Attacks! was* willfully quirky and everyone involved was upfront about that from the start. Therefore, it was pretty much an established fact before it came out that *Mars Attacks!* would be offbeat, to say the least. As the disappointing release failed to gain momentum with filmgoers, the word "disaster" was frequently applied to it—something that had never before been said of any Tim Burton picture.

In reality, the reviews for *Mars Attacks!* were far from universally negative, but few of them were unqualified raves, either. *Boxoffice* gave it a three-star rating and, understanding the essential problem with the movie, noted that "while *ID4* was an overblown, special-effects-driven, factory-generated formula blockbuster playing on patriotism and America's kick-ass mentality, *Mars Attacks!* is a Tim Burton—brand dark satire freakshow, overall more much more interesting and entertaining, but likely with a much more limited appeal as well." In the *San Francisco Chronicle,* Peter Stack came down squarely against the movie. "This messy science fiction comedy blows most of its inspired moments because of its mean-spirited, deafening siege mentality, which turns rich promise into a tiresome parade of half-baked skits. Hilarity never seemed so tedious." The *Washington Post's* Desson Howe merely found it "moderately amusing." Jack Garner of the Gannett News Service was less kind, flatly declaring, "Tim Burton doesn't have a clue how to make a comedy," going on to call the screenplay "superficial and utterly predictable," and remarks that "Burton has mistakenly directed all the actors to deliver hammy, way-over-the-top performances."

Also weighing in against *Mars Attacks!* was Abbie Bernstein in *Drama-Logue,* saying the movie "essentially replays the same gag over and over: Fatuous, self-involved humans, unable to recognize danger when they see it, keep making friendly overtures and getting themselves incinerated or blown-apart." *People* magazine's Ralph Novak opined, "On every level, whether it's acting, humor, action, or special effects, it is consistently disappointing." Janet Maslin singled out Lisa Marie's sequence for praise in the *New York Times,* only to note that "it's one of the rare occasions where his star-filled, prankish new film doesn't misfire," and complained that overall the film is "just a parade of scattershot gags, more often weird than funny and most often just flat."

After praising *Nightmare Before Christmas* and *Ed Wood,* Roger Ebert (*Chicago Sun-Times*) was far less enthused with *Mars Attacks!,* which he saw as Burton's own attempt at making an Ed Wood film (a not uncommon view). He concluded, "Ed Wood himself could have told us what was wrong with this movie: The makers felt superior to the material." Chiming in on the Ed Wood bandwagon was Terrence Rafferty in *The New Yorker.* "After the slick, impersonal stupidity of this summer's alien-invasion extravaganza *Independence Day,* the self-conscious stupidity of Tim Burton's *Mars Attacks!* should be terrifically refreshing," he wrote, going on to explain Burton's approach ("Cheesiness is next to godliness"). He declared that *Mars Attacks!* makes clear why "someone as gifted as Burton" would "rhapsodize over a filmmaker who lacked even the most rudimentary skills" in *Ed Wood.* "At the time, the notion seemed entirely disingenuous," Rafferty continues, "but it now appears that Burton's admiration was sincere—that, perversely, he wished he *were* Ed Wood. With *Mars Attacks!* he comes perilously close to getting his wish."

While Rafferty's critique in *The New Yorker* seems lamentably wide of the mark in terms of understanding *Ed Wood* and the rationale behind it, he gets very near the truth when he writes, "*Mars Attacks!* is *meant* to be a kind of anti-entertainment: a subversion of major-studio production values, of star power, of the sleek illusionism that pictures like *Independence Day* represent. In a sense, this movie, along with *Ed Wood,* is Tim Burton's declaration of independence from the expectations created by the success of the Batman pictures." Rafferty is on target concerning the film's subversive side. However, Tim is too canny a Hollywood businessman and too responsible a person to deliberately make a $73 million "anti-entertainment."

A few critics, however, actually did understand the concept of *Mars Attacks!* In the Los Angeles *New Times,* Peter Rainer was very enthusiastic: "Forget *Independence Day.* If you really want to see Earth get it, you can't do any better than Tim Burton's *Mars Attacks!* It's a destruction orgy orchestrated without any phony-baloney sanctimony about the fellowship of man—or spaceman." *Time* magazine's Richard Schickel was entranced by Burton brazenly killing off his big-name cast, which he found "curiously refreshing." He lauded "everyone's chutzpah: the breadth of Burton's [and writer Jonathan Gems's] movie references, which range from [Akira] Kurosawa to [Stanley] Kubrick; and above all their refusal to offer us a single likable character." Beth Pinsker, in the *Dallas Morning News,* was equally enthusiastic if a little less cheerfully nihilistic, saying that Burton's filmmaking offers "proof that there is intelligent life on this planet," and enthusiastically endorses all the kitsch he poured into the film, while bemoaning the fact that the similarity to *Independence Day* is going to hurt the film at the box office. Frequent Burton champion Kim Newman wrote in the British *Sight and Sound* that the film's commitment to chaos is "the sort of thing that alienates far more people than it converts, but it has so much sheer verve packed into its admittedly incoherent frame that it's hard not to take something cherishable away from it."

The critical voices raised in favor of *Mars Attacks!* were scarcely enough to prevent it from clocking in as Tim Burton's first big Hollywood failure. *Ed Wood* may not have made money, but it certainly didn't cost so much, and was, at least, a critical success. In contrast, *Mars Attacks!* cost a great deal and was garnering very mixed reviews by critics who, by and large, just couldn't figure the film out at all.

One of the people who was there during the making of *Mars Attacks!* was special movement choreographer Dan Kamin. He feels the entry was "a disaster," and has his own insider's take on what went wrong and where and why. Commenting on Burton's strong visual sense as a director and noting instances of beautiful images in *Mars Attacks!,* he told this author, "I have nothing but high praise for Tim and the atmosphere and his professionalism . . . but visual doesn't ultimately matter unless it supports content, as it has in all of his previous films so well." Further, Kamin recalls, "Surprisingly, Martin Short was very funny on the set—just cracking everybody up—he was doing all this stuff, putting his finger on the corner of his mouth like he had herpes, just making the character comically very sleazy, and it was very funny to watch, but when I saw the film it didn't work even slightly. It was too over-the-top for the film. He was coming off as if he was on a *Saturday Night Live* [TV] sketch."

Kamin also suggests that the broad humor of *Mars Attacks!* may have played worse than it actually was, due to the context of Burton's career, coming as it does right after *Ed Wood,* which was "so clever and so sly." In the end, Kamin believes that the script just wasn't there and that the Topps trading cards (which inspired the film), while interesting in themselves, were not enough to support a large-scale feature movie. However, at the time *Mars Attacks!* got under way, everyone, Kamin included, believed that Tim was going to do something so magically visual that it would overcome these inherent problems. "People's faith in him was such that Glenn Close and [Jack] Nicholson and these other folks were just perfectly contented to put themselves in his hands. Glenn Close was also very funny in her performances on the set, but it didn't come off quite right on film. Again, the Nancy Reagan parody she was doing just didn't come off—and I have to fault Tim with that. It just wasn't filmed in such a way that even what humor was there in the script was fully realized. Comedy is a very elusive animal to trap and I don't know what he had in mind. And I was sorry because it was such a lovely experience. There was such a spirit of kindliness on that set. There was a gentleness that permeated that set. It's unfortunate that the end result wasn't pleasing to everyone."

Dan Kamin's sentiments about the atmosphere on the set were by no means isolated. Everyone who appeared in *Mars Attacks!* seems to have had nothing but a good time on the film. Sylvia Sidney, in fact, a veteran of nearly seventy years of filmmaking, enthused that Burton "*really* made me feel like a movie star!" Unfortunately, the fun of the enterprise, of the making of the movie, didn't quite convey itself to the majority of the ticket-buying audience.

In the end, *Mars Attacks!* may be a film that cannot be fully appreciated until its place in Burton's work is established by the productions that follow it. It is clearly a much more personal work than is casually assumed, and there is more of Burton in it than there isn't. The aesthetic question that arises at this point is whether the picture is a less self-pitying, less isolated Burton entry, an idea that was established by *Nightmare Before Christmas* and made clear by *Ed Wood;* or is it, instead, merely an aberration—a dazzling, frequently brilliant tangent, destined to remain on the fringes of a moviemaking career that has already proven to be one of the richest in modern times.

21 | A JOB FOR SUPERMAN?

The English have Shakespeare, the Greeks have their myths, and America has Batman, Superman, and Mickey Mouse.

NICOLAS CAGE, 1997

FOR ITS OVERSEAS RELEASE, *MARS ATTACKS!* WAS decked out with a fresh advertising campaign. It was sold outside the United States as a comic romp and hip experience, rather than a big-star, big-budget, big-effects sci-fi film, as had been done domestically. With this approach *Mars Attacks!* opened much more lucratively abroad, pulling in $19.3 million in its first week, somewhat increasing Burton's luster with the film's distributor, Warners Bros. It was not, in the long run, however, sufficient to keep the film out of the red, nor was it enough to reestablish Burton as the hottest director around. Something more would have to do that, or at least afford the opportunity for that to happen. Burton certainly wasn't in serious professional trouble yet—he'd had too strong a record as a hitmaker for that—but the days when he could seemingly do no wrong were over. His next career move had to be a good one.

As always, Burton's name became attached to numerous projects during this time: *Sweeney Todd, The Demon Barber of Fleet Street* (variously reported as both being *and* not being a film version of Stephen Sondheim's musical!); *Dinosaurs Attack!* (a singularly unlikely project in the wake of *Mars Attacks!*); *House of Usher* (though a movie from another Jonathan Gems screenplay also seemed unlikely at that point); a film version—or versions—of the Goosebumps horror novels for children; *Catwoman* (yet again); a remake of Roger Corman's *X: The Man with X-Ray Eyes* (1963); and, the most likely sounding of all, *Superman Lives,* or *Superman Reborn,* as it was sometimes called.

The Superman property had been in development before Tim Burton's name was attached to it. Producer Jon Peters was at the helm of the concept, which was to have a blockbuster Superman picture in the theatres by the summer of 1998. It was to tie in with the sixtieth anniversary of the famed comic-book character. Created in 1938 by writer Jerry Siegel and artist Joe Shuster, Superman—much like Batman the following year—immediately entered the American consciousness in the pre–World War Two era and was quickly absorbed into popular culture. Soon Superman would be a Max Fleischer cartoon character, spawn a radio series, become a movie serial, and so on, before becoming indelibly etched into our collective minds by George Reeves in the early-1950s TV series. That Reeves *was* Superman, there was no doubt. However, the popular series of big-budget *Superman* features with Christopher Reeve in the late 1970s and 1980s proved that the public would accept another actor in the larger-than-life role. Considering that the success of those *Superman* movies had been the inspiration for what would become Burton's *Batman* in 1989, it was perhaps inevitable that Peters himself would latch on to the Man of Steel, hoping that lightning would strike twice. Certainly that was what Warner Bros.' co-chairman Terry Semel was counting on when the studio purchased the screen rights to *Superman* from producer Alexander Salkind in 1993.

Much like *Batman, Superman Lives* was inspired by the success of the newer breed of comic book—the darker, more adult-oriented works that had helped to regenerate interest in the long-lasting character and boost sales of the magazine. In the case of *Superman,* the inspiration was the hugely popular comic book series, *The Life and Death of Superman.* The screenwriter brought in by Peters was Jonathan Lemkin, a Warner Bros. staff scripter who'd done the first draft of *Lethal Weapon 4* (1998). Lemkin based his Superman scenario on the new-breed comic-book approach. Peters at once put the pressure on, for the simple reason that toy manufacturers were clamoring for a look at the script before committing to the project.

Not surprisingly, a large part of the appeal of a potential new batch of *Superman* motion pictures lay less in the actual movies themselves than in the even-more-lucrative merchandising deals to be struck globally with toy manufacturers and fast-food franchises. These financial enterprises may have little to do with moviemaking, but they are essentials today to movie studios, and a very real business concern. (Not a little of the furor over whether *Batman Returns* was suitable for children stemmed directly from the film's merchandising tie-in with McDonald's.) *Superman* looked to be just as marketable as *Batman* in that regard.

As it turned out, Lemkin's script was apparently a little too radical for the studio's tastes. His Superman actually dies *at the beginning* of the film, but not before somehow passing his "spirit" on to Lois Lane, who gives birth to Superman's son, who quickly inherits his father's mantle. Peters was unhappy with this approach (which, according to Lemkin, had underlying themes that were too close to the upcoming *Batman Forever* [1995], though what these themes were, he didn't reveal). Peters brought in Gregory Poirier for a second attempt. This version apparently better pleased the studio, but not so much that they didn't bring in yet another writer. The newcomer to the project was the up-and-coming Kevin Smith, whose low-budget feature, *Clerks* (1994), had proved a major success, and who is now better-known for the brilliantly funny, moving, and quirky film, *Chasing Amy* (1997).

Kevin Smith is known for his passion for comic books (all the main characters in *Chasing Amy*, in fact, are connected with the comic-book world) and it seemed reasonable that he could improve on Poirier's scripting effort. Reportedly, Smith's job originally was merely to offer his input. This he did quite simply by rejecting the whole thing, which he thought completely misrepresented the original comic books and the character. Remembering the backlash—and threatened backlash—from comic-book fans over the casting of Michael Keaton as Batman in Burton's 1989 film, the studio then decided to offer the scripting job to Smith, since presumably he could get it right from that perspective.

The resulting script, *Superman Lives*, retained some of the basic story line, but otherwise went its own way—or ways, since the story of *Superman Lives* is all over the map. Smith not only brings on two villains (Lex Luthor and Brainiac), but various sidekicks (Brainiac has a long-suffering robot called L-Ron), monsters, wild incidents, and even Batman, who appears briefly to deliver a eulogy for the "dead" Superman. The plot puts Brainiac and Lex Luthor in cahoots with each other against Superman. According to the new script, Superman derives his energy from the sun. This leads Brainiac to cause the sun to be blocked out by technical jiggery-pokery. (Ostensibly this is done to hide the Earth from a fleet of spaceships piloted by hostile alien invaders. Shades of *Mars Attacks!*) Now without his power source, Superman is killed in a battle with Brainiac's monster, Doomsday, and is entombed with all the ceremony expected for a fallen hero. This proves to be merely part of Brainiac's scheme. What he is really after is a creation called the "Eradicator," a sort of supercomputer-robot of almost limitless power, which Superman's father, Jor-El, had linked to his son's life force. Luthor knows the Eradicator will come to the fallen hero's aid and revive him.

Convoluted, expensive to make, and with some genuinely atrocious dialogue (is the world really ready for a Superman who calls Lois Lane "babe"?), not to mention an occasional bad case of terminal plot compressions, Kevin Smith's version was mystifyingly considered the best yet—mostly because it appears that this was the screenplay that supposedly attracted Burton to the *Superman* project.

Superman, at least on the surface, seemed like a natural subject for Burton. He had, after all, made *Batman* and *Batman Returns,* and any reservations Warners Bros. may have had about the trouble with the latter were fairly minor, since Burton was credited—rightly or wrongly—with what had made the first film such an unqualified success. Hollywood logic, therefore, dictated that reteaming the director with Jon Peters was the proper thing to do, especially since the project was revisionist in tone (a Burton specialty) with the casting of Nicolas Cage as Superman. Burton's *Batman* had ushered in the1990s superhero— mightn't he be just the director to close out the decade with a bang in the same department? In theory, it sounded very promising.

The prevalent notion that Burton undertook the epic project because of Kevin Smith's screenplay is open to question and is hardly supported by subsequent events. It appears far more probable that Tim saw the offer as a vehicle that would regain him much of the industry power he had earned with *Batman.*

By the time Burton's name was attached to the *Superman* project, *Mars Attacks!* was a "disaster." Thus, despite Tim's statement to *Starlog* magazine that he only goes into projects "hoping that anybody gets the same enjoyment out of it that I get," his interest in *Superman* seemed just good business sense on his part. Moreover, the fact that the first thing he did upon signing to do the picture was to reject the Smith script and bring in screenwriter Wesley Strick (who wrote *The Saint*, 1997) scarcely makes it look like Smith's participation in *Superman* was the inducement to bring Burton aboard!

None too surprisingly, Kevin Smith was furious over this turn of events, even though he was himself the third writer to tackle the *Superman* project and had certainly not been reticent in his own criticism of the Poirier screenplay. "I was under the impression that Burton would at least have the courtesy to sit down and talk with me," Smith complained to *Entertainment Weekly* (May 29, 1998), apparently ignorant of Burton's long-standing tendency to avoid confrontation. A year earlier in the same publication (May 16, 1997), Smith had remarked, "Burton wants to Hollywood it out," suggesting that Burton wanted something lighter and campier in the scenario. "Maybe mine just didn't have enough quirk. Maybe not enough people wore black," he mused. An independent filmmaker, unused to the kind of studio interference and infighting surrounding a mammoth Hollywood production, Smith was simply unprepared for this kind of professional treatment. "I was told, 'This is a corporate movie.' Nobody is treating this like a $100 million art film," he concluded.

Burton negotiated an amazingly good deal for himself on *Superman Lives*— a guaranteed $5 million just for signing, whether the picture is ultimately made or not. And, in light of subsequent events, this may have been a financially slick move, since the project has had nothing but bad luck. Part of the impetus behind the new *Superman* entry was the popularity of the ABC-TV series, *Lois and Clark—The New Adventures of Superman,* which debuted in September 1993 with Teri Hatcher (as Lois Lane) and Dean Cain (as Superman/Clark Kent). When the series suddenly took a dive in the ratings and was quickly yanked from the network schedule, it shook Warner Bros.' faith in the public's appetite for the Superman character. As estimated costs on the big-screen project mushroomed from $100 million to somewhere between $140 million and a mind-boggling $190 million, the studio's interest dwindled even further. Then, on

April 15, 1998, Warner Bros. unceremoniously put the planned film on hiatus, and on May 1, shut down the production offices. While the film project was not canceled as such, the prospects were not good, despite the fact that Tim Burton was then still working on the screenplay with yet another screenwriter, Dan Gilroy, and Warners' president of production Lorenzo DiBonaventura was still being quoted as saying that he'd be "shocked" if the movie didn't ultimately get made. Whether or not it will ever be done—and whether or not it will be made by Burton—remains to be seen.

Upon examination, it is debatable whether or nor Superman really is a good choice for a Tim Burton feature film. The original equation—Burton plus Jon Peters plus a comic-book superhero equals big box office—is fine *to a degree*. Not all comic-book heroes are created equal, and years earlier Burton had gone on record as not even being much of a comic-book fan. Rather, he had been able to connect with the specific Batman character—a darker, more potentially dangerous, and, as he saw it, even slightly warped hero—one who dressed up and played a role. (This aspect of Burton and Burton's films makes Kevin Smith's statements that his script was too dark for Burton sound peculiarly hollow.)

In other words, Batman already *was* a Tim Burton character. Superman is rather different—more traditional. When Tim was being interviewed by James Ryan in the *New York Times* to help promote his book, *The Melancholy Death of Oyster Boy and Other Stories* (1997), the writer noted that the Superman story "might not seem as well suited to Mr. Burton's esthetic as that of the brooding figure of Batman." Burton explained—perhaps *rationalized* would be a better term—"You strip away everything, all the surface things, and what you have is a man from another planet who's unlike anyone else on earth." In a strict sense, this is unarguable, but he's unlike anyone else on earth in a way that can hardly be called Burtonesque. Yet, this probably is exactly the approach Burton planned (or *plans*, should the movie still be made) to bring to *Superman*. Would it work? That's a hypothetical question that cannot be answered. However, it would seem that it's about an even chance that it would succeed beautifully, or evolve as if Burton had simply grafted his own concerns on top of an already existing character.

While *Superman Lives* was still "in the works," Burton's book, *Oyster Boy and Other Stories,* finally made its bow. This slim volume, weighing in at a scant 113 pages, was, as previously noted, generally received by the critics with the vague air of condescension usually associated with artists who dare to step out of their respective areas of expertise. *Harper's Bazaar* (October 1, 1997) reviewed the publication in the context of two other books by filmmakers, Gus Van Sant and Oliver Stone. The review styled Burton's book as being the "least ambitious of the three," but the "most successful." This was not exactly high praise, though; the review's summation said, "It's hard to misfire when all you're striving for is Edward Goreyesque oddball cartoons and doggerel." *Oyster Boy* is a book that no doubt would never have existed had Tim not been a successful and famous filmmaker. However, that hardly invalidates it from the onset; it should merely invite a degree of healthy skepticism. While it is possible to question the book's slightness, it is impossible not to admit that it is also very clearly related to Burton's other work. It neither enlightens nor informs those works, but is very much an extension of them: charming, quirky, a little self-indulgent, and ultimately strangely moving. It may not be successful as literature, but it is certainly successful Burtonia.

Also in the midst of the *Superman Lives* fracas, development proceeded on the remake of *X: The Man with X-Ray Eyes,* which looks like it may well yet become a Tim Burton film property after all. In many ways it is a good fit for Burton's sensibilities—the story of a man who falls prey to his own obsessions. However, the only problem with it lies in the fact that it draws from schlock filmmaking. It is apt to raise the specter of Burton supposedly wanting to be Ed Wood all over again and, subsequently, bring the *Mars Attacks!* disaster back to the forefront. However, the film will be buffeted from *Mars Attacks!* by what is actually turning out to be Burton's next feature, *Sleepy Hollow.*

Burton was approached with Andrew Kevin Walker's adaptation of Washington Irving's classic ghost horror story, "The Legend of Sleepy Hollow," by producer Scott Rudin at Paramount Pictures. Walker, one of Hollywood's hotter screenwriters thanks to *Se7en* (1995), appears to have created a fairly loose adaptation of the classic story that emphasizes the horror element beyond earlier film or TV versions of the work. Upon reading the script, Burton agreed to do the film. Making the project just that much more enticing, Johnny

Depp has signed for the lead, Christina Ricci (an actress who seems born to grace a Tim Burton film) contracted for the romantic role, and Casper Van Dien was Depp's on-camera rival.

In this new adaptation, Ichabod Crane, according to the Reuters Entertainment News Wire, is presented as "a professor whose wild theories get him discredited and exiled to an upstate New York hamlet where he happens on a myth come to life of a headless horseman who has taken the heads of four people trying to find the one that fits him perfectly." The concept would seem perfect for Burton. It is certainly in keeping with his earlier entries. (What, after all, is Ichabod Crane but *the* original geek?) Also, its more flat-out horror elements could well provide the kind of artistic stretching that Burton had hoped for in *Mars Attacks!* and did not quite find. It may, in fact, be the perfect cinema opportunity for Tim to make the transition from macabre humor to more-seriously-intended macabre storytelling. He certainly has the aptitude for it. Burton may have the talent, in fact, to make what could be one of the great Hollywood horror films.

To help launch the film's production—and to honor the genre he will be working in—Burton agreed to play host to the American Movie Classics cable channel's special Halloween "horrorthon," called *Monsterfest with Tim Burton.* It was a week (October 26–November 1, 1998) of airing classic (and some not-so-classic) horror movies. The approach was more elaborate than might be expected. Rather than have Burton merely sit in the cable studio and film brief introductions and exits to the movies, AMC traveled around the Northeast and shot the intros at various "haunted houses" and other bizarre sites.

The normally withdrawn Burton actually seems to relish the "new" business of playing at being a horror-movie host, although he had done something similar on a much smaller scale in 1994 to promote *Ed Wood.* Talking to film historian and writer David J. Skal about this fall 1998 TV chore, Tim enthused over the TV horror-movie hosts of his childhood: "Every town had its own regional host. In L.A., it was this guy called Seymour. He was like a corpse, and came from behind a slimy wall. He did the same kind of bad jokes that I'm doing today. Somehow bad jokes seem to go with the territory." Burton should know. After all, he featured perhaps the best known of all horror-film TV hosts, Vampira, in *Ed Wood,* and the jokes he lovingly reproduced for her there were certainly bad. The kind of jokes he makes here, though, are more personal and savvy. The one promo quoted by Skal includes Burton announcing, "I've made a living scaring people, especially studio executives and people giving me money for my movies."

Burton also confided to Skal, "One of the reasons I wanted to do this was because I was such a fan of these movies. They helped me get from childhood to adulthood." Indeed, the movies being aired on AMC include two of Burton's special favorites, Mario Bava's *Black Sunday* (1961) and William Castle's *House on Haunted Hill* (1958), neither choice being much of a surprise to Burton admirers.

With *Monsterfest* behind him, Burton has tackled *Sleepy Hollow* (and once again indicated a desire to finally complete *Conversations with Vincent*) and, with it, undertakes to make the journey into his full adulthood as a filmmaker. However, it seems more than likely that Burton will always retain something of that alienated wonder that has made his films so unique and frequently so powerful and moving. Burton himself offered the best and most poignant image of himself—possibly another bit of his own myth, but shot through with an undeniable reality—in *The Melancholy Death of Oyster Boy and Other Stories*. The final "story" in the book is a single sentence that, in fact, could well be read as a comment on Burton's entire life and his feeling of where he belongs in the world: "For Halloween, Oyster Boy decided to go as a human." It is at once absurd and yet utterly Burtonesque (the misfit donning the mask of normalcy)—and finally almost heartbreaking and telling. Perhaps we might as well read it as, "For life, Tim Burton decided to go as a myth of his own creation."

FILMOGRAPHY

Short Films

VINCENT
(1982, WALT DISNEY PRODUCTIONS)

CREDITS: Directed by Tim Burton; screenplay: Tim Burton; producer: Rick Heinrichs; music: Ken Hilton; cinematography: Victor Abdalov; production designer: Tim Burton; animator–technical director: Stephen Chiodo; sculptor and additional designer: Rick Heinrichs. Running time: 6 minutes.

CAST: Vincent Price (narrator).

FRANKENWEENIE
(1984, WALT DISNEY PRODUCTIONS)

CREDITS: Directed by Tim Burton; screenplay: Leonard Ripps; producer: Julie Hickson; associate producer: Rick Heinrichs; music: Michael Convertino, David Newman; cinematography: Thomas E. Ackerman; costume designer: Jack Sandeen; film editor: Ernest Milano; art director: John B. Mansbridge; makeup: Marvin McIntyre, Robert J. Schiffer. MPAA Rating: PG; running time: 27 minutes.

CAST: Shelley Duvall (Susan Frankenstein); Daniel Stern (Ben Frankenstein); Barret Oliver (Victor Frankenstein); Joseph Maher (Mr. Chambers); Roz Braverman (Mrs. Epstein); Paul Bartel (Mr. Walsh); Domino (Ann Chambers); Jason Hervey (Frank Dale); Paul C. Scott (Mike Anderson); Helen Boll (Mrs. Curtis); Sparky (Himself).

Feature Films

PEE-WEE'S BIG ADVENTURE

(1985, WARNER BROS./ASPEN FILM SOCIETY)

CREDITS: Directed by Tim Burton; screenplay: Phil Hartman, Paul Reubens, Michael Varhol; producers: Richard Gilbert Abramson, Robert Shapiro; executive producer: William E. McEuen; original music: Danny Elfman; cinematography: Victor J. Kemper; costume designer: Aggie Guerard Rodgers; production designer: David L. Snyder; film editor: Billy Weber; first assistant director: Robert P. Cohen; second assistant directors: Robert Engelman, Harvey Waldman; set decorator: Thomas Roysden; second second assistant director: Willie F. Simmons Jr.; music editor: Bob Badami; supervising sound editors: Cecelia Hall, David B. Cohn; sound editors: Denise Horta, Joey Ippolito, David Pettijohn; musical arrangements: Steve Bartek; rerecording mixers: Terry Porter, David J. Hudson, Neil Brody; special-effects supervisor: Chuck Gaspar; special-effects coordinator: Joe Day; set designer: James F. Tocci; illustrator: Paul H. Chadwick; gaffer: Earl Gilbert; best boy: Rhio Haessig; rigging gaffer: Patrick H. Marshall; stunt coordinator: Paul Baxley; men's costumers: Don Vargas, Richard Little; women's costumer: Sandy Berke Jordan; makeup artist: Frank Griffin; animated-effects supervisor: Rich Heinrichs; cel animation: Jorgen Klubein; animated-effects consultants: John Scheele, Stephen Chiodo; special visual effects: Dream Quest Images; color timer: Dick Richie; main titles designed by Anthony Goldschmidt; stunts: Corey Eubanks, Trace Eubanks, Steve Mack, Bob Hierron, Troy Melton, Alonzo Brown, Angelo Lamonea, Solomon I. Marx, Russell Solberg, Amanda Baxley, P. J. Amateau, Stagg Summers, Patrick Romano, Joe Margucci, Fred Scheiwiller, Don Happy, Jeff Imada, Mary Albee, Marian Green, Shelly Hoffman, Theresa Eubanks, Suzanne Harvey. Recorded in Dolby Stereo; lenses and Panaflex cameras by Panavision; color by Technicolor; projection ratio: 1.85:1. MPAA Rating: PG; running time: 90 minutes.

CAST: Paul Reubens (Pee-Wee Herman); Elizabeth Daily (Dottie); Mark Holton (Francis); Diane Salinger (Simone); Judd Omen (Mickey); Irving Hellman (Neighbor); Monte Landis (Mario); Damon Martin (Chip); David Glasser (BMX Kid #1); Gregory Brown (BMX Kid #2); Mark Everett (BMX Kid #3); Daryl Roach (Chuck); Bill Cable (Policeman #1); Peter Looney (Policeman #2); Starletta DuPois (Sergeant Hunter); Professor Toru Tanaka (Butler); Ed Herlihy (Mr. Buxton); Ralph Seymour (Francis's Accomplice); Lou Cutell (Amazing Larry); Raymond Martino (Gang Member); Erica Yohn (Madam Ruby); Bill W. Richmond (Highway Patrolman); Alice Nunn (Large Marge); Ed Griffith (Trucker); Simmy Bow (Man in Diner); Jon Harris (Andy); Carmen Filpi (Hobo Jack); Jan Hooks (Tina); John Moody (Bus Clerk); John O'Neill (Cowboy #1); Alex Sharp (Cowboy #2); Chester Grimes (Biker #1); Luis Contreras (Biker #2); Lonnie Parkinson (Biker #3); Howard Hirdler (Biker #4); Cassandra Peterson (Biker Mama); Jason Hervey (Kevin Morton); Bob McClurg (Studio Guard); John Paragon (Movie Lot Actor); Susan Barnes (Movie Lot Actress); Zachary Hoffman (Director);

Lynne Marie Stewart (Mother Superior); George Sasaki (Japanese Director); Richard Brose (Tarzan); Drew Seward (Kid #1); Brett Fellman (Kid #2); Bob Drew (Fireman); John Gilgreen (Policeman at Pet Shop); Noreen Hennessey (Reporter); Phil Hartman (Reporter); Michael Varhol (Photographer); David Rothenberg, Patrick Cranshaw, Sunshine Parker (Hoboes); Gilles Savard (Pierre); James Brolin (Himself, as "P. W."); Morgan Fairchild (Herself, as "Dottie"); Tony Bill (Terry Hawthorne) Dee Snider (Himself); Milton Berle (Himself).

BEETLEJUICE

(1988, WARNER BROS./GEFFEN FILMS)

CREDITS: Directed by Tim Burton; screenplay: Michael McDowell and Warren Skaaren; story: Larry Wilson, Michael McDowell; producers: Richard Hashimoto, Michael Bender, Larry Wilson; original music: Danny Elfman; cinematography: Thomas E. Ackerman; costume designer: Aggie Guerard Rodgers; production designer: Bo Welch; film editor: Jane Kurson; first assistant director: Bill Scott; second assistant directors: K. C. Colwell, Jerry Fleck; assistant producer: June Petersen; art director: Tom Duffield; set decorator: Catherine Mann; production sound mixer: David Ronne; costume supervisors: Linda Henrikson, Chuck Velasco; wardrobe: Betty Jean Slater; makeup: Ve Neill, Steve LaPorte; stunt coordinator: Fred Lerner; choreographer: Chrissy Bocchino; special-effects supervisor: Chuck Gaspar; special effects: Joe Day, Elmer Hut, William Lee, Tom Mertz, Jeff Wischnak; special-effects supervisor: Alan Munro; visual-effects consultant: Rick Heinrichs; creatures and makeup effects: Robert Short; visual effects by VCE, Inc./Peter Kuran; optical effects: Beverly Bernacki, Spencer Gill, Sarah Pasanen, Jo Martin, William Conner; miniature production: James Belohovek, Thomas Conti; animation production: Jammie Friday, Mark Myer; supervising sound editor: Richard Anderson; sound editors: David Stone, Warren Hamilton, Mark Pappas; supervising ADR editor: Mary Andrews; music editors: Nancy Fogarty, Bob Badami; re-recording mixers: Gregg Landaker, Steve Maslow, Kevin O'Connell; music recording mixer: Bob Fernandez; orchestration: Steve Bartek; title design: Pablo Ferro; puppeteers: Fred Spencer, Kevin Carlson, Van Snowden, James McGeachy, Mark Brian Wilson, Sandy Grinn; stunts: Fred Waugh, Mike Cassidy, Carl Ciarfalio, Di Ann Lerner, Shinko Isobe, Pat Puccinelli, Mary Peters, James Lerner, Maria Kelly, Noon Orsatti, Fred Lerner, Cris Thomas Palomino, Anthony Schmidt, Beth Nufer; lenses and Panaflex cameras by Panavision; color by Technicolor; projection ratio: 1.85:1. Recorded in Dolby Stereo; MPAA rating: PG; running time: 92 minutes.

CAST: Alec Baldwin (Adam Maitland); Geena Davis (Barbara); Annie McEnroe (Jane Butterfield); Maurice Page (Ernie); Hugo Stanger (Old Bill); Michael Keaton (Betelgeuse); Rachel Mittelman (Little Jane); Catherine O'Hara (Delia Deetz); J. Jay Saunders (Moving Man #1); Mark Ettlinger (Moving Man #2); Jeffrey Jones (Charles Deetz); Winona Ryder (Lydia Deetz); Glenn Shadix (Otho); Patrice Martinez (Receptionist); Cynthia Daly (Three-fingered Typist); Douglas Turner (Char Man);

Carmen Filpi (Messenger); Simmy Bow (Janitor); Sylvia Sidney (Juno); Robert Goulet (Maxie Dean); Dick Cavett (Bernard); Susan Kellerman (Grace); Adelle Lutz (Beryl); Gary Jochimsen (Dumb Football Player #1); Bob Pettersen (Dumb Football Player #2); Duane Davis (Very Dumb Football Player); Maree Cheatham (Sarah Dean); Tony Cox (Preacher); Jack Angel (Preacher [voice]).

BATMAN

(1989, WARNER BROS.)

CREDITS: Directed by Tim Burton; screenplay: Sam Hamm and Warren Skaaren, based upon the DC Comics character created by Bob Kane; story: Sam Hamm; producers: Jon Peters, Peter Guber; co-producer: Chris Kenny; executive producers: Benjamin Milniker, Michael E. Uslan; music: Danny Elfman; songs: Prince; cinematography: Roger Pratt; costume designers: Linda Henrikson, Bob Ringwood; production designer: Anton Furst; film editor: Ray Lovejoy; second unit director/cameraman: Peter MacDonald; special visual effects: Derek Meddings; first assistant director: Derek Cracknell; associate producer: Barbara Kalish; supervising art director: Les Tomkins; set decorator: Peter Young; special-effects supervisor: John Evans; supervising sound editor: Don Sharpe; rerecording mixer: Bill Rowe; sound mixer: Tony Dawe; second assistant directors: Melvin Lind, Julian Wall; project consultant: Bob Kane; art directors: Terry Ackland-Snow, Nigel Phelps; wardrobe supervisor: Annie Crawford; chief makeup artist: Paul Engelen; Joker makeup design: Nick Dudman; prosthetic-makeup artist: Suzanne Reynolds; stunt coordinator: Eddie Stacey; sound editor: Eddy Joseph; visual-effects editor: Russ Woolnough; Foley editor: Rocky Phelan; dialogue editor: Paul Smith; additional sound editor: Derek Trigg; music supervisor: Michael Dilbeck; music editors: Bob Badami, Robin Clarke; orchestrations: Steve Bartek; conductor: Shirley Walker; visual-effects coordinator: Peter Watson; second-unit assistant director: Steven Harding; second-unit second assistant director: Nikolas Korda; second-unit third assistant director: Steve Millson; visual effects by the Meddings Magic Camera Co, a member of the Lee Group of Companies; MMCC visual-effects unit/production manager: Susan Ford; visual-effects art director: Peter Chiang; produced in association with Polygram Pictures; title sequence: Plume Partners; lenses and Panaflex cameras by Panavision; color by Technicolor; projection ratio: 1.85:1. Recorded in Dolby Stereo; MPAA rating: PG-13; running time: 126 minutes.

CAST: Michael Keaton (Batman/Bruce Wayne); Jack Nicholson (The Joker/Jack Napier); Kim Basinger (Vicki Vale); Pat Hingle (Commissioner Gordon); Robert Wuhl (Alexander Knox); Michael Gough (Alfred Pennyworth); Billy Dee Williams (Harvey Dent); Jack Palance (Carl Grissom); Jerry Hall (Alicia Tracey); Walter (Bob the Goon); Lee Wallace (Mayor Borg); William Hootkins (Lieutenant Eckhardt); Richard Strange, Carl Chase, Mac MacDonald, George Lane Cooper, Terence Plummer, Philip Tan (Goons); John Sterland (Accountant); Edwin Craig (Ratelli); Joel Cutrara (Crimelord #2); John Dair (Ricorso); Vincent Wong (Crimelord #1); Christopher Fairbank (Nic);

George Roth (Eddie); Kate Harper (Anchorwoman); Bruce McGuire (Anchorman); Richard Durden (TV Director); Kit Hollerbach (Becky); Lachelle Carl (TV Technician); Del Baker, Jazzer Jeyes, Wayne Michaels, Valentino Musetti, Rocky Taylor (Napier Hoods); Keith Edwards, Leon Herbert (Reporters); Steve Plytas (Doctor); Anthony Wellington (Patrolman at Party); Amir M. Korangy (Wine Steward); Hugo Blick (Young Jack Napier); Charles Roskilly (Young Bruce Wayne); Philip O'Brien (Maître D'); Michael Balfour (Scientist); Liza Ross (Mom); Garrick Hagon (Dad); Adrian Meyers (Jimmy); David Baxt (Dr. Wayne); Sharon Holm (Mrs. Wayne); Clyde Gatell (Mugger); Jon Soresi (Medic); Sam Douglas (Lawyer); Elliott Stein (Man in Crowd); Denis Lill (Bob the Cartoonist); Paul Birchard (Another Reporter); Paul Michael (Cop); Carl Newman (Movement Double); Bob Kane (Bit).

EDWARD SCISSORHANDS

(1990, TWENTIETH CENTURY-FOX)

CREDITS: Directed by Tim Burton; screenplay: Caroline Thompson; story: Tim Burton, Caroline Thompson; producers: Tim Burton, Denise DiNovi; executive producer: Richard Hashimoto; associate producer: Caroline Thompson; music: Danny Elfman; cinematography: Stefan Czapsky; costume designer: Colleen Atwood; production designer: Bo Welch; film editor: Richard Halsey; first assistant director: Jerry Fleck; second assistant director: Francis Conway; special makeup and Scissorhands effects created at Stan Winston Studio by art-department coordinators John Rosengrant and Shane Patrick Mahan, and mechanical-department coordinator Richard J. Landon; art director: Tom Duffield; set decorator: Cheryl Carasik; set designers: Rick Heinrichs, Paul Sonski, Ann Harris; effects director of photography: Bill Neill; film editor: Colleen Halsey; main title sequence designed by Robert Dawson; music editor: Bob Badami; assistant music editor: Margie Goodspeed; sound mixer: Peter Hliddal; supervising sound editors: Warren Hamilton Jr., Michael J. Benavente, James Christopher; ADR editor: Mary Andrews; second second assistant director: Margaret Nelson; costume supervisor: Ray Summers; women's key costumer: Nancy McArdle; men's key costumer: David Davenport; women's wardrobe: Kathryn "Bird"; department head makeup: Ve Neill; special-effects supervisor: Michael Wood; special effects: Michael Arbogast, James Reedy, Gary Schaedler, David Wood, Brian Wood; visual effects: VCE/Peter Kuran; special-effects production assistant: Michael Umble; stunt supervisor: Clyde Zimmerman; art department sculptor: Leo Run; stunt coordinator: Glenn R. Wilder; animal trainers: Sled Reynolds, David Allsberry, Boone Nar; orchestrations: Steve Bartek; conductor: Shirley Walker; music scoring mixer: Shawn Murphy; Foley: Vanessa T. Ament, Heather McPherson; Foley mixer: Robert Deschaine; Foley editor: Mike Chock; sound effects recording: Eric Potter; rerecording mixers: Steve Maslow, Stanley Kastner; miniature effects provided by Stetson Visual Services, Inc., Robert Spurlock, Mark Stetson; chief model maker: George Trimmer; lead sculptor: Jaroslaw G. Alfer; lead miniature special effects: Terry King; stunts: Greg Anderson, Todd Bryant, Gary Rev. Price, Gar Stephen, Scott Wilder, Tammy

Brady-Conrad, David Burton, Lori Lynn Ross, Bill Suiter, John Zimmerman; lenses and Panaflex cameras by Panavision; color by Deluxe; projection ratio: 1.85:1. Titles composited by Cinema Research Corporation; recorded in Dolby Stereo and Cinema Digital Sound. MPAA rating: PG; running time: 100 minutes.

CAST: Johnny Depp (Edward Scissorhands); Winona Ryder (Kim Boggs); Dianne Wiest (Peg Boggs); Anthony Michael Hall (Jim); Kathy Baker (Joyce Monroe); Robert Oliveri (Kevin Boggs); Conchata Ferrell (Helen); Caroline Aaron (Marge); Dick Anthony Williams (Officer Allen); O-Lan Jones (Esmeralda); Vincent Price (The Inventor); Alan Arkin (Bill Boggs); Susan Blommaert (Tinka); Linda Perri (Cissy); John Davidson (TV Host); Biff Yeager (George); Marti Greenberg (Suzanne); Bryan Larkin (Max); John McMahon (Denny); Victoria Price (TV Newswoman); Stuart Lancaster (Retired Man); Gina Gallagher (Granddaughter); Aaron Lustig (Psychologist); Alan Fudge (Loan Officer); Steven Brill (Dishwasher Man); Peter Palmer (Editor); Marc Macaulay, Carmen J. Alexander, Brett Rice (Reporters); Andrew B. Clark (Beefy Man); Kelli Crofton (Pink Girl); Linda Jean Hess (Older Woman/TV); Rosalyn Thomson (Young Woman/TV); Lee Ralls (Red-Haired Woman/TV); Eileen Meurer (Teenage Girl/TV); Bea Albano (Rich Widow/TV); Donna Pieroni (Blonde/TV); Ken DeVaul (Policeman); Michael Gaughan (Policeman); Tricia Lloyd (Teenage Girl); Kathy Dombo (Other Teen); Rex Fox (Police Sergeant); Sherry Ferguson (Max's Mother); Tabetha Thomas (Little Girl on Bike); Neighborhood Extras: Tammy Boalo, Jackie Carson, Carol Crumrine, Suzanne Chrosniak, Ellin Dennis, Kathy Fleming, Jalaine Gallion, Miriam Goodspeed, Dianne L. Green, Mary Jane Heath, Carol D. Klasek, Laura Nader, Doyle Anderson, Harvey Billman, Michael Brown, Gary Clark, Roland Douville, Russell F. Green, Cecil Hawkins, Jack W. Kapfhamer, Bill Klein, Phil Olson, Joe Sheldon, James Spicer.

BATMAN RETURNS

(1992, WARNER BROS.)

CREDITS: Directed by Tim Burton; screenplay: Daniel Waters, Wesley Strick (uncredited), based on characters appearing in DC Comics created by Bob Kane; story: Daniel Waters, Sam Hamm; producers: Tim Burton, Denise Di Novi; co-producer: Larry Franco; production manager/associate producer: Ian Bryce; associate producer (4-Ward Productions): Holly Borradaile; line producers (4-Ward Productions): Robin D'Arcy, Jenny Fulle; executive producers: Jon Peters, Peter Guber, Benjamin Melniker, Michael E. Uslan; music: Danny Elfman; cinematography: Stefan Czapsky; costume designers: Bob Ringwood, Mary Vogt; production designer: Bo Welch; film editor: Chris Lebenzon; first assistant director: David McGiffert; second assistant director: Carla Corwin; second second assistant director: Marge Piane; supervising art director: Tom Duffield; art director: Rick Heinrichs; assistant art director: Richard Mays; set decorator: Cheryl Carasik; set designers: Nick Navarro, Sally Thornton; visual-effects supervisor: Michael Fink; production sound mixer: Petur Hliddal; project consultant: Bob Kane;

stunt coordinators: Max Kleven, Charlie Croughwell; special-effects supervisor: Chuck Gaspar; special effects: Jan Aaris, Karl Nygren, Elmer Hui, Scot Forbes, Bruce Robles, Mike Weaver, Andy Evans, Ken Clark, Dan Gaspar; men's costume supervisor: Norman Burza; women's costume supervisor: Oda Groeschel; visual and technical costume effects supervisor: Vin Burnham; makeup supervisor: Ve Neill; penguin makeup design: Shane Mahan, John Rosengrant, Mark "Crash" McCreety; head animal trainer: Gary Gero; animals and Blackfeet penguins provided by Bird and Animals, Inc.; King penguins provided by Birdland; film editor: Bob Badami; visual-effects coordinator: Erik Henry; supervising sound editors: Richard L. Anderson, David Stone; sound editors: Julia Evershade, Michael J. Benavente, Warren C. Hamilton Jr., John C. C. Dunn; sound effects: Jim Pospisil; dialogue editors: Jim Christopher, Stephen Hunter Flick, Mike Chock; ADR supervisor: Mary Andrews; ADR editor: Jessica Gallavan; Foley mixer: David Miranda; sound effects recordist: Eric Potter; ADR mixer: Thomas J. O'Connell; music editors: Bob Badami, Bill Bernstein; rerecording mixers: Steve Maslow, Jeffrey J. Haboush; music produced by Danny Elfman, Steve Bartek; orchestrator: Steve Bartek; conductor: Jonathon Sheffer; music recording engineer: Shawn Murphy; additional orchestrations: Mark McKenzie; main title sequence designed by Robert Dawson; special visual effects in VistaVision by Boss Film Studios; visual-effects supervisor: John Bruno; visual-effects co-supervisor/art director: Brent Boates; visual-effects supervisor: Ellen Somers; director of photography/miniatures: Garry Waller; director of photography/plates: Neil Krepela; editorial supervisor: Michael Moore; digital-effects supervisor: Jim Rygiel; matte camera: Alan Harding; visual-effects supervisor: Robert Skotak; supervising director of digital photography: Dennis Skotak; directors of photography: James Belkin, George Dodge; Matte World Visual Effects—visual-effects supervisors: Michael Pangrazio, Craign Barron; digital bats and Batmobile shields by Video Image; video image: Rhonda C. Gunner, Richard E. Hollander, Gregory L. McMurry, John C. Walsh; "Old Zoo" miniature effects by Stetson Visual Services, Inc.; effects supervisors: Mark Stetson, Robert Spurlock; chief model maker: Ian Hunter; "Old Zoo" visual effects by the Chandler Group; effects supervisors: Don Baker, John Scheele; director of photography: Tim Angulo; second-unit directors: Billy Weber, Max Kleven; second-unit first assistant director: Artist Robinson; second-unit second assistant director: Kevin Duncan; second-unit director of photography: Paul Ryan; production sound mixer: Roger Pietschmann; stunts: Scott Sproule, Patricia M. Peters, Brian Smrz, Mike Cassidy, Kathy Long, David Lea, Heather Ann Ryan, Richard Drown; produced in association with Polygram Pictures; lenses and Panaflex cameras by Panavision; color by Technicolor; projection ratio: 1.85:1. Recorded in Dolby Stereo; MPAA rating: PG-13; running time: 126 minutes.

CAST: Michael Keaton (Bruce Wayne/Batman); Danny DeVito (Oswald Cobblepot/Penguin); Michelle Pfeiffer (Selina Kyle/Catwoman); Christopher Walken (Max Shreck); Michael Gough (Alfred Pennyworth); Michael Murphy (Mayor); Cristi Conaway (Ice Princess); Andrew Bryniarski (Chip Shreck); Pat Hingle (Commissioner Gordon); Vincent

Schiavelli (Organ Grinder); Steve Witting (Josh); Jan Hooks (Jen); John Strong (Sword Swallower); Rick Zumwalt (Tattooed Strongman); Anna Katerina (Poodle Lady); Gregory Scott Cummins (Acrobat Thug #1); Erika Andersch (Knifethrower Dame); Travis McKenna (Fat Clown); Doug Jones (Thin Clown); Branscombe Richmond (Terrifying Clown #1); Paul Reubens (Penguin's Father); Diane Salinger (Penguin's Mother); Stuart Lancaster (Penguin's Doctor); Cal Hoffman (Happy Man); Joan Jurige (Happy Woman); Rosie O'Connor (Adorable Little Girl); Sean Whalen (Paperboy); Erik Onate (Aggressive Reporter); Jocy DePinto (Shreck Security Guard); Steven Brill (Gothamite #1); Neal Lerner (Gothamite #2); Ashley Tillman (Gothamite #3); Elizabeth Sanders (Gothamite #4); Henry Kingi (Mugger); Joan Giammarco (Female Victim); Lisa Coles (Volunteer Bimbo); Frank DiElsi (Security #1); Biff Yeager (Security #2); Robert Gossett (TV Anchorman); Adam Drescher (Crowd Member); Niki Botelho (Emperor Penguin/Baby Penguin); Robert N. Bell, Susan Rossitto, Margarita Fernández, Denise Killpack, Felix Silla, Debbie Lee Carrington (Emperor Penguins); Anthony DeLongis (Terrifying Clown #2); Leticia Rogers (Reporter); Nathan Stein (Uncle Sam on Stilts); Andy Schoneberg, Len Burge III, Karen Mason, Ian Stevenson, Jeffrey Edwards, Craig Canton-Largent (Puppeteers).

TIM BURTON'S THE NIGHTMARE BEFORE CHRISTMAS

(1993, TOUCHSTONE PICTURES)

CREDITS: Directed by Henry Selick; screenplay: Caroline Thompson, based on a story and characters by Tim Burton; adaptation: Michael McDowell; music and lyrics: Danny Elfman; produced by Tim Burton, Denise Di Novi; co-producer: Kathleen Gavin; associate producer: Danny Elfman; associate producers: Philip Lofero, Jill Jacobs, Diane Minter; animation supervisor: Eric Leighton; storyboard supervisor: Joe Ranft; cinematographer: Pete Kozachik; original score: Danny Elfman; animators: Trey Thoms, Timothy Hittle, Michael Belzer, Anthony Scott, Owen Klatte, Angie Glocka, Justin Kohn, Eric Leighton, Paul Berry, Joel Fletcher, Kim Blanchette, Loyd Price, Richard C. Zimmerman, Stephen A. Buckley; art director: Deane Taylor; editor: Stan Webb; visual consultant: Rick Heinrichs; armature supervisor: Tom St. Amand; mold-maker supervisor: John A. Reed III; character fabrication supervisor: Bonita De Carlo; storyboard artists: Miguel Domingo Cachuala, Bob Pauley, Jorgen Klubein, Steve Moore. Art department—assistant art directors: Kendal Cronkhite, Kelly Adam Ashbury, Bill Boss; artistic coordinator: Allison Abbate; sculptors: Norm DeCarlo, Greg Dykstra, Shelley Daniels, Randal M. Dutra; additional character design: David Cutler, Barry Jackson, Jorgen Klubein. Set construction—set designer and dressing supervisor: Gregg Olsson; background design: B. J. Fredrickson; production coordinator: George Young. FX Animation—effects animators: Gordon Baker, Miguel Domingo Cachuala, Chris Green; digital effects provided by Walt Disney Feature Animation; digital-effects supervisor: Ariel Velasco Shaw. Post-production—post-production supervisor: Sara Duran;

visual-effects supervisor: Pete Kozachik; additional optical effects: Harry Walton/Image FX, Michael Hinton/Interformat; vocal and song arrangements: Steve Bartek; song orchestrations: Steve Bartek; score orchestrations: Mark McKenzie; song conductor: Chris Boerman; score conductor: J. A. C. Redford; music editor: Bob Badami; music recorded by Shawn Murphy, Bobby Fernandez; song vocals recorded by Bill Jackson; sound editing: Weddington Productions; supervising sound editor: Richard L. Anderson; special sound effects: John Pospisil; dialogue editors: Mary Andrews, Joe Dorn; sound effects editors: Michael Chock, James Christopher; Foley: Joan Rowe, Hilda Hodges; Foley mixer: Ezra Dweck; re-recorded at Warner Hollywood Studios; rerecording mixers: Terry Porter, Shawn Murphy, Greg P. Russell; original dialogue recording: Samuel Lehmer; dubbing recordists: Tim Webb, Tony Araki; ADR mixer: Thomas J. O'Connell; ADR recordist: Rick Canelli; color timer: Dale E. Grahn; titles: Buena Vista Optical; post-production administration: Jeannine Berger; post-production assistant: Tracy Barber; color by Monaco Film Lab; prints by Technicolor; produced and distributed on Eastman Film; projection ratio: 1.66:1. Recorded in Dolby Stereo; MPAA rating: PG; running time: 76 minutes.

CAST: (Voices): Danny Elfman (Jack Skellington [singing] and Barrel); Chris Sarandon (Jack Skellington [speaking]); Catherine O'Hara (Sally and Shock); William Hickey (Dr. Finklestein); Glenn Shadix (Mayor); Paul Reubens (Lock); Ken Page (Oogie Boogie); Ed Ivory (Santa); Susan McBride (Big Witch); Debi Durst (Corpse Kid, Corpse Mom, Small Witch); Greg Proops (Harlequin Demon, Devil, Sax Player); Kerry Katz (Man under Stairs, Vampire, Corpse Dad); Randy Crenshaw (Mr. Hyde, Behemoth, Vampire); Sherwood Ball (Mummy, Vampire); Carmen Twillie (Undersea Gal, Man under the Stairs); Glenn Walters (Wolfman); Additional Voices: Mia Brown, Ann Fraser, L. Peter Callender, Jesse McClurg, Robert Olague, Jennifer Levey, Elena Praskin, Judi M. Durand, John Morris, Daamen J. Krall, David McCharen, Bobbi Page, David J. Randolph, Trampas Warman, Doris Hess, Christina MacGregor, Gary Raff, Gary Schwartz.

CABIN BOY

(1994, TOUCHSTONE PICTURES)

CREDITS: Directed by Adam Resnick; screenplay: Adam Resnick; story: Adam Resnick, Chris Elliott; producers: Tim Burton, Denise Di Novi; executive producers: Barry Bernardi, Steve White; music: Steve Bartek; cinematography: Steve Yaconelli; costume designer: Colleen Atwood; production designer: Steven Legler; film editor: Jon Poll; first assistant director: Thomas A. Irvine; second assistant director: Seth Cirker; animator: Doug Beswick; set designer: Stephen Alesch; art directors: Daniel A. Lomino, Nanci Roberts; set decorator: Roberta J. Holinko; wardrobe supervisor: Kenn Smiley; set costumer: Marci R. Johnson; visual-effects consultant: Rob Hummel; visual-effects supervisor: Michael Lessa; visual-effects producer: Lynda Lemon; special-effects coordinator: Robert Knott; stunt coordinator: Ben Scott; unit production manager/second unit director:

John Engel; orchestrations: Marc Mann, Edgardo Simone; music editor: Alex Gibson; supervising sound editor: C. T. Welch; rerecording mixers: Dean A. Zupancic, Dean Ash; production sound mixer: Edward Tise; supervising ADR editor: Avram D. Gold; ADR mixer: Doc Kane; Foley walkers: Jeffrey Wilhoit, James Moriana, David Gertz; post-production supervisor: Steven Tyler Sahlein; key makeup artist: Mindy Hall; additional editor: Greg Hayden; lenses and Panaflex cameras by Panavision; color by Technicolor; projection ratio: 1.85: 1. Recorded in Dolby Stereo; MPAA rating: PG-13; running time: 80 minutes.

CAST: Chris Elliott (Nathaniel Mayweather); Ritch Brinkley (Captain Greybar); James Gammon (Paps); Ricki Lake (Figurehead); Brian Doyle-Murray (Skunk); Brion James (Big Teddy); Melora Walters (Trina); I. M. Hobson (Headmaster Timmons); Alex Nevil (Thomas); David Sterry (Lance); Bob Elliott (William Mayweather); Edward Flotard (Limo Driver); Jim Cummings (Cupcake); Ann Magnuson (Calli); Russ Tamblyn (Chocki); Mike Starr (Mulligan); Andy Richter (Kenny); David Letterman [as Earl Hofert] (Old Salt in Fishing Village).

ED WOOD
(1994, TOUCHSTONE PICTURES)

CREDITS: Directed by Tim Burton; screenplay: Scott Alexander, Larry Karazewski, based on the book *Nightmare of Ecstasy* by Rudolph Grey; producers: Tim Burton, Denise DiNovi; co-producer: Michael Flynn; executive producer: Michael Lehmann; music: Howard Shore; cinematography: Stefan Czapsky; costume designer: Colleen Atwood; production designer: Tom Duffield; film editor: Chris Lebenzon; first assistant director: Michael Topodzian; second assistant director: Gregory Ken Simmons; art director: Okowita; assistant art director: Keith Neely; set decorator: Cricket Rowland; key makeup artist: Ve Neil; makeup: Carrie Angland; Bela Lugosi makeup designed and created by Rick Baker; costume department supervisor: Nancy McArdle; men's costume supervisor: Kenn Smiley; costumer: Stephanie Colin; production sound: Edward Tise; additional editor: Tom Seid; assistant editors: Pam Di Fede, Sandra Kaufman; music editor: Ellen Segal; supervising sound editor: John Nutt; dialogue editors: Joan E. Chapman, Patrick Dodd, Scott Levitin; sound effects editors: Ernie Fosselius, Sam Hinkley; rerecording mixers: David Parker, Michael Semanick, Richard Schirmer; ADR mixers: Jeff Courtie, Brian Rubero, Paul Zydell; Foley artists: Maggie O'Malley, Jennifer Myers; Foley recording engineers: Richard Quarte, Linda Lew; post-production sound editing and rerecording: The Saul Zaentz Film Center; special-effects coordinator: Howard Jensen; special effects: J. Kevin Pike; motion-control photography and special visual effects: Boyington Film Productions, Inc.; visual-effects supervisor: Paul Boyington; model production designer: Jeryd Pojawa; director of photography: Alan Blaisdale; octopus by Sota Effects; stunt coordinator: John Brannagan; second second assistant director: Michael McCue; set designers: Chris Nushawg, Bruce Hill; illustrator: James Carson; music scoring mixer: John Kurlander; orchestrations: Howard Shore; opticals: Reel Effects; negative cutter: J. G. Films; main titles composite: Cinema Research Corporation; main title sequence designers: Robert Dawson, Paul Boyington; visual consultant: Richard Hoover; dailies processing by DuArt Laboratories; lenses and Panaflex cameras by Panavision; print by Technicolor; produced and distributed on Eastman Film; projection ratio: 1.85: 1. Recorded in Dolby Stereo Digital; MPAA rating: R; running time: 127 minutes.

CAST: Johnny Depp (Ed Wood); Martin Landau (Bela Lugosi); Sarah Jessica Parker (Dolores Fuller); Patricia Arquette (Kathy O'Hara); Jeffrey Jones (Criswell); G. D. Spradlin (Reverend Lemon); Vincent D'Onofrio (Orson Welles); Bill Murray (Bunny Breckenridge); Mike Starr (Georgie Weiss); Max Casella (Paul Marco); Brent Hinkley (Conrad Brooks); Lisa Marie (Vampira); George "The Animal" Steele (Tor Johnson); Juliet Landau (Loretta King); Clive Rosengren (Ed Reynolds); Norman Alden (Cameraman Bill); Leonard Termo (Makeup Man Harry); Ned Bellamy (Dr. Tom Mason); Danny Dayton (Soundman); John Ross (Camera Assistant); Bill Cusack (Tony McCoy); Aaron Nelms (Teenage Kid); Biff Yeager (Rude Boss); Joseph R. Gannascoli (Security Guard); Carmen Filpi (Old Crusty Man); Lisa Malkiewicz (Secretary #1); Melora Walters (Secretary #2);Conrad Brooks (Bartender); Don Amendolia (Salesman); Tommy Bertelsen (Tough Boy); Reid Cruickshanks (Stage Guard); Stanley DeSantis (Mr. Feldman); Lionel Decker (Executive #1); Edmund L. Shaff (Executive #2); Gene LeBell (Ring Announcer); Jesse Hernandez (Wrestling Opponent); Bobby Slayton (TV Show Host); Gretchen Becker (TV Host's Assistant); John Rice (Conservative Man); Catherine Butterfield (Conservative Wife); Mary Portser (Backer's Wife); King Cotton (Hick Backer); Don Hood (Southern Backer); Frank Echols (Doorman); Matthew B. Barry (Valet); Ralph Monaco (Waiter); Anthony Russell (Busboy); Tommy Bush (Stage Manager); Gregory Walcott (Potential Backer); Charles C. Stevenson Jr. (Another Backer); Rance Howard (Old Man McCoy); Vasek Simek (Professor Strowski); Alan Martin (Vampira's Assistant); Salwa Ali (Vampira's Girlfriend); Rodney Kizziah (Vampira's Friend); Korla Pandit (Indian Musician); Hannah Eckstein (Greta Johnson); Luc De Schepper (Karl Johnson); Vinny Argiro (TV Horror Show Director); Patti Tippo (Nurse); Ray Baker (Doctor); Louis Lombardi (Rental House Manager); James Reid Boyce (Theatre Manager); Ben Ryan Ganger (Angry Kid); Ryan Holihan (Frantic Usher); Marc Revivo (High School Punk); Charlie Holliday (Tourist); Adam Drescher (Photographer #1); Ric Mancini (Photographer #2); Daniel Riordan (Pilot/Strapping Young Man); Mickey Cottrell (Hammy Alien); Christopher George Simpson (Organist); Robert Binford, Herbert Boche, Linda Rae Brienz, Marlene Cook, Sylvia Coussa, Audrey Cuyler, Joseph Golightly, Carrie Starner Hummel, Ramona Kemp-Blair, Carolyn Kessinger, Nancy Longyear, Matthew Nelson, Robert Nuffer, William Michael Short, Susan Eileen Simpson, George F. Sterne, Charles Alan Stephenson, Cheri A. Williams, Cynthia Ann Wilson (Choir Members); Maurice LaMarche (Orson Welles' Voice [uncredited]).

BATMAN FOREVER

(1995, WARNER BROS.)

CREDITS: Directed by Joel Schumacher; screenplay: Lee Batchler, Janet Scott Batchler, Akiva Goldsman; story: Lee Batchler, Janet Scott Batchler; producers: Tim Burton, Peter MacGregor Scott; executive producers: Benjamin Melniker, Michael E. Uslan; associate producer: Mitchell E. Dauterive; music: Elliot Goldenthal; cinematography: Stephen Goldblatt; costume designers: Ingrid Ferrin, Bob Ringwood; production designer: Barbara Ling; film editor: Dennis Virkler; assistant directors: Alan Edmistein, William M. Elvin, Joseph P. Lucky; project consultant: Bob Kane; art director: Christopher Burian-Mohr; set designers: Thomas Betts, Sean Haworth; set decorator: Cricket Rowland; set dresser: Ari David Schwartz; special makeup effects: Rick Baker; key makeup artist: Ve Neill; sound design: Lance Brown; visual-effects supervisors: John Dykstra, Boyd Shermis; visual-effects editor: Kate Crossley; digital visual-effects producer: Andrea D'Amico; special-effects supervisor: Thomas L. Fisher; second unit director: David Hogan; second unit director of photography: Gary Holt; stunt coordinator/underwater unit director: Conrad E. Palmiano; director of photography/underwater unit: Pete Romano; music supervisors: Leslie Reed, Jolene Cherry; music editor: Zigmund Gron; orchestrations: Robert Elhai; sound editors: Jay Nierenburg, Bruce Stambler; rerecording mixers: Donald O. Mitchell, Frank A. Montano, Michael Herbick; sound mixer: Petur Hliddal; Foley mixer: Mary Jo Lang; ADR editors: Zack Davis, Josh Leveque; special effects: Pacific Data Images, Rhythm and Hues, Effects Associates Ltd., Composite Images Systems; lenses and Panaflex cameras by Panavision; color by Technicolor; projection ratio: 1.85:1. Recorded in Dolby Stereo Digital; MPAA rating: PG-13; running time: 121 minutes.

CAST: Val Kilmer (Batman/Bruce Wayne); Tommy Lee Jones (Harvey Dent/Two-Face); Jim Carrey (Edward Nygma/The Riddler); Nicole Kidman (Dr. Chase Meridian); Chris O'Donnell (Dick Grayson/Robin); Michael Gough (Alfred Pennyworth); Pat Hingle (Commissioner Gordon); Drew Barrymore (Sugar); Debi Mazar (Spice); Elizabeth Sanders (Gossip Gerty); Rene Auberjonois (Dr. Burton); Joe Grifasi (Bank Guard); Philip Moon (Newscaster); Jessica Tuck (Newscaster); Dennis Paladino (Crime Boss Moroni); Kimberly Scott (Margaret); Michael Paul Chan (Executive); Jon Favreau (Assistant); Greg Lauren (Aide); Ramsey Ellis (Young Bruce Wayne); Michael Scranton (Thomas Wayne); Eileen Seeley (Martha Wayne); David U. Hodges (Shooter); Jack Betts (Fisherman); Tim Jackson (Municipal Police Guard); Daniel Reichert (Ringmaster); Glory Fioramonti (Mom Grayson); Larry A. Lee (Dad Grayson); Bruce Roberts (Handsome Reporter); George Wallace (Mayor); Bob Zmuda (Electronic Store Owner); Rebecca Budig (Teenage Girl); Don "The Dragon" Wilson (Gang Leader); Sydney D. Minckler (Teen Gang Member); Maxine Jones, Terry Ellis, Cindy Herron, Dawn Robinson (Girls on Corner); Gary Kasper (Pilot); Amanda Trees (Paparazzi Reporter); Andrea Fletcher (Reporter); Ria Coyne (Socialite); Jed Curtis (Chubby Businessman); William Mesnik

(Bald Guy); Marga Gómez (Journalist); Kelly Vaughn (Showgirl); John Fink (Deputy); Noby Arden, Marlene Bologna, Danny Castle, Troy S. Wolfe (Trapeze Act); Chris C. Caso, Gary Clayton, Oscar Dillon, Keith Graham, Kevin Grevioux, Mark A. Hicks, Corey Jacoby, Randy Lamb, Maurice Lamont, Sidney S. Liufau, Brad Martin, Deron McBee, Mario Mugavero, Joey Nelson, Jim Palmer, Robert Pavell, Pee Wee Piemonte, Peter Radon, François Rodrigue, Joe Sabatino, Mike Sabatino, Ofer Samra, Matt Sigloch, Mike Smith (Harvey's Thugs); Katrina Fisher (Wig Lady); Stunts: John Ashker, Keith Campbell, Dana Hee, Jim McConnell.

JAMES AND THE GIANT PEACH

(1996, TOUCHSTONE PICTURES)

CREDITS: Directed by Henry Selick; screenplay: Steven Bloom, Karey Kirkpatrick, Jonathan Roberts, based on the book by Roald Dahl; producer: Tim Burton; co-producers: Henry Selick, John Engel; executive producer: Jake Eberts; music and songs: Randy Newman; cinematography: Pete Kozachik (animation), Hiro Narita (live action); production designer: Harley Jessup; film editor: Stan Webb; assistant directors: Lisa Davidson, Kat Miller, Kendal Cronkhite; art directors: Lane Smith, Blake Russell; set dresser: Nanci Noblett; scenic artist: Robert L. Peden; animation supervisor: Paul Berry; special-effects/visual-effects supervisor: Scott E. Anderson; visual-effects supervisor: Dorne Huebler; visual-effects producer: Lynda Lemon; visual-effects executive producer: George Merkert; makeup: Richard Snell; Foley artists: Dennis Thorpe, Jana Vance; rerecording mixer/sound designer: Gary Rydstrom; entomologist consultant: Steven R. Kutcher; supervising sound editor: Tim Holland; consulting editor: Robert Grahamjones; orchestrations: Chris Boardman, Don Davis; stunt coordinator: Rocky Capella; special effects: Sony Pictures Image Works, Buena Vista Visual Effects, Hybrid Technologies; lenses and Panaflex cameras by Panavision; color by Technicolor; projection ratio: 1.66:1. MPAA rating: PG; running time: 79 minutes.

CAST: Simon Callow (Grasshopper [voice]); Richard Dreyfuss (Centipede [voice]); Jane Leeves (Ladybug [voice]); Joanna Lumley (Aunt Spiker); Miriam Margolyes (The Glowworm [voice]/Aunt Sponge); Pete Postlethwaite (Old Man); Susan Sarandon (Spider [voice]); Paul Terry (James); David Thewlis (Earthworm [voice]); J. Stephen Coyle (Reporter #2); Steven Culp (James's Father); Cirocco Dunlap (Girl with Telescope); Michael Girardin (Reporter #1); Tony Haney (Reporter #3); Katherine Howell (Woman in Bathrobe); Chae Kirby (Newsboy); Jeff Mosely (Hard Hat Man); Al Nalbandian (Cabby); Mike Starr (Beat Cop); Susan Turner-Cray (James's Mother); Mario Yedidia (Street Kid); Emily Rosen (Bit).

MARS ATTACKS!

(1996, WARNER BROS.)

CREDITS: Directed by Tim Burton; screenplay: Jonathan Gems, Tim Burton (uncredited), based on the Topps Trading Cards by Len Brown, Woody Gelman, Wally Wood, Bob Powell, Norman Saunders; producers: Tim Burton, Larry Franco; associate producers: Paul Deason, Mark S. Miller; music: Danny Elfman; cinematography: Peter Suschitzky; costume designer: Colleen Atwood; production designer: Wynn Thomas; film editor: Chris Lebenzon; first assistant director: Tom Mack; second assistant director: David Kelley; special-effects supervisor: Michael Lantieri; supervising art director: James Hegedus; art director: John Dexter; set decorator: Nancy Haugh; set dresser: Richard Berger; second second assistant directors: C. C. Barnes, Paul Bernard, Cathy Bond; visual-effects editor: David Dresher; special effects: Tom Pank, Loue Lantieri, Dan Ossello, Brian Tipton, Tom Tokunaga; costume supervisor: Sue Moore; key makeup: Valli O'Reilly; Mr. Nicholson's Makeup: Ve Neill; makeup: Julie Hewitt, Robin Neal; body makeup: Julie Steffes; sound designer: Randy Thom; supervising sound editor: Richard Hymns; sound effects editors: Ken Fischer, Frank Eulner; supervising dialogue ADR editor: Michael Silvers; dialogue editors: Sara Bolder, Ewa Sztompke Oatfield; Foley editor: Sandina Baulo Lape; music editors: Bob Badami, Ellen Segal; rerecording mixers: Gary Summers, Shawn Murphy, Randy Thom; music score produced by Danny Elfman, Steve Bartek; music score recorded and mixed by Shawn Murphy; conductor: Artie Kane; orchestrations: Steve Bartek; animal trainers: Animals R Us; negative cutting: Donah Bassett and Associates; titles and opticals: Pacific Title; title design: Robert Dawson. Washington, D.C.—art director: Hugo Santiago; set decorator: Katherine Lucas; Martian visual effects and animation by Industrial Light and Magic; associate effects supervisor: Ellen Poon; visual-effects art director: Mark Moore; computer graphics supervisors: Roger Guyett, Andy White; computer graphics sequence supervisors: Joel Aron, David F. Horsley, Barbara L. Hellis, Ben Snow; miniature director of photography: Patrick Sweeney; digital armature designer: Tim Waddy; senior visual-effects coordinator: Jill Brooks; chief digital character modeler: Tony Hudson; editorial supervisor: Dan McNamara; visual-effects editors: Bill Kimberlin, Greg Hyman; inferno supervisor: Victor Jimenez; design supervisors: Peter Saunders, Ian MacKinnon; costume supervisor: Geraldine Corrigan; mechanic design: Stuart Sutcliffe, Georgina Mayns; stunt coordinator: Joe Dunne; aerial coordinator: Cliff Fleming; stunt pilots: Craig Hoskins, Dirk Vahle, Ken Viera, John T. Scanlon, David G. Mills, Sich Shuster, Christopher Saunders, Glenn J. Smith; filmed with Panavision cameras and lenses; camera dollies: J. L. Fisher; camera cranes and dollies by Chapman; color by Technicolor; Kodak Motion Picture Products; projection ratio: 2.35:1. Recorded in Dolby Digital Surround Sound; MPAA rating: PG-13; running time: 106 minutes.

CAST: Jack Nicholson (President Dale/Art Land); Glenn Close (Marsha Dale); Annette Bening (Barbara Land); Pierce Brosnan (Donald Kessler); Danny DeVito (Rude Gambler); Martin Short (Jerry Ross); Sarah Jessica Parker (Nathalie Lake); Michael J. Fox

(Jason Stone); Rod Steiger (General Decker); Tom Jones (Himself); Lukas Haas (Richie Norris); Natalie Portman (Taffy Dale); Jim Brown (Byron Williams); Lisa Marie (Martian Girl); Sylvia Sidney (Grandma Norris); Paul Winfield (General Casey); Pam Grier (Louise Williams); Jack Black (Billy Glenn Norris); Janice Rivera (Cindy); Ray J (Cedric); Brandon Hammond (Neville); Joe Don Baker (Glenn Norris); O-Lan Jones (Sue Ann Norris); Christina Applegate (Sharona); Brian Haley (Mitch); Jerzy Skolimowski (Dr. Zeigler); Timi Prulhiere (Tour Guide); Barbet Schroeder (French President); Chi Hoang Cai (Mr. Lee); Tommy Bush (Hillbilly); Joseph Maher (Decorator); Gloria M. Malgarini, Betty Bunch, Gloria Hoffmann (Nuns); Willie Garson (Corporate Guy); John Roselius (GNN Boss); Michael Reilly Burke, Valerie Wildman, Richard Irving (GNN Reporters); Jonathan Emerson (Newscaster); Tamara "Gingir" Curry, Rebecca Broussard (Hookers); Vinny Argiro (Casino Manager); Steve Valentine (TV Director); Coco Leigh (Female Journalist); Jeffrey King (NASA Technician); Enrique Castillo (Hispanic Colonel); Don Lamoth (Colonel #2); C. Wayne Owens (Stranger); Joseph Patrick Moynihan (Stranger); Roger Peterson (Colonel #1); John Finnegan (Speaker of the House); Ed Lambert (Morose Old Guy); John Gray (Incredibly Old Guy); Gregg Daniel (Lab Technician); J. Kenneth Campbell, Jeanne Mori (Doctors); Rance Howard (Texan Investor); Richard Assad (Saudi Investor); Velletta Carlson (Elderly Slots Woman); Kevin Mangan (Trailer Lover); Rebeca Silva (Hispanic Woman); Josh Weinstein (Hippie); Julian Barnes (White House Waiter); Ken Thomas (White House Photographer); Darelle Porter Holden, Christi Black, Sharon Hendrix (Tom Jones Backup Singers); Frank Welker (Martian vocal effects); Roger L. Jackson (Translator Device voice); Walt G. Ludwig (Tank Gunner); Stunts: Perry Barndt, Daniel W. Barringer, George Chelung, Mark Donaldson, Corey Eubanks, Tanner Gill, Sherry Ham-Bernard, Steven Ito, Hannah Kozak, John Moio, Sean B. Murphy, Jim Palmer, Tricia Peters, Darrin Prescott, Thomas Rosales Jr., Lynn Salvatori, Lincoln Simonds, Mark Stefanich, Neil Summers, George P. Wilbur, Stanton Barrett, Joey Box, Phil Chong, Richard Duran, George Fisher, Gary L. Guercio, Dick Hancock, Jesse Johnson, Julius LeFlore, Bennie E. Moore, Jimmy Ortega, Victor Paul, Dan Plum, George Robotham, George Marshall Ruse, Dennis R. Scott, Erik Stabernau, Jim Stephan, Clark Tucker, Brian J. Williams, Danny Wong.

Television Films

HANSEL AND GRETEL

(1982, WALT DISNEY PRODUCTIONS, FOR THE DISNEY CHANNEL)

CREDITS: Directed by Tim Burton; producer: Julie Hickson; teleplay: Julie Hickson. Running time: 45 minutes.

CAST: Michael Yama, Jim Ishida.

ALADDIN AND HIS WONDERFUL LAMP

(1984, PLATYPUS PRODUCTIONS/LION'S GATE FILMS/SHOWTIME)

CREDITS: Directed by Tim Burton; screenplay: Mark Curtiss, Rod Ash; producers: Bridget Terry, Fredric S. Fuchs; associate producer: Sandra Pearson; executive producer: Shelley Duvall; music: David Newman, Michael Convertino; production designer: Michael Erler; costume designer: Terry Tam Soon; makeup designers: Sheryl Leigh Shulman, Ron Figuly; video effects consultant: Chuck Cirino; art directors: Jane Osmann, Richard Greenbaum; costumer: Beth Alexander; technical director: Jim Ralston; lighting director: Mark Levin; audio: Ron Cronkhite; video: Ros Harmon; special effects: Jeff Jackson, Al Kidd; videotape editor: Marco Zappia; video effects: Cause & EFX; music produced by Rob Meurer; music recorded and mixed by Lee Hirschberg, Chet Himes; videotaped at ABC Television Center. Running rime: 47 minutes.

CAST: Valerie Bertinelli (Princess Sabrina); Robert Carradine (Aladdin); James Earl Jones (Genie of the Lamp/Genie of the Ring); Leonard Nimoy (Evil Magician); Ray Sharkey (Grand Vizier); Rae Allen (Aladdin's Mother); Joseph Maher (Sultan); Jay Abramowitz (Habibe); Martha Velez (Lady Servant); Bonnie Jefferies, Sandy Lenz, Marcia Gobel (The Three Green Women); John Salazar (Servant).

THE JAR

(1985, NBC-TV/UNIVERSAL/ALFRED HITCHCOCK PRESENTS)

CREDITS: Directed by Tim Burton; teleplay: Larry Wilson, Michael McDowell, based on a story by Ray Bradbury; producer: Alan Barnette; supervising producer: Andrew Mirisch; executive producer: Christopher Crowe; associate producer: Daniel Sackheim; music: Danny Elfman, Steve Bartek; director of photography: Mario DiLeo; production designer: Dean Edward Mitzner; editor: Heather MacDougall; first assistant director: Doug Metzger; second assistant director: Lonnie Steinberg; set decorator: Victoria Hugo; sound: Jim Alexander; costume designer: Sharon Day; color by Technicolor; titles and optical effects: Universal Title; Panaflex cameras and lenses by Panavision; sound editor: Burness J. Speakman; music editor: Dino A. Moriana. Running time: 24 minutes.

CAST: Griffin Dunne (Noel); Fiona Lewis (Erica); Laraine Newman (Periwinkle); Stephen Shellen (Justin); Paul Bartel (The Art Critic); Paul Werner (Nazi); Sunshine Parker (Texan); Eileen Barnett (Texan's Wife); Peter D. Risch (Happy Kaufman); Regina Richardson (Female Art Type); Susan Moore (Female Fashion Victim); Nathan LeGrand (Male Fashion Victim); Roy Fegan (Person #1); Leah Kates (Person #2); Lori Lynn Lively (Frail Woman); Jeffrey Steven Kramer (Guest #1).

BIBLIOGRAPHY

Sources of Chapter Opening Quotes

1. Salisbury, Mark, and Tim Burton. *Burton on Burton*. London: Faber and Faber, 1995, p. 75.

2. Indiana, Gary. "Into the Wood." *Village Voice*, October 4, 1994.

3. Breski, David. "Tim Burton." *Rolling Stone*, July 9, 1992.

4. Morgenstern, Joe. "Tim Burton, Batman, and the Joker." *New York Times*, April 9, 1989, *Magazine* section.

5. Paul Reubens in *Pee-Wee's Big Adventure* (1985).

6. Paul Reubens in *Pee-Wee's Big Adventure* (1985).

7. Winona Ryder in *Beetlejuice* (1988).

8. Michael Keaton in *Batman* (1989).

9. Michael Keaton in *Batman* (1989).

10. Rose, Frank. "Tim Cuts Up." *Premiere*, January 1991, pp. 96–102.

11. TV audience member in *Edward Scissorhands* (1990).

12. Danny DeVito in *Batman Returns* (1992).

13. Danny DeVito in *Batman Returns* (1992).

14. Santa Claus in *Tim Burton's The Nightmare Before Christmas* (1993).

15. Edelstein, David. "Tim Burton's Hollywood Nightmare." *Vanity Fair*, November 1994.

16. Bela Lugosi in *Glen or Glenda* (1952).

17. Bela Lugosi in *Bride of the Monster* (1955).

18. Ferrante, Anthony C. "Duck for Cover When *Mars Attacks!*" *Fangoria*, #159, January 1997.

19. Pierce Brosnan in *Mars Attacks!* (1996).

20. Warren, Bill. "Tim Burton Attacks!" *Starlog*, January 1997.

21. Gross, Edward. "Super Duper." *Cinescape*, September–October, 1997.

Books

Burton, Tim. *The Melancholy Death of Oyster Boy and Other Stories*. New York: Rob Weisbach Books, 1997.

Griffin, Nancy, and Kim Masters. *Hit and Run: How Jon Peters and Peter Guber Took Sony for a Ride in Hollywood*. New York: Simon and Schuster, 1996.

Salisbury, Mark, and Tim Burton. *Burton on Burton*. London: Faber and Faber, 1995.

Thompson, Frank. *Tim Burton's The Nightmare Before Christmas: The Film, the Art, the Vision*. New York: Hyperion, 1993.

Periodicals

Adams, Doug. "Tales from the Black Side: An Interview with Danny Elfman." *Film Score Monthly*, June 1997, pp. 20–26.

Allman, Kevin. "A Little Nightmare Music." *Details*, December 1993.

Ansen, David. "The Disembodied Director." *Newsweek*, January 21, 1991, pp. 58–60.

———. "Kitsch as Kitsch Can." *Newsweek*, October 10, 1994, pp. 71–72.

Ascher-Walsh, Rebecca. "Cape Fear." *Entertainment Weekly*, May 29, 1998, pp. 16–18.

Avens, Mimi. "Ghoul World." *Premiere*, November 1993, pp. 102–108.

Benson, Sheila. "Bat*angst* in Basic Black." *Los Angeles Times*, June 23, 1989.

Bernstein, Abbie. "*Mars Attacks!*" *Drama-Logue*, December 19, 1996, p. 36.

Brennan, Judy. "Ed Wood: A Man, a *Plan*, a Banal . . . " *Los Angeles Times*, October 2, 1994, "Calendar" section, pp. 27, 29.

Breski, David. "Tim Burton." *Rolling Stone*, July 9, 1992.

Brown, Colin. "Burton Sets Sights on Corman's X-Ray Eyes." *Screen International*, April 25, 1997.

Busch, Anita M. "Warners' *Superman* Gaining Strength." *Daily Variety*, April 7, 1997.

Byrge, Duane. "*Edward Scissorhands*." *Hollywood Reporter*, December 3, 1990.

Canby, Vincent. "*Beetlejuice* Is Pap for the Eyes." *New York Times*, May 8, 1988.

———. "Nicholson and Keaton Do Battle in *Batman*." *New York Times*, June 23, 1989.

Christy, George. "The Great Life." *Hollywood Reporter*, August 7, 1985, p. 15.

Clark, John. "The Wood, the Bad, and the Ugly." *Premiere*, October 1994, pp. 90–94, 96.

Clark, Mike. "The Intricate Recipe for Making *Giant Peach*." *USA Today*, October 29, 1997.

_____. "*Mars Attacks!* But Doesn't Quite Triumph." *USA Today*, October 29, 1996.

Corliss, Richard. "A Monster to Be Despised!" *Time*, October 10, 1994.

_____. "Murk in the Myth." *Time*, June 19, 1989, pp. 60–61.

Counts, Kyle. "*Beetlejuice*." *Hollywood Reporter*, March 28, 1988.

Daly, Steve. "Ghost in the Machine: Tim Burton's Animated *Nightmare* Haunts Disney with the Question, Can Naughty Be Nice?" *Entertainment Weekly*, October 29, 1993.

_____. "Sets Appeal: Designing *Batman Returns*." *Entertainment Weekly*, June 19, 1992, p. 24.

_____. "Unhappy *Returns* Batlash." *Entertainment Weekly*, July 31, 1992.

_____. "Video Features Source." *Entertainment Weekly*, April 10, 1992, p. 65.

Dargis, Manhola. "*Batman Forever*." *Sight and Sound*, August 1995, pp. 40–41.

De Vries, Hilary. "The Normalization of Johnny Depp." *Los Angeles Times*, December 1, 1993, "Calendar" section, pp. 3, 42–46.

_____. "Ready or Not It's Back to Tim Burton's World." *Los Angeles Times*, June 14, 1992, "Calendar" section.

Denby, David. "Babes in Cinema Land." *Premiere*, July 1989.

Dunkley, Cathy, and Stephen Galloway. "Burton House Scaling Back." *Hollywood Reporter*, August 3, 1995.

Easton, Nina J. "For Tim Burton, This One's Personal." *Los Angeles Times*, August 12, 1990, "Calendar" section.

Ebert, Roger. "The Batbrain Director." *Los Angeles Daily News*, June 21, 1992, p. 3.

_____. "*Batman*." *Chicago Sun-Times*, June 23, 1989.

_____. "*Batman Forever*." *Chicago Sun-Times*, June 16, 1995.

_____. "*Batman Returns*." *Chicago Sun-Times*, June 19, 1992.

_____. "*Ed Wood*." *Chicago Sun-Times*, October 7, 1994.

_____. "*Edward Scissorhands*." *Chicago Sun-Times*, December 14, 1990.

_____. "*Mars Attacks!*" *Chicago Sun-Times*, December 13, 1996.

_____. "*Tim Burton's The Nightmare Before Christmas*." *Chicago Sun-Times*, October 22, 1993.

Edelstein, David. "Mixing *Beetlejuice*." *Rolling Stone*, June 2, 1988, pp. 51, 53, 76.

_____. "Tim Burton's Hollywood Nightmare." *Vanity Fair*, November 1994, pp. 124, 129–34.

Ehrman, Mark. "Attack of Martians Who Ate Hollywood." *Los Angeles Times*, December 16, 1996.

Ferrante, Anthony C. "Duck for Cover When *Mars Attacks!*" *Fangoria*, # 159, January 1997, pp. 30–35, 79.

Ferrara, Denis, and St. Clair Pugh. "Sidney: To *Mars* and Back." *Los Angeles Times*, June 24, 1996.

Fine, Marshall. "*Mars Attacks!* Trades Too Much for Too Little." Gannett News Service, December 13, 1996.

Fleming, Michael. "Burton Set for *Todd* Feature." *Daily Variety*, May 23, 1995.

Garfield, Simon. "Life Is Something to Avoid." *The Independent on Sunday*, October 23, 1994, pp. 16–18.

Garner, Jack. "*Mars Attacks Is a Belly Flop of a Comedy.*" Gannett News Service, December 10, 1996, p. S12.

Gaydos, Steven. "On Location: *Edward Scissorhands.*" *Hollywood Reporter*, July 31, 1990.

Gelmis, Joseph. "Manchild in Suburban Fantasy Land." *Newsday*, December 2, 1990.

Gleiberman, Owen. "The Awful Truth in *Ed Wood*, His Delightfully Strange Biography of the Worst Director Ever, Tim Burton Pays Affectionate Tribute to the Tattered Fringes of '50s Hollywood." *Entertainment Weekly*, September 30, 1994, p. 36.

_____. "*Ed Wood.*" *Entertainment Weekly*, October 14, 1994, p. 40.

_____. "Holloween Tim Burton's *Nightmare Before Christmas* Is Technically Amazing But Devoid of Feeling." *Entertainment Weekly*, October 22, 1993, p. 82.

_____. "Revenge of the Nerds." *Entertainment Weekly*, June 16, 1992, pp. 90–91.

Gliatto, Tom, and Lois Armstrong. "*Ed Wood.*" *People*, October 10, 1994.

_____. "Master Ed." *People*, October 31, 1994, pp. 87–88, 90.

Gordinier, Jeff. "News and Notes: Jack's Back." *Time*, 1996.

Gross, Edward. "Super Duper." *Cinescape*, September-October, 1997, pp. 50–53.

Grove, Martin A. "Hollywood Report." *Hollywood Reporter*, April 6, 1988.

Groves, Don. "*Mars* Out of This World: Burton Pic Hits Stride at O'seas B.O." *Daily Variety*, March 10, 1997, pp. 12, 14.

Handelman, David. "Auteurs Turned Authors." *Harper's Bazaar*, October 1, 1997, pp. 142–43.

Hoberman, J. "*Ed Wood* . . . Not." *Sight and Sound*, May 1995, pp. 10–12.

Hofman, Adina. "Close Encounters of the Satirical Kind." *Jerusalem Post*, March 1997.

Indiana, Gary. "Into the Wood." *Village Voice*, October 4, 1994.

Johnson, Ted. "Burton Returns to William Morris." *Daily Variety*, July 22, 1996.

Kael, Pauline. "Boo!" *The New Yorker*, April 18, 1988, pp. 119–20.

_____. "*Edward Scissorhands.*" *The New Yorker*, December 17, 1990.

Kaplan, Michael. "Ryder Storm." *Movieline*, November 1990, pp. 29–34, 86–87.

Kipen, David. "Bela of the Ball." *Los Angeles Daily News*, September 28, 1994.

Klawans, Stuart. "*Ed Wood.*" *The Nation*, October 17, 1994, pp. 433–34.

Klein, Andy. "The Famous Mr. Ed." *Los Angeles Reader*, September 30, 1994, pp. 66, 68.

Koltnow, Barry. "Elfman's Split Personality." *Los Angeles Daily News*, October 31, 1993.

Kuklenski, Valerie. "Any *Good Will* for Composer?" *Los Angeles Daily News*, March 8, 1998.

Lahr, John. "Tim Burton's Dark Knight." *Fame*, August 1989, pp. 24–25, 28.

LaSalle, Mick. "*Batman Forever* Goes On and On." *San Francisco Chronicle*, June 16, 1995.

Marich, Robert. "Fox Positions *Scissorhands.*" *Hollywood Reporter*, November 14, 1990, p. 9.

"*Mars Attacks!*–More Weird from Tim Burton." Gannett News Service, December 13, 1996.

Maslin, Janet. "And So Handy Around the Garden." *New York Times*, December 7, 1990.

_____. "The Moral: Be Careful of Aliens." *New York Times*, December 13, 1996, p. B3.

Matthews, Jack. "A Good Ed Wood Movie." *Newsday*, September 28, 1994, pp. B2–B3.

_____. "Xmas Marks the Spot for a *Nightmare.*" *Newsday*, 1993.

Morgenstern, Joe. "Tim Burton, Batman, and the Joker." *New York Times*, April 9, 1989, *Magazine* section, pp. 45–46, 50, 53, 59–60.

Newman, Kim. "*Batman Returns.*" *Sight and Sound*, August 1992, pp. 48–49.

_____. "*Ed Wood.*" *Sight and Sound*, May 1995, pp. 44–45.

_____. "*Mars Attacks!*" *Sight and Sound*, March 1997, pp. 53–54.

_____. "*Tim Burton's The Nightmare Before Christmas.*" *Sight and Sound*, December 1993, pp. 53–54.

Nichols, Natalie. "Dark Knight Lite." *Los Angeles Reader*, June 16, 1995, pp. 28–29.

Novak, Ralph. "*Mars Attacks!*" *People*, December 23, 1996, pp. 17–18.

Pennington, Ron. "*Batman.*" *Hollywood Reporter*, June 15, 1989, pp. 4, 22.

Pinsker, Beth. "*Mars Attacks!*— Sci-Fi Spoof Is Spectacular Comic-Book Fun." *Dallas Morning News*, December 13, 1996, p. 1C.

Pye, Michael. "A Walk on the Weird Side." *Hot Air*, January-March 1995, pp. 16, 18–20.

Rafferty, Terrence. "Lost in the Stars." *The New Yorker*, December 16, 1996, pp. 116–18.

Rainer, Peter. "It's Topps!" *Los Angeles New Times*, December 12, 1996, pp. 26, 30.

Rebello, Stephen. "Danny Elfman's Nightmare." *Movieline*, November 1993, pp. 55–58, 86–87.

_____. "In Depp." *Movieline*, October 1994, pp. 40–45, 81–82.

_____. "Johnny Depp Lets Down His Hair." *Movieline*, April 1993, pp. 31–36, 78.

Rhodes, Joe. "Mad Love: The Curious and Captivating Romance of Tim Burton and Lisa Marie." *Us*, August 1997.

Rose, Frank. "Tim Cuts Up." *Premiere*, January 1991, pp. 96–102.

Rugoff, Ralph. "Shot Through the Heart: Director Burton Expresses His Interest in Photography with Rare Polaroid Camera." *Harper's Bazaar*, September 1, 1994, pp. 418–24.

Ryan, James. "In the Studio with Tim Burton: *Oyster Boy* and Other Misfits." *New York Times*, November 2, 1997.

Ryon, Ruth. "Director Cuts His Ties to Ojai." *Los Angeles Times*, June 28, 1998.

Scheck, Frank. "*Ed Wood.*" *Hollywood Reporter*, September 23, 1994, pp. 10, 20.

Schruers, Fred. "Batmitvah." *Premiere*, July 1992, pp. 56–64.

Shaw, Jessica. "A Super Look, Up in the Sky, It's a Multimillion-Dollar Feature Film Franchise. Or Is It Just Superman?" *Entertainment Weekly*, May 16, 1997.

Schickel, Richard. "Spaced Invaders: *Mars Attacks!*" *Time*, December 23, 1996.

Skal, David J. "On the Set with Tim Burton, Monster Man." *American Movie Classics Magazine*, October 1998, pp. 4, 6.

Smith, Laurie Halpern. "Look, Ma, No Hands—or Tim Burton's Latest Feat." *New York Times*, August 26, 1990.

Smith, Liz. "Depp-Burton Reteaming." *Los Angeles Times*, March 4, 1993.

Strick, Philip. "*Edward Scissorhands.*" *Sight and Sound*, July 1991, pp. 42–43.

Thompson, Anne. "After *Batman*: Anatomy of a Deal." *Los Angeles Weekly*, November 23, 1990.

Travers, Peter. "Auteur in Angora." *Rolling Stone,* October 20, 1994. pp. 153, 155.

"Tribute: *Batman's* Architect." *People*, December 9, 1991, p. 55.

Turan, Kenneth. "*Ed Wood*: '50s Blithe Spirit." *Los Angeles Times*, September 28, 1994, pp. F1, F12.

_____. "*Mars Attacks!*: Tim Burton's *Plan 9.*" *Los Angeles Times*, December 13, 1996, "Calendar" section, p. 14.

"Up from Transylvania: Interview with Martin Landau." *The Valley Vantage*, October 13, 1994.

Warren, Bill. "Tim Burton Attacks!" *Starlog*, January 1997.

Williams, Stephen. "Extreme Measures." *Newsday*, December 1996.

Willman, Chris. "Back to Boingo." *Los Angeles Times*, May 15, 1994, *Calendar* section, pp. 55, 62, 66.

Wilmington, Michael. "A Modern Fairy Tale." *Los Angeles Times*, December 7, 1990.

Young, Paul F. "Burton Taps Parker Prez of His Warner-Based Firm." *Daily Variety*, March 16, 1995.

INDEX

ABOUT THE AUTHOR

KEN HANKE IS A FREELANCE WRITER, photographer, and filmmaker. His previous books include *Ken Russell's Films* (Scarecrow Press, 1984), *Charlie Chan at the Movies* (McFarland and Co., 1989), and *A Critical Guide to Horror Film Series* (Garland Publishing, 1991). In addition to these, he served as a contributing essayist on *The Fearmakers* (St. Martin's Press, 1994) with entries on James Whale, Roman Polanski, David Cronenberg, and Stuart Gordon, and *The Sleaze Merchants* (St. Martin's Press, 1995). He is a frequent contributor to such magazines as *Films in Review, Filmfax,* and *Video Watchdog,* and has recently joined the staff of writers for *Scarlet Street.* He lives in south Florida with his wife, Shonsa, and their daughter, Jeanne.